CONCORDIA
UNIVERSITY

A gift to
Concordia University Library
by Mrs. Diane Koch
in memory of

Dr. Raymond P. Koch

D0758963

OREGON CITY, OREGON

SMALL BOAT ON THE UPPER RHINE

Some other books by Roger Pilkington

SMALL BOAT THROUGH BELGIUM
SMALL BOAT THROUGH HOLLAND
SMALL BOAT TO THE SKAGERRAK
SMALL BOAT THROUGH SWEDEN
SMALL BOAT TO ALSACE
SMALL BOAT TO BAVARIA
SMALL BOAT THROUGH GERMANY
SMALL BOAT THROUGH FRANCE
SMALL BOAT IN SOUTHERN FRANCE
SMALL BOAT ON THE MEUSE
SMALL BOAT ON THE THAMES
SMALL BOAT TO LUXEMBOURG
SMALL BOAT ON THE MOSELLE
SMALL BOAT TO ELSINORE
SMALL BOAT TO NORTHERN GERMANY
SMALL BOAT ON THE LOWER RHINE
WORLD WITHOUT END
HEAVEN'S ALIVE

For Younger Readers

Adventures in Boats
THE MISSING PANEL
THE DAHLIA'S CARGO
DON JOHN'S DUCATS
NEPOMUK OF THE RIVER
THE EISENBART MYSTERY
THE BOY FROM STINK ALLEY

Non-fiction
THE GREAT SOUTH SEA

SMALL BOAT ON
THE UPPER RHINE

BY
ROGER PILKINGTON

Illustrated by David Knight

MACMILLAN
ST MARTIN'S PRESS

914.3
PIL

© St Aubin's Productions Ltd 1971

All rights reserved. No part of this publication
may be reproduced or transmitted, in any form or
by any means, without permission.

SBN Boards: 333 12590 8
Library of Congress Catalog Card No: 71–125603

First published 1971 by
MACMILLAN LONDON LTD
London and Basingstoke
Associated companies in New York Toronto
Dublin Melbourne Johannesburg & Madras

Printed in Great Britain by
ROBERT MACLEHOSE AND CO LTD
The University Press Glasgow

This book is dedicated to all those who have travelled
the upper reaches of the Rhine aboard the *Thames
Commodore*: my son Hugh and daughter Cynthia; Brian
Dodds; Florence Wheelock; Hubert and Agnes
Conover; Joanna Ide; Jan Pilkington-Miksa; Richard
Jaboor; Christine Craig; Fred and Lisa Doerflinger;
Fritz, Else and Irmel Hockenjos; Bill Gardam; and
especially to the ship's mate, my wife Miriam.

CONCORDIA UNIVERSITY LIBRARY
PORTLAND, OR 97211

Kennt Ihr den schönen goldnen Rhein
mit seinem Duft und Sonnenschein,
mit prächt'ger Stromung seiner Wogen,
von Berg und Felsen kühn umzogen?

Know ye the beauty of the golden Rhine,
its perfumed breeze and summer sunshine's gleam,
the mighty current of its wave-tossed flow,
and cliff-perched castles proud above its stream?

Otto Roquette.

LIST OF MAPS

A 2

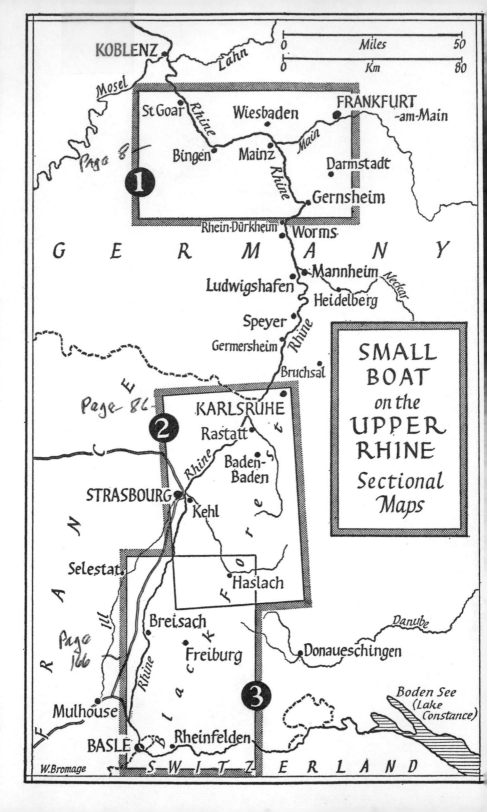

KOBLENZ

Lahn

Mosel

0 ___ Miles ___ 50
0 ___ Km ___ 80

St Goar

Rhine

Wiesbaden

FRANKFURT
-am-Main

Bingen

Mainz

Main

Darmstadt

Page 8

①

Rhine

Gernsheim

Rhein-Dürkheim

Worms

G E R M A N Y

Mannheim

Neckar

Ludwigshafen

Heidelberg

Speyer

Rhine

Germersheim

Bruchsal

SMALL
BOAT
on the
UPPER
RHINE
*Sectional
Maps*

Page 86

②

KARLSRUHE

Rastatt

Rhine

Baden-
Baden

STRASBOURG

Kehl

B l a c k

F o r e s t

F R A N C E

Selestat

Haslach

Page 166

Breisach

Danube

Freiburg

Donaueschingen

ill

Rhine

③

Mulhouse

*Boden See
(Lake
Constance)*

BASLE

Rheinfelden

S W I T Z E R L A N D

W. Bromage

FOREWORD

THIS is the seventeenth book of inland voyaging which I have written. The main *dramatis personae* are as before – that is to say myself as the skipper or ancient mariner, my wife Miriam as mate, the five-year-old *Thames Commodore* and the shade of her departed elder sister as the young ladies of virtue who, unlike so many heroines of the Rhine itself, are not going to be cut short in their prime by jealous rivals, heartless husbands, or foolish fathers. But the journey itself is unusual in that it begins in midstream, half way up the splendid if forbidding castled gorge of the middle section of Europe's greatest river, the Rhine. By greatest I do not mean that the Rhine delivers more water into the sea than do the Vistula or the Danube (for which in any case I have no figures of discharge), nor that it exceeds other rivers in length, height, depth, or any other creature, but just that in history, majesty and sheer shipping there is nothing in all the world as splendid as the Rhine, on which thousands of powerful vessels ceaselessly churn the water as they thrust upstream beneath the frowning remains of castle keeps built long ago as strong-points from which archi-episcopal or baronial customs men might sally out under armed guard to hold up the shipping to ransom.

The Rhine is busy and in certain reaches it is highly industrial, but that is not to say that the smoke-laden stretches of river through Duisburg and Mannheim are unattractive. They have a new, technological romance of their own, and the colours in the coppery sky of Ruhr industry may be so breathtakingly beautiful that one can only regret not having a Turner aboard to paint it. More familiar is the Rhine of the gorge where this tale is to start, the river of crags and cliffs each bearing a ruin around which is woven a legend of some Knight or Baron, noble or villainous. Beneath them the vineyard terraces are cramped against the hillsides, golden with the autumn leaves of wines famous the world over, and at the very foot runs the river itself, the line of which has for centuries been the scene of bloody battles. Even now there are three stretches of the Rhine where sovereign states face each other across the water, although they do so without the hostility of former times.

Then there is the Rhine of the summer visitors who come to stay in the same inns and hotels as were the very height of fashion in the grand tour years or were perhaps the scene of notable romances such as that of Victoria and Albert, and of fateful meetings like that of Chamberlain and Hitler in the Hotel Dreesen. And a short way downstream of our mid-river starting point the alluring form of the spirit of the Lorelei may still be seen sitting up aloft to comb her locks with a golden comb and entice to destruction a barge of some coal magnate of the Ruhr – though I think this is less likely now that the navigation authority has been hard at work to dynamite all the more notable rocks and reefs so that ships may pass up and down the river in greater safety.

All up the river, plaques in village inns announce that Goethe slept there (or had lunch there, or maybe just used the toilet, for all I know). If plates were cast with the words *'Thames Commodore liebte hier zu weilen'* then to erect enough would be a difficult task indeed, and few villages or creeks along the course of the Rhine would be without one, for she and her skipper and mate have indeed loved the river in all its guises, in summer sun and spring showers and in the driving snow of a winter blizzard. They have loved it for its beauty and its romance, but also as a challenging river to navigate, its phenol-scented waters heaving in the throes of a traffic that never quite ceases even on Christmas Day.

If this present voyage begins not only in midstream but halfway up the river, that is because the Rhine is too powerful a stream to be contained in one book. When first I began to write of it, the spirit of the Rhine himself came and sat on the corner of my desk, cross-legged and wet and smelling just a bit of coal-tar derivatives, and intervened continually in my narrative to ask whether I had remembered about Anne of Cleves, and Stinnes the barge-owner, and had I forgotten Roland and his arch, or my Neanderthal relatives, and what about the Templars of Lahneck, and the nun of Oranienstein. And as I always had to give way and listen to his tales and agree to set them down rather than offend him and risk being wrecked on the Unkelstein or the Goat's Back, by the time I had written as much as Macmillan could handle and a reader digest we had got no further than the bend above Oberwesel, and that book had to become *Small Boat on the Lower Rhine*. So there remained half of the voyage still to be told, and to do so is the object of this present book, which will take us up to the limit of navigation in Switzerland.

A speed-boat owner once told me that he had knocked back the whole of the Rhine in a day and a half. Perhaps he was in a hurry to get home, but in any event I am glad I was not with him. Such velocity is a desecration of all that voyaging means, an insult to the river itself. The *Thames Commodore* would never be so brash, unladylike, and even dangerous. She is more likely to chug contentedly from early morning until lunch and then sidle into a harbour and relax.

Sometimes I have a suspicion that with increasing age I become more long-winded. If that is so, I do not regret it. There is much to be said for taking things slowly, and that is why I prefer to travel the Rhine upstream, against the current, and aboard a ship which cruises at a modest nine knots rather than to flash down the river so fast that there is no time to see what lies to port and starboard. But one should not remain made fast in a harbour or in a foreword indefinitely, and the time has come to check over the engines and get under-way, heading up the stream towards its fleetest passage in the defile below Bingen.

St Aubin, 1971   ROGER PILKINGTON

I

*The earliest ships – from rafts to horse-haulage – Hermann
of Stahleck – Hilchen's betrothal – murder of Wiltrud – the
blind marksman – Klemenskapelle – Gerda's betrothal – the
Mouse Tower – Bingen rapids – battle of the barge dog*

Warum *ist es am Rhein so schön?* Why is it so schön, so lovely
on the Rhine? So asks the Rhenish song that pours from the
windows of the inns along the valley, and it supplies an answer,
too. Because the girls are so gay and the boys so thirsty.

Maybe. But there is feminine gaiety and male thirst in many a
place without the environment thereby becoming something that
would entrance Victor Hugo, inspire Heinrich Heine and Clemens
Brentano, lure Schumann to his death, bring Goethe to sleep in
one hotel after another, and draw the *Thames Commodore* to join
the throng of shipping thrusting up the stream, criss-crossing with
the approaching traffic as she makes up from one little river port
to the next. For her at least there is a fascination which goes far
beyond the gay girls and thirsty boys. Besides, she has never been
up or down the gorge without young friends aboard who are quite
as lively as any to be found ashore, and just as thirsty too.

There is a wildness about the river which has always appealed
to me. Of course the Rhine is no longer so unbridled as in the old
days when, diffuse and uncontrolled, it flowed from Switzerland
to the sea just as it wished. But it still has a will of its own. In the
last year for which I have the complete figures there were 952
accidents upon the river, most of them occurring within the three
or four kilometres of the stretch immediately below the Mouse
Tower, which we shall be entering before the end of this chapter.
Indeed, I have never yet been on the Rhine without seeing a
lighter stranded on a reef because of a broken tow-cable, or a
powerful and expensive ship broken in half by the sheer force of
the river running past the shoal on which it has stranded, and if

two tugs are kept permanently at the ready at Assmannshausen they are by no means relics of the past, like the tug at London's Tower Bridge. At any moment they may be called to race to a ship in danger from the sheer force of the Rhine.

For myself the Rhine also has a strange appeal which comes from the fact that one is following in the wake of generations of worthy ships. Whether regulated and dredged or not, its course has been run by vessels in their hundreds or thousands since earliest times – since men could make even the simplest kind of craft. The first ships (if one may so describe them) to navigate the Rhine were the heavy rafts of the German tribes, steered downstream with sweeps and broken up when they reached their destination.

The same peoples had dug-outs too, and perhaps some of these could be paddled upstream against the current if they took the slack water on the inside of the bends and kept where possible to the creeks and marshy loops. Ferries already existed, small and light, a wooden framework covered with the stretched skins of animals.

Then came the Romans with their new-style ships constructed by the shipbuilders they brought with them from the Mediterranean, long-oared craft of the galley type but with only one bank of oars. The oldest Rhine barge of which precise details exist is that shown in the museum at Mainz on the tomb of Blussus, a member of a Roman guild of shippers. It had considerable freeboard and was operated by a crew of four. There were two rudders aft and one at the bow, and sail could be mounted on a short mast. It was certainly a local type of boat, quite unlike the Mediterranean craft, and in fact the shipwrights of the German tribes absorbed into the Roman empire were in some ways technically ahead of those brought in from beyond the Alps – for example in knowing how to bend planks by steaming them.

The Rhine was of course the great route by which goods were brought from beyond the Alps to the colonies as far away as the Netherlands, and so most of the transport was in a downstream direction. Yet the Romans were able to work cargoes upstream too, and the remains of a Roman barge laden with millstones from the Eiffel hills has been found in a minor channel near Strasbourg, hundreds of miles upstream of the area where the stone was quarried. Such cargo-ships not only had sail to help whenever possible but mounted awnings to protect the merchandise. There were also armed patrol vessels, forerunners of the *Wasserschutz-polizei* of modern times, and from their build one can assume that they could have made a speed of six knots. Indeed, in Roman times the Rhine was so thoroughly exploited as a transport route that there were probably more ships upon the river than there were at any other time up to 1900, the difference being in the slower speed and lower carrying capacity.

After the collapse of Rome the trade upon the Rhine very naturally declined. The imports from the south dried up and the great river became almost deserted through the dark ages of tribal migration. It was only when Europe became more stable that the shipping could blossom and flourish again under the flags of the Hanseatic cities, whose rich merchants had narrow-built sailing vessels of such design that they could even manage the voyage upstream under their own power if the wind was in the most favourable quarter. Otherwise it was a case of slow, plodding haulage by the teams of rough men who strained, often up to their waists in the water, to drag the vessels yard by yard through the hundreds of miles of the upstream voyage.

The next improvement came with the tow-horses and their drovers, the *Halfen*, such as one sees in the sketches drawn by Wenceslas Hollar when he accompanied the Duke of Albermarle up the river on his way to Vienna. Ships up to one hundred tons lading were hauled upstream by ten or twelve horses, each horse costing about 10 thalers for the whole journey from Cologne to Mainz, though the charge might be half as much again in times when fodder was expensive. In addition the skipper had to provide free board and lodging for the *Halfen*, who numbered one to every two or three horses. Because the drink was free these men were rarely sober, and the sharp knives they carried to sever the traces instantly in case of danger were sometimes used upon each other. Nevertheless these vessels managed the upstream journey in eight to seventeen days according to the lading and the current, and the return in a mere three, without the aid of the drovers – who rode the horses back down the riverside path or by the tracks which

In the Rhine gorge

led from village to village. It was a laborious system and yet it was the means by which the trade of Europe flowed – and flowed to such an extent that in the fourteenth century there were eleven hundred barges and two hundred passenger vessels on the stretch between Cologne and Mainz alone.

Modern shipping on the Rhine is certainly very different. Yet in the gorge section of the river between Koblenz and Bingen the course itself has hardly changed over the centuries. The crag-top castles have fallen into decay and tough knights no longer sally forth with their men-at-arms to hold up the vessels and plunder the cargoes, but the vintners still climb up to their patches of terrace to tie and stake the vines in much the same way as they did in the days of Charlemagne. As the *Thames Commodore* headed upstream from Oberwesel the sun was baking the brown shale, warming the roots and flinging back enough radiant heat to raise hopes that this particular year would bring the sort of vintage always longed for but rarely achieved.

4

Up past the ship-like form of the Pfalzgrafenstein on its midstream rock we were already in sight of the curving line of trees on the island below Bacharach, and then the town itself opened up to starboard, the hill behind it crowned by the massive ruin of Burg Stahleck, now a youth hostel but once the main seat of the counts palatine and a very suitable point from which they could raid the convoys of goods upon the river. The first of these counts was Hermann von Stahleck, nephew of the Emperor Conrad III, who somewhat unwisely appointed him to a position of trust and authority over the imperial domains while he himself went off to the Middle East on one of those perennial and age-long attempts to settle the hash of the Arabs.

Hermann's rapacity came up against the difficulty that most of the lands on which he had designs belonged to abbeys, deans and chapters. However, there was no shortage of robber barons who disliked the clergy as much as he, so Hermann mustered a force which included the Counts of Leiningen and Kirchberg, Deidesheim and Sponheim, Nidda and Katzenellenbogen, as well as a host of minor nobility, most of them veterans of Palestine campaigns. He first led this mighty army against the domains of the Archbishop of Trier, but the prelate delivered a rousing speech to his supporters and himself led a counter-attack to rout the invaders. Hermann had to flee for his life to Stahleck.

His second attempt had to wait for the absence in Italy of the new emperor Friedrich Barbarossa. This time Hermann and his friends attacked the sees of Worms and Speyer, and finally the lands of Archbishop Arnold of Mainz, a prelate who was hated even by his own clergy. The archbishop announced a wholesale excommunication of Hermann and his followers, but none of them fell down dead as a result of his displeasure. Instead they ravaged his territories and had sacked all but Mainz itself when Barbarossa returned from Italy. Furious that Arnold had excommunicated a prince of the Holy Roman Empire without his permission, and equally enraged that the same prince should have invaded the lands of the various sees, the emperor called an immediate diet or meeting at Worms, at which both sides were duly pronounced guilty.

The sentence, from which only the archbishop himself was

excused on account of his age and infirmity, was for every one of
the leading participants to appear before the peers and people with
a dog on his back – this being by common consent the ultimate in
degradation. Certainly it must have been so considered, for if
Hermann had survived excommunication unscathed the cur-
carrying so broke his tough nature that a few days after returning
to Stahleck he summoned his retainers, gave them all his belong-
ings and left for the depths of the forest, where he ended his days
as an impoverished hermit.

As for the archbishop, although he had escaped having to carry
a dog on his shoulders he found that his subjects hated him more
than ever before. Deciding to take himself off to Rome he foolishly
imposed a new tax to pay for his travel expenses, and had it levied
with exceptional harshness. The result was that the people marched
upon his palace and set it ablaze, together with the houses of all
the clergy known to have supported him. The emperor had to
march from Worms to restore order, but he could not be prevailed
upon to punish the rioters beyond banning some of their leaders
from the city.

As soon as Barbarossa had retired from Mainz the ringleaders
returned to the city and began to organise once again an uprising.
Archbishop Arnold was informed, but he disdained to take
precautions.

'The people of Mainz are dogs,' he declared. 'They bark, but
cannot bite. I have no fear of them, for I despise them.'

Perhaps he did, but when he at last decided to visit again his
own city and spent the night in one of the monasteries the people
silently surrounded the place and launched an attack.

'The noise, the tumult, the confusion of the fray, the whizzing
of arrows, the hissing of fire-brands, the clash of arms and armour
aroused the archbishop from a troubled sleep' wrote Joseph
Snowe. 'He was soon seized and his death was dreadful. He was
torn to pieces by the mob.'

Below Stahleck and set on a mound against the backdrop of
trees stands the delicate shape of the Werner Chapel, put up in
memory of the glass-blower apprentice said to have been murdered
by a Jew who hung him up by the heels till he died. Such tales
were often put about to discredit the Jews, even in our own

century, though once in a while they may well have been true. Jews never had a monopoly of wickedness, nor of virtue.

Whatever may have happened to young Werner, Bacharach is nowadays more noted for wine than murder, and even its name carries a hint of the fact, for a rock covered with water was known locally as the Altar of Bacchus (Bacchi Ara). When it was visible there had of course been exceptionally little rain, which in itself was a sign that a good vintage was likely. Certainly the appearance of the rock was considered as a harbinger of excellent Bacharacher, a wine so prized that the Emperor Wenceslas chose four barrels of it rather than ten thousand florins offered him by the city of Nürnberg to redeem their privileges, which he had sequestered; and the Pope Pius II had a 250 gallon cask transported every year to Rome for his own personal consumption. As for the stone itself, the Romans are said to have offered sacrifices to Bacchus on the rock, and in later days the vintners of the town would row out to it and set up a figure of rags and straw, a sort of scare-crow which they would call by the name of Bacchus.

Across the river on the port hand stands Burg Nollig, and below it the little village of Lorch, a place which owes its existence less to the flavour of the wine from the hillsides above than to the obstacle of the Binger Loch upstream, where the Rhine current has always been at its strongest. At Lorch the goods of the medieval bank-hauled craft would be off-loaded into much smaller boats to pass the rapids, or perhaps transferred to carts which would climb up the trail of the Wispertal, wind across the plateau of the Westerwald, and rejoin the Rhine further upstream. When the channel was improved and ships had no longer to stop, the villagers had to find a new trade, but it cannot have been difficult to make the change to the wine-growing which is now its mainstay.

When Hilchen von Lorch followed a call to arms and went off to the Holy Land to cut the Saracens down to size, he left behind him his fiancée. But he had hardly reached the Middle East before his neighbour von Nollig decided that he would have her for himself. He fired the castle at Lorch, stormed it, killed the staff and even murdered the girl's father before taking her off. Curiously, this treatment did not endear him to her, so he locked her up in Castle Nollig until she should be willing to marry him.

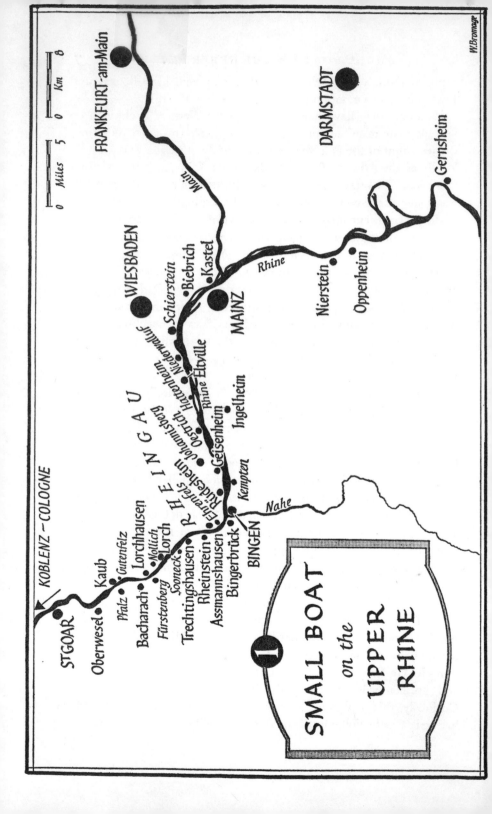

News of this deed reached Hilchen by a vision – or by E.S.P. as we might nowadays say. With a final cut or two at the Saracens he raced back to the Rhine, and drawing rein before Castle Nollig he demanded that his bride should be returned to him. Nollig's lord laughed loudly and taunted him that if he could jump his horse up the cliff into the walls, then certainly he could take the girl away. Hilchen realised that he could no more do this than capture the place by storming it, and he was just about to give up the girl and ride sorrowfully home when a face peered out of the bushes beside him.

'Psst! You want a horse to jump into the castle? O.K. It's yours. Just sign this contract note.'

The speaker was of course the devil, who was often to be found going his rounds of the Rhineland castles. Hilchen was at once aware of his identity, but thinking of his terrified girl-friend he nobly decided to sacrifice his own soul for her freedom. He signed on the dotted line, and at once a splendid black horse was provided for him. At a single bound he was up the crag and over the walls to cut down the guards and sever the ropes of the drawbridge for his waiting men to pour in. Roused from his sleep, the abductor of Nollig perished in the fighting, lamented by none.

Hilchen's young lady was as delighted as she was astonished at such a rescue, and had just begun kissing him when the devil hopped in through the window and thumped the contract on the table. It was time to be going to Hell, he said peremptorily.

But Hilchen's bride had great presence of mind. Snatching the crucifix that hung on a light golden chain around her neck she tossed it on the contract, which of course immediately burst into flames. The devil flew out again with a horrible oath and a smell of sulphur dioxide. Hilchen congratulated her upon her promptitude, and shortly afterwards they were married.

If Hilchen's romance ended happily, the same could hardly be said of the marriage of Lambert and Wiltrud, lord and lady of the mighty Fürstenberg, the next castle upstream on the starboard hand. Not that Lambert was anything but loving by nature; indeed he seems to have been a model husband, kindly if perhaps a shade susceptible. Indeed it was his generous nature which led him to agree to the suggestion of his delicate wife Wiltrud that they should share their good fortune with those less happy, and take into their home a girl called Luckharde, orphaned daughter of a neighbouring noble family. She was only eighteen, but as Dr Ruland in his *Rheinsagen* states that she 'possessed a lascivious beauty very dangerous to men' we can rightly suspect that she is going to wheedle her way easily enough into Lambert of Fürstenberg's susceptible heart, and bed.

Poor Wiltrud. The fact that she actually produced a son for Lambert seems to have been too much for the jealous Luckharde, who crept into her bedroom one night and smothered her with the goose-down pillows, and as Wiltrud had long been of a weak constitution there was no reason at all for the servants to believe that she had died of anything other than natural causes, particularly if one extended the term to include a broken heart.

Luckharde was now mistress of the Fürstenberg, and at least she did not murder the infant child of her predecessor. Perhaps it would have been wiser to do so, but Luckharde disposed of him simply enough by handing him over to an old woman who lived in one of the more remote parts of the servants' quarters. This same aged woman awoke one night and beheld with very under-standable terror a white woman bending over the cot and kissing the boy. When she sat up in bed the apparition vanished, but in the morning the woman asked to be admitted to the new mistress of Fürstenberg to tell her what she had seen. Luckharde was distressed indeed, because the explanation that occurred to her was that maybe she had not completely asphyxiated Wiltrud, who had been hidden away in safety and had now recovered. She therefore decided to try to murder her rival a second time, and having sent the old woman to sleep elsewhere she herself took up her station in the nursery, a dagger concealed in her nightgown.

Sure enough, at midnight a woman appeared, silent and swathed in white, but instead of bending over the cot she came straight towards Luckharde herself and leaned over her bed. It was enough to terrify even the boldest adventuress, but Luckharde steeled herself and suddenly leaped up to stab. The dagger went right through the apparition, and so did her arm. When Lambert awoke next morning he dressed and went down to breakfast as usual, but his beautiful young wife was not there. Instead there was a note addressed to him in which she confessed to Wiltrud's murder, told him of what had occurred during the past night, and added that the sense of her guilt was so tremendous that she had left the Fürstenberg to enter a convent. And because at least in his heart Lambert had been an accessory, she thought he should do likewise.

So Lambert handed over Fürstenberg and his own infant to the care of an upright and virtuous brother. He did not go into a monastery but lived as a hermit in a cave on a crag overlooking the Rhine. And there among his memories he eventually died.

Thick and fast the castles succeed each other on the long curve to starboard before the Bingen defile with its famous rapids. There the *Thames Commodore* will have to have her wits about her, but already the stream is so strong that it will take her a whole hour to force her way up from the Fürstenberg past the Heimburg to abeam of the tall tower of Castle Sooneck, below Trechtingshausen. There is more than time enough for her crew – who at this stage of the voyage are requested to leave the steering to the skipper – to read the story of that castle, and certainly the tale of the banquet at Sooneck must rank as one of the greatest epics of the Rhine.

Hans Veit of Fürsteneck was the champion marksman of all the Rhineland and none could equal him at drawing the crossbow. It was therefore natural enough that the lord of Sooneck should be roused to cnvious enmity, should storm the quiet castle of this worthy man and put out his eyes before having him thrown into the dark, damp dungeon underneath Sooneck's keep. The young son of Veit managed to escape in the attack upon the castle, and fled for his life.

The years passed, and poor old Veit was forgotten. Somehow he still clung on to life itself, but he was an old and bent man when the night of the great party came, the occasion when – to quote Dr Ruland and his equally enthusiastic translator – 'wanton women with showy apparel and painted cheeks lolled in the arms of tipsy cavaliers'. It was into such a scene in the great hall of Sooneck's castle that there was ushered a minstrel to strike up his lays of chivalry, and love, and valour. He performed so excellently that Sooneck himself applauded loudly and drunkenly, and asked the singer what favour he would wish as a reward. The troubadour bowed and said he had no very great favour to ask, but he had heard that there was an old, blind prisoner somewhere down below. He would like to have him brought up.

'A good idea!' Sooneck exclaimed. 'Have the dog hauled up and brought in.'

So old Veit was lifted from the dungeon and brought into the hall. 'See,' roared Sooneck, 'See, ladies and gentlemen. There, in that bent and filthy creature you have one who fancied himself as having the best eye of all the marksmen of the Rhineland. Haha!' He filled a goblet with wine and held it up. 'Hey, you there who are such a good shot, why don't you see if you can shoot the goblet from my hand?'

Wanton women and tipsy cavaliers alike must have thought it a great joke indeed when Sooneck called for a crossbow to be given to the blind man. The minstrel proffered the one he was carrying, which in fact was Veit's own bow – for, as the reader will surely have guessed, the singer was none other than Veit's own son. Veit's aged fingers felt the taut string, and he took the bolt which was placed in his hand. He had recognised the weapon by its feel, he knew the voice of the minstrel, and he trembled with emotion as with all his remaining strength he drew back the string.

Once again the lord of Sooneck shouted down the hall. 'When I say shoot, shoot!' But the instruction ended in a gurgle and choking of blood, for without waiting the old crossbowman had taken aim just below the sound of Sooneck's voice and a little to the right. From the furthest end of the hall he had shot him through the heart.

Flinging off his cloak, young Veit drew his sword and rushed upon those who were nearest. But there was no resistance. As Dr Ruland put it, 'Like a flock of frightened crows the knights and their paramours fled, and only a few terrified squires and servants muttered prayers over the body of the Lord of Sooneck.' Sword in hand the son now ran to the gate, cut down the guard and slashed the ropes of the drawbridge to admit his own men who were waiting outside. There was a brief skirmish, and that was the end of the Soonecks. What became of all the wanton women I am not sure, but there were plenty of other castles where they would no doubt have been sure of a welcome.

Probably this tale borrows heavily from other and older stories – the home-coming of Odysseus, for instance. Yet in essence it might even be true, for life was hard and cruel in the castles that looked down over the vineyards to the river below, and there were villains as well as men of courage and true valour. And certainly there were travelling minstrels who could take the flimsiest of events and embroider them to become just such a tale as would enthrall the knights and their ladies in the great halls all along the river – a story such as that of the Feast at Sooneck, which even now must rank as one of the most gripping that ever a troubadour sang.

We are now bearing up to Trechtingshausen, and ahead in the stream several tugs are hovering, hoping perhaps that we shall signal one of them to come to our assistance, for we are now approaching the fastest reach of all the Rhine, where the river cuts through between the rocky uplands on either side. There are two channels; on the right the Neues Fahrwasser, diked off and racing round the bend from the Mouse Tower, the compulsory channel for all passenger vessels and tow-trains, and for down-coming barges. On the left the water seethes and boils through a gap between the rocks and here and there a stone breaks the surface. The buoys lie almost horizontal with the force of the flow, and already the *Thames Commodore* has put her engines up to full speed and yet she is not making walking pace against the land. But the Binger Loch will not stop her any more than the swift current round the end of the Pont d'Avignon on the Rhône. She will not need to take a tug in harness in front, a *Vorspann-schlepper*, to pull her through the gap. Nor will all the barges need one, though many will pay a few pounds for a haul of a quarter of an hour so that they will run no risk of being swept round at the critical moment and cast on the rocks.

Assmannshausen is now close to port, not twenty yards from our side as we edge across to steal some slacker water. It is a pretty village and it produces a red wine which I for one consider has no equal in all the vineyards of France. Perhaps that is because my wife and I usually drink it at Limburg's Weinhaus Schultes, for to some extent the flavour of any wine must depend in part upon the associations in the bottle. Yet Assmannshäuser is an excellent wine with steak and onions, and if it were not as good as it is the enterprising villagers would undoubtedly have started exporting it to Britain instead of keeping it for themselves. But for all that, its name on a label will always conjure up for me that pretty village with the villainous offshore rocks, and the two tugs lying at the jetty, ready to race to the help of any ship which is in distress – for as I have mentioned, more than half the accidents on all the Rhine occur at this point in the defile.

Across the river Castle Rheinstein stands magnificent, even if only a shadow of what it was in the years of highway robbery of the shipping. Below it and right against the shore stands a chapel, the Clemenskapelle. Standing on its own it is a memorial to yet another deed of medieval violence. The lord of Rheinstein had put into a state of imminent maternity a virtuous girl who lived in a valley on the further side of the river and for some reason which I have never fully understood this caused him to be ridiculed by his neighbours who, one would have thought, might have been expected to regard this as the most commonplace situation. The Rheinsteiner was stung by their taunts and decided to show that he was capable of going further than a mere clandestine meeting by night. He would seize the girl and carry her off to Rheinstein.

With an adequate force of toughs he crossed the Rhine and abducted her, but on the return voyage the poor girl stood up in the boat and called upon St Clement, promising him a new chapel if he would rescue her. And lo, in a moment the saint appeared on the water, scaring the robbers out of their wits with his unearthly shining light. Clement took the girl by the hand, and she stepped out of the boat to walk over the water with him to the bank. As for her captors, the boat was overset and every one of them was drowned. Which I think probably served them right.

However, another tale of its building is less romantic. When the unauthorised tolls levied by the gangsters in their Rhine castles had become too oppressive to be borne any longer, the Emperor Rudolph of Hapsburg decided to have done with these aristocratic brigands for ever. After his warnings had been disregarded with contempt, he appeared in the Rhineland with a mighty force of men swelled by the burghers of the towns which suffered at the hands of the robbers. His system was not to storm the castles but to fire incendiary materials into them until they were well ablaze. From Reichenstein, from Sooneck and the Heimburg the clouds of smoke drifted down into the valley, and as the robber lords issued from their burning nests they were seized and taken for trial, then led through the streets of Assmannshausen amid the cheers of the merchants and vintners (and particularly the women, I imagine) to a place of execution on the bank of the Rhine.

It seems that the relatives of these men were very naturally concerned about the fate of their souls, and a priest advised them to cut down the trees on which their fathers and husbands had been hanged, and to use the timber together with stones from the burned castles to build a chapel of expiation for their misdeeds. When it was finished, the bodies were all exhumed and brought up the river in a macabre procession of barges, to be buried a second time in the Clemenskapelle under the special grace of an absolution pronounced over them by the Archbishop of Mainz.

But this little chapel on the river bank is also connected with another of the most dramatic tales of the Rhine gorge, for it became the burial place also of Gerda of Rheinstein and Helmbrecht of Sterrenberg. Gerda's father Diethelm was a highly successful robber baron, and he did not confine himself to plundering Rhine barges. On one of his forays he abducted a beautiful girl named Jutta, a girl of such winning ways and golden character that, according to Dr Ruland, 'as the delicate ivy twines itself round the rough oak and clothes its knotty stem with shimmering velvet, so in time the gentle conduct of this maiden changed the coarse baron to a noble knight who eschewed pillaging and carousing' – and actually married her. But alas, she died when her baby was born; and that baby was Gerda. Needless to say she was wondrous fair, so that those familiar with the Rhineland will already suspect that she was destined to have the most alarming experiences, which are almost certain to end in either defenestration or suicide.

Old Diethelm wanted to marry his daughter to anyone who had enough money (the ivy which had twined itself round the rough oak being now dead) and he was not at all averse to the suit of Helmbrecht of Sterrenberg, who had fallen in love with Gerda when she appeared as Beauty Queen at a tournament at Rheinstein.

Gerda was in love with Helmbrecht also, so everything seemed set fair for a wedding approved by all. But in those days it was the curious custom to urge one's suit through a relative who was a contemporary of the bride's father, and so Helmbrecht of Sterrenberg put his uncle to work on his behalf. Needless to say, the man was a wicked uncle, and as he was also very rich he easily persuaded the rough oak Diethelm that it would be much better if he married Gerda himself. The girl had no great wish to be espoused to this crafty old schemer instead of to the man of her own choice, but in those days young ladies were rarely consulted as to their desires. She was bluntly informed that she was to be married to Helmbrecht's uncle.

Looking up from the river towards the ruin of the great castle one can even now imagine the events of the fateful day and see the wedding procession winding its way down the steep track from the Rheinstein towards the Clemenskapelle on the shore, the chapel in which so many noble brigands lie interred. None can now intervene to save the lovely girl from the wicked uncle of her lover. No mere human, that is, can stop the train of events. But insects are a different matter, and suddenly a squadron of horse-flies buzzes out of the bushes and collectively they bite Gerda's horse on the rump. The steed rears and breaks away, racing down the dangerous path ahead. Gerda screams, the wicked uncle puts spurs to his charger to save his precious bride. So does old Diethelm.

There is a clatter of hoofs, then the uncle's horse trips on a stone and goes over the edge of the cliff with its rider still in the saddle. There is a crashing from below as rider and steed bounce from rock to rock, but the wedding party is more worried about Gerda's fate. Her father has now nearly reached the bridle of the fleeing animal but before he can seize the reins the steed rears, raises a hoof, and lodges a well-aimed blow upon his leg. Moaning, the knight is carried back to the castle, and the doctor is called.

Gerda's horse is now out of sight, the wedding guests and horse-flies all left behind. Nor has the animal any inclination to stop its wild galloping. And then as it careers round a bend a man bursts from the wayside bushes and grabs the reins. It is – as the reader will have guessed – the faithful Helmbrecht, who was lying in wait to have a farewell glance at the bride who was not to be his. Gerda has already swooned away with fright and when she awakes it is in the strong arms of her own dear, dear Helmbrecht.

I am glad to say that after a few days in bed nursing his bruised leg old Diethelm came to his senses enough to decide that Helmbrecht was not such a bad young fellow after all. Besides, one must assume that he had inherited his uncle's wealth. The old man gave the youngsters his blessing and rode in their wedding procession to the Clemenskapelle, accompanied by his sister Notburga from the Nonnenwerth convent – who must surely have been there to see that he behaved himself.

To-pocherti-pocherti-pocherti, the motor of a fat Belgian barge just ahead of us is turning as fast as it can. A smell of hot oil drifts from her sky-lights as we creep up to her stern and begin to edge past her. She has a tug ahead of her on a long line but we shall just be able to overhaul the two craft before the foaming surge up the final step into the slacker water beyond. Ehrenfels castle is frowning down on us from the top of the vineyards on the port hand, and to starboard the signal flags on the Mouse Tower out in the stream at the head of the Neues Fahrwasser announce a single ship descending. She is one of the giant passenger vessels of the Cologne–Düsseldorf line and she shoots past us like an express train to fade away past the Clemenskapelle.

As for the Mouse Tower, tall and thin and battlemented, the story of Bishop Hatto is probably the best known of all the Rhineland tales. In fact the tower was not a refuge for the wicked prelate but was built as a toll station to work in conjunction with Castle Ehrenfels across the river. In those days the toll went by the name of *Maut*, close enough to *Maus* to set the scene for the dreadful story so often told, and perhaps most vividly of all by Victor Hugo, who embroidered it with great skill. Hatto, 'the greedy prelate whose hand was more often stretched out to bless than to give' (whereas in fact he was really a very reasonable bishop) made a corner in grain when it was in short supply so that he could sell it at an advanced price. But the poorer people could not pay, and when they begged for food the bishop rounded them up, packed them into the barn at Mainz, and set it on fire. 'It was a spectacle to make the stones weep,' added Hugo for good measure.

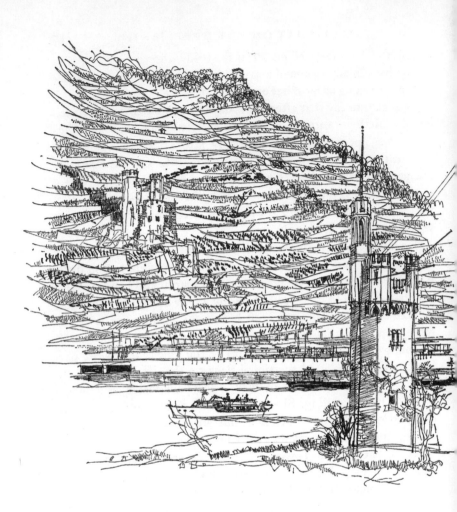

Mouse Tower and Ehrenfels

But Hatto only laughed. '*Haha! Haha! Entendez vous siffler les rats?*'

It should, I think have been *souris*, but however that may be the very next day saw countless rats (or mice) 'pullulating in the ashes of the barn like the maggots in the ulcers of Ahasuerus', a nice simile indeed. They even emerged from the plaster, to reproduce in the streets and the episcopal palace itself. No wonder Hatto fled before the scourge. Yet even as he reached Bingen the pursuing rodents swarmed over the town walls. Swiftly – very swiftly, it would seem – Hatto had a tower built in the river and fled thither. During the short voyage across to it ten of his men had continually to beat on the water around the boat to keep the rats and mice at bay.

But it was in vain that Bishop Hatto reached his island refuge. The beasts climbed the tower, gnawed through doors and ceilings, floors and all, moving from room to room and setting upon the costly tapestries (for Hatto had evidently furnished the place in style) to gnaw out every place where his name was woven, or carved in the woodwork. At last they reached the lowest dungeon, where the bishop himself was cowering in understandable terror. There they devoured him *'tout vivant'*. That was long, long ago, but according to Hugo sometimes at night one may see rising from the tower a strange reddish vapour like the smoke of a furnace. That is the soul of Hatto, returning to the scene of his frightful ending.

The *Maut* or toll levied where the Mouse Tower guarded the entrance to the safe channel past the reefs of the Binger Loch was in fact the mainstay of the finances of the see of Mainz. Originally the excuse for tolls had been that the money would be used to keep the channel and towpath in order, and for the same reason the electors of Cologne, Trier and the Palatinate were also empowered to collect dues. But, like Britain's Road Fund, the tax very quickly came to be regarded merely as a useful source of revenue.

The tower was admirably situated, for the only way to avoid the toll was to choose a course which led to almost certain destruction on the rocks. Even within the channel the rapids were always dangerous, but that did not mean that travellers necessarily avoided them. In some respects one was safer on the water than travelling a narrow track by the riverside. Boniface shot the Bingen rapids on his fateful voyage from Mainz to the land of the rough Frisians. Louis the Pious tossed down them on his way to Koblenz. It was not until 1720 that the first improvements were undertaken by a Frankfurt firm of contractors, who widened the narrow navigation gap to 45 feet at the surface so that their own rafts could pass down. A century later the Prussian engineers dynamited some more of the rocks, but it was only in the 1890s that the reefs were carefully blown up to provide two separate fairways, each

B

one hundred yards broad. This was the condition in which the Binger Loch (or Gap) still remained as the *Thames Commodore* came panting upstream to tackle it herself and move out into the broader, tranquil waters above. And in so doing she passed close beside a cross set in a rock a little way from the port or right bank of the river. This unexpected mark is not an aid to navigation but marks the place where a small casket was cemented into a hole in the stone in order to carry out part of the wishes expressed in the will of Niclas Vogt, a writer who loved the Rhine above all else, a desire that after his death the great stream might still flow over his heart. The rest of the poet was buried further upstream in the chapel of the Johannisberg where, I suppose, the tomb was more likely to be submerged by wine than by mere water.

Schiff leut sin brave leut – boating men are good men. Naturally I agree with this old saying of the Rhineland. Besides, a ship is no place for a crook or misanthrope. But the saying implied something more than mere unviciousness and included a degree of piety which came naturally to the skipper who had to steer his ship – and his family and all his worldly wealth – through swift and often dangerous waters. It was rare for a captain in times gone by to start a fresh voyage without having the priest or pastor come down to the ship to invoke a blessing upon it, and every ship would have in addition to its dog or cat and canary a statue of St Nicholas of Myra (patron of bargemen) or of St John Nepomuk, one who was supposed specially to watch over those in danger of falling into mill-races or off bridges. One or the other is still to be seen on many a bridge in Europe, and St Nicholas can yet be found set on the rocks beside what used to be particularly dangerous passages. At these the skipper would also light dedicated candles to see him through, but nowadays there is a tendency to rely more upon diesel than the deity.

Yet barge-skippers are not necessarily men to lie down under a sense of injustice, as is shown by the extraordinary events which once occurred in the town of Bingen, which lies just above the rapids and on the starboard side. Bingen is nowadays a peaceable and not very beautiful town, a place of transhipment and the supply port for the United States Air Forces. Like every other place along the Rhine it has known sieges and sackings, but in 1324 it had a private disturbance without the aid of any invader from outside. A dog – and I do not know what kind of dog, but merely that it belonged to a barge as so many maladjusted or psychopathic dogs do today – a dog jumped ashore, walked into the main street and snicked a joint of meat from one of the stalls in the market. The good butcher snatched up a broom or a cudgel or some other weapon that lay to hand, and running after the dog he gave it a good thrashing. Whereupon the bargemaster in turn took up a broom or a cudgel or some equally serviceable weapon and beat the butcher. The forces of law and order were invoked, and the magistrates found the butcher guilty of assaulting the dog, and sent him to prison. I think this was surely unjust, and I cannot blame the members of the Worshipful Guild of Butchers if they rushed the gaol and retrieved their unfortunate fellow-member. Yet this goaded the united bargemen to action, and soon Bingen was torn between the pro-butcher and the pro-skipper elements who set about each other so violently that shops were wrecked, men were slain in the streets and others injured. It was now time for the forces of law and order to make themselves felt a second time. Peace was quickly restored by the simple expedient of executing the ring-leaders on either side and bringing out the chopper and block to cut off the hands of any others who were implicated. As for the dog, he seems to have been forgotten. Probably he was enjoying the joint of beef on the fore-deck of his ship.

A more genial and pleasant tale of Bingen concerns the town council, at a meeting of which the twenty-one elected representatives discussed some unusually weighty matter. When they were agreed upon a resolution the Mayor decided to write it down so that it might be recorded in proper form. However, he had left his pencil behind, and so he asked that one of the councillors would lend him one. All felt in their pockets, but not one of the members could produce a writing implement.

'In that case, gentlemen, we'll conclude our session with a couple of bottles,' said the mayor. 'Has anybody a corkscrew?'

Twenty-one corkscrews were immediately whipped out of the councillors' pockets. From which time forward a corkscrew has been known in the Rheingau as a 'Bingen pencil'.

II

*Rüdesheim – Charlemagne and the vines – Brömser the
hard-headed – Germania the thirty-tonner – friend of the
hawks – Rüdesheim brandy – buried wine – tasting across a
century – the Rhine in winter – Ingelheim and the
Emperor's daughter – the nun of Oestrich*

B INGEN is famous for its wine. It also has a harbour and a
useful quayside in the river from which the ferries and trip-
boats run ceaselessly to Assmannshausen downstream and
Rüdesheim above. At the edge of the town the shallow little Nahe
runs into the Rhine from its own pleasant valley of vineyard slopes,
but Bingen is a little too large and somewhat too industrial for my
liking. Besides, the harbour cannot compare with the quiet one
tucked away behind the blackberry thickets at the upstream side
of Rüdesheim, a tree-edged lagoon which provides a home only
for moorhens, water police-boats, a survey vessel and a cluster of
rusty work-boats. A mile of leaf-shaded promenade along the river
bank separates this dreamy little port from the bustle of the town
and the jetties where the large passenger vessels are disembarking
another thousand visitors to taste the Rüdesheim wines.

The waterfront of Rüdesheim is pleasantly stately, and the
hotels beloved of the English grand tour travellers still have an air
of superiority, hardly deigning to notice the railway which so
unfortunately thunders past them on the other side of the riverside
road. A little further back stands the amorphous and rather ugly
ruin of the Brömserburg, now a museum with a fine collection of
ancient wine-presses, pruning-knives and drinking glasses from
Roman times onwards. Certainly the Romans had plenty of
vineyards in the Rheingau, even if they may not necessarily have
developed the slopes at the back of Rüdesheim itself. Locally it is
asserted that it was Charlemagne who was responsible for
Rüdesheim's rise to fame as a wine village. He often resided at

22

In the Rheingau

Ingelheim, a little further upstream on the other shore, and as he froze in the winter wind which drove the snow around his quarters he noticed that the hill across the river faced south and was free of snow, basking instead in the winter sunshine. As this happened regularly it occurred to the great Emperor that the slope would be an excellent one for viticulture, and he despatched riders to Orleans to fetch some stocks. Sure enough, the vines flourished, and three years later the first grapes were pressed. The vintage proved an excellent one, as have hundreds of others in the succeeding eleven centuries. Rüdesheimers used also to claim that whenever a year was to be a good one for its wine the Emperor would rise from his tomb in Aachen and transport himself to Rüdesheim, where he would stride up and down the river bank blessing the vines which had originally been established there at his command.

The solid and rather featureless remains of the Brömserburg recall the very human story of Engelhard Brömser, a stubborn but upright man whose lot it was to live at the time when Bernard of Clairvaux was stumping Western Europe to raise a force for a determined attempt to wrest Jerusalem from the dreadful Saracens.

Every man of honour or money or property was obliged to swell the ranks of the crusaders, and no doubt most of them did so very willingly. Yet in the case of Brömser the anticipation of slaughtering the infidel was slightly dulled by his having to leave behind him his only child, the fair Mechthild whose mother had recently died. After much deliberation he decided to place her in the care of his friend and neighbour at Castle Falkenstein, and then he rode away to Regensburg on the Danube to join the seventy thousand other mounted knights who were massing for the campaign.

After much savage fighting beneath the hot sun of the Middle East, Brömser of Rüdesheim was captured alive, and as a prisoner of war he became a slave. In his despair he made the usual vows to encourage the Almighty to arrange his deliverance, promising that he would build at Rüdesheim a church to the Virgin and the Apostle James the Elder, and also a chapel to recall the agony on the Mount of Olives. He repeated these vows over and over again, then as a final bait he added that he would place his only daughter Mechthild in a convent.

Shortly afterwards, a new invading wave of European knights bore down upon the Holy Land. Quickly the Saracens drove their prisoner slaves far into the interior, but in the confusion Brömser escaped and hid in a disused sepulchre until the fresh force of crusaders had overrun his place of hiding. Free at last, he did not hasten home to the Rhineland until he had again fought the Saracens in bloody contests, and it was some years before he came riding across the low hills of the Rheingau to his castle at the entrance to the river gorge, and to his own daughter Mechthild. At once he gave a banquet to all his friends and neighbours, and in his after dinner speech he told them of his stirring adventures at the hands of the infidel, of his vows, and how he now had no thought but to put them into practice at once. There was to be a church for Rüdesheim, a chapel also, and he had promised his daughter to a convent.

The shriek with which Mechthild greeted this last item caused a chill to fall over the company. At once the young Falkenstein stepped forward, said that he and Mechthild had been in love for years, were engaged, and intended to marry at the earliest possible moment. He was sorry, but that last bit of his host's vows would not, could not be fulfilled.

Brömser was silent for a moment. In his anxiety to be free he had never even considered that his daughter was growing up and might have developed a will of her own. But he was an obstinate man, and soon he was declaring to the company that no Brömser had ever broken his vows, least of all to the Almighty, and as last of the line he certainly was not going to do so. To which his daughter replied that precisely the same went for her. She had promised to marry the young Falkenstein and she did not wish to be the first Brömser girl to break her word. As for the convent, her father could keep it. And she swept out of the room, followed by the Falkensteins and their friends.

For two days the obstinate man argued with his equally obdurate daughter. Neither would move from their intentions. In the third night an ingenious idea came to Brömser. He would agree to the engagement in principle and then travel to Rome to ask the Pope to annul the part of his vow which related to putting his dear Mechthild into a convent. It might cost a little – such favours were rarely obtained free – but the Pope would surely agree to the request of a stalwart and faithful crusader. Then the wedding could take place, and everyone would be happy. Even he himself.

Brömser jumped out of bed and sent a servant to fetch Mechthild. But the maid came back and reported that the daughter of the house was not in her room. Her bed had not been slept in.

Those confounded Falkensteins, Brömser thought. Unable to get Mechthild by fair means they had obviously contrived to take her by stealth. Girding on his sword he galloped off to Castle Falkenstein and hammered furiously on the door. But the Falkensteins were so genuinely surprised that they quickly convinced him that they knew nothing of Mechthild's disappearance, and they roused their own men to join in the search. No trace of Mechthild was found. It was two days later that her body was washed up on the shore below Assmannshausen.

How Mechthild had come to be drowned was never known. It might have been an accident, but I doubt it – just as in his heart Brömser doubted it, too. The girl was just one more victim of the perennial problem that nearly every family has to face. Nowadays we call it the Generation Gap. In the middle ages – for it was in 1147 that Brömser rode off to the Crusade – it may have gone by some other name, but then as now it was the simple clash of inflexible wills which led to a tragedy that none could undo.

Brömser built his church, and his chapel too. And every day the villagers would see the old man, grey and broken, ride or walk from the Brömserburg to pray there for the soul of his daughter. And, I hope, for forgiveness.

Rüdesheim is not everybody's choice. Not everybody's but very nearly so, to judge from the scores of thousands of visitors from Britain and the Netherlands who are brought there on package tours. A representative of the place told me how many visitors spent the night in the village during the year, and though I rarely remember such statistics I know it was a very large number indeed. More than three million, if I recollect rightly, and when one considers that nearly all of them arrive during the brief summer months one can see that Rüdesheim is hardly the place in which to seek solitude. Its few streets are thronged with the English indulging their favourite interest of looking in the shop windows, laboriously calculating the prices into sterling, and then deciding that a packet of cigarettes, or a bottle of beer, a jar of mustard or a pair of socks is either a tremendous bargain because it is a few pence cheaper or outrageously expensive because it is slightly dearer than its counterpart in Britain.

The village is famous for its Drosselgasse (Thrush Alley), a passage lined from end to end with pubs and wine-bars, some of which are very much better than one would expect. There is music and dancing, mostly of a rather old-fashioned kind because on the whole it is the tired middle-aged English and the solid retired Dutch or Scandinavians who come there to drink the wine. Over all the din the little carillon on the Schloss inn just makes itself heard as several times each day it sends the melody of the Lorelei or some other folk tune to tinkle away pleasantly over the grey slated roofs. And up at the back of the town there is a cable-lift to the top of the Niederwald, where stands the truly astounding figure of Germania.

'The visitor will hardly waste his time in going up the cogwheel railway to see the Denkmal of Germania above Rüdesheim', wrote

Baring Gould. 'From a distance it looks like a shattered windmill. The absurdity of putting a huge elaborate piece of sculpture halfway up a mountain could hardly be surpassed.' But the fact remains that the Kaisers often did just that, and in the case of the Niederwald memorial there were no half measures.

Hurra, du stolzes schönes Weib, Hurra, Germania! Wie kühn mit vorgebeugtem Leib am Rheine stehst du da!

Proud she certainly is, but I am not so sure that Ferdinard Freiligrath was correct when he described her as beautiful, though it is perhaps difficult to judge the charm of a lady of such unusual size. For the figure of Germania is huge. She weighs 30 tons; and I hope it is not immodest to say that she measures just over 23 feet round the hips. She is not quite so spiky and masculine as the Germania on the old pre-1914 German stamps, who was modelled on Anna von Strantz-Führing, an actress of some renown and not the all-in wrestler one might have thought from her portrait. The postal Germania shared with the Marianne of France a curious embattled sexlessness, but the Germania of the Niederwald monument is definitely feminine, although in a rather militant suffragette way. It is surprising to discover that she was in fact modelled from a Bad Ems bath attendant who was renowned for her beauty; but maybe even one of Rüdesheim's graceful wine queens might appear rather overpowering if blown up to such dimensions.

Kaiser William I unveiled the mighty Watch-on-the-Rhine memorial, and in so doing he had a surprisingly near escape, though probably the 30-ton Germania was in fact too heavy to have been toppled by the bottle of nitro-glycerine carefully buried beside it by two anarchists. Leading to the flask was a buried fuse-cord with only the tip protruding from the ground, and the plotters had merely to set this alight and the fuse would burn swiftly to its destination. And that would be the end of the Hohenzollerns.

Or so they thought, but unfortunately for the anarchist cause the night before the opening was one of incessant rain. Their Excellencies and the other important personages took their seats, and still the police had not so much as noticed any interference with the ground where the fuse had been laid. One of the men lit a cigar and touched the end of the cord. Nothing happened. He

B2

puffed to a red heat and tried again, but in vain. The fuse was too wet to light. Still the police were unaware of any plot, and they remained so until fifteen months later, when the two men were foolish enough to try and claim their travelling expenses at a workers' meeting in Elberfeld. A police agent noted what they said, and one of the men was executed for treason; the other, being then only twenty years of age, received a life sentence. And in Germany a lifer meant a lifer.

Swinging from pylon to pylon in the little two-seater carriage of the cable-lift one is swiftly removed from the noisy bustle of Rüdesheim to look down upon the peaceful vineyards, on the ruins of the Brömserburg, and the wide expanse of river above the gorge. Every hour during the summer the lift carries several thousands to the hill top and hundreds more arrive by coach and car. Just occasionally some old-fashioned German may even arrive on foot. Yet few stray beyond the terrace from which they can stare up with a cricked neck at the immense display of the life-sized Prussian general staff cast in bronze around Germania's base, and the pathways which run through the thickets over towards Assmannshausen are deserted. Yet as a boatman I found myself irresistibly drawn to the little ruined tower above the Ehrenfels, from where I could look right down upon the actual passage between the rocks and see the ships labouring through the gap which the *Thames Commodore* had just passed. It is as splendid a sight as the Rhine has to offer, and it is one reserved mainly for the sun-tanned vinedressers who patiently hoe the steep upper slopes or work at whatever is next on the list of demands made by the vine – binding and tying-in, spraying for pests, or carefully pulling away those leaves which may rob a bunch of grapes of the vital sunshine of September.

In the woodland above the Germania memorial I came to where a hawker had his establishment, not an itinerant vendor but a man who looks after hawks. Goshawks and falcons, a peregrine and an eagle, a harrier or two, a dapper little kestrel and a surly-looking buzzard, the birds were sitting on their low perches, each with a thong attached to one leg. They were casualties, birds shot by hunters and left disabled with a broken wing, nestlings left to die when sportsmen had killed their parent on the nest, birds with legs broken in snares or bodies torn by barbed wire when raiding a hen-run. It was a strange but kindly occupation, I thought, to act the Samaritan to these robbers among the birds, and I wondered how he came by the patients he was nursing.

'Nature-lovers bring them,' he said. 'Or somebody may telephone and say there is a hawk caught in netting or a trap. Sometimes I fetch them in myself, but usually there is a sensible man in the nearby village who can take the bird without himself being injured or damaging the invalid even more. Yes, I have a pleasant little colony of these birds of prey. People pay to see them, but that doesn't cover the cost. Hawks are expensive on food, you know, when they can't hunt for themselves.'

His real enemies were the *Halbstarke*, the 'half-strongs' as the Germans so succintly term their vandals. A bird of prey firmly attached to a lead and unable to escape was too much of a temptation for the half-strongs. Only a week before, he said, some lads had come up in the evening and flung stones at a tethered buzzard which was recovering from a broken wing. One stone smashed a leg, another stunned the bird – and that, he thought, was fortunate, for the youths probably assumed they had killed it and ran off. No, there was no point in telling the police. The magistrates would merely give the young brigands a pious lecture and send them off to smash up something else.

'Ah, Germany, Germany,' he sighed. 'To what depths you have sunk when lads can come up to my enclosure in broad daylight and attack the birds, defying me to retaliate because I should get a prison sentence for assaulting them if I did. It would not be like that in Britain.'

So, to cheer him up, I had to tell him of my old friend Frank Barker who kept the Six Hills Nursery at Stevenage. It was, I suppose, as good an alpine nursery as one could have found anywhere. Every year Frank would go off, rucksack on back, and explore the Carpathians, the Alpes Maritimes or some other mountain fastness, bringing back many choice discoveries to pot up and propagate. For years I contributed a small sum to this venture and so did others. Months later we had our reward in the form of a parcel of exciting little plants, new to the catalogue.

One night two young half-strongs broke in, took all the pots of prize specimens which Frank had made ready for the Chelsea show, and used them as missiles to smash the greenhouses. Afterwards the place looked as though it had been severely hit in an air-raid, but the noise involved in breaking several thousand square feet of glass panes was not inconsiderable, and a neighbour ran out and caught the lads. At Stevenage juvenile court they were asked whether they had in fact caused the destruction; and having actually been caught in the act they admitted that they had. Frank told me that the bench then called in the parents and congratulated them on having brought up their boys to tell the truth. The lads left the court in honour and glory. As for Frank Barker he just went out of business. The six hillocks which gave their name to the nursery were bulldozed out of the way, and a soulless piece of Stevenage New Town was raised over the site. I never bought any more alpines, even elsewhere. Somehow I had lost heart.

The mere name of Rüdesheim conjures up wine – good, bad and indifferent. The town is also so much the home of German brandy that half the total export comes from there. Personally I do not particularly like brandy, but I make an exception in the case of Asbach Uralt, which tastes pleasant to my palate and somehow lacks the overtones of microscope slides which seem to haunt so many brands. No doubt this is the fault of my upbringing, in which alcohol was something in which one dipped the glass-mounted microtome slices before finishing them off with Canada balsam and a glass cover-slip. I liked the clean, crisp, dehydrating smell of the alcohol jars, but ever since the time when I worked in a laboratory I have never been able really to enjoy spirits. They are reagents, and that is that. However, the Asbachs (and they are not paying me to say so) have succeeded where others have failed and I can drink their stuff without looking for a window through which to tip it when my host is not looking; and that is why I phoned them from Oberwesel and asked if the *Thames Commodore*'s crew might see the works.

Brandy, *Brandtwein*, or burnt wine, was originally made for medicinal use only, and it is still kept for such specialised purposes in the *Thames Commodore*'s medicine chest. Ancient decrees reserved it to apothecaries and prescribed suitable punishments for innkeepers who actually sold it as a drink. At least, that was the case in Germany. But in the sixteenth century some of the distillers in the Low Countries fled from the tyranny of the Spaniards and began to turn their hand to 'burning' wine instead of grain, and soon they were showing the Germans how to do it.

There is really very little to see in a brandy factory. At one end are the huge copper stills, at the other the bottling machine. I am sure it is really much more complicated than that, but we were shown round by a grammar-school lad from the North of England who was acting as guide for a holiday job and knew what he had learned to say but otherwise understood little about the mysteries. Yet there was something awe-inspiring about the great vats, the stacks of little 'barriques' of Limousin oak in which the distillate ripened and acquired its bouquet – caused, no doubt by formation of esters and also by absorption from the wood itself. One could admire the precision of the machine which put the flasks in the cartons, and realise that somewhere behind the scenes there was a blender who could 'marry' the distillates of a number of different years so that whatever the weather and the vintage of the Rhine-land wines Asbach Uralt would eternally taste precisely the same. In any one country, I should add, for Asbach Uralt in Belgium and Mexico, the Lesser Antilles and Britain are not identical. Governments must always interfere, just to keep their customs clerks occupied, so the percentage of alcohol has to be varied from one country to the next.

Our other call was at the Adlerturm cellars, where the crew was received by experts highly scientific who knew all about trace elements and aromatic essences. Yet in spite of this, there was something curiously eerie about the place and after a while I realised that it was because we were sipping our excellent samples of wine among the tombs. Certainly there were tuns, finely carved and stately in the flickering candle-light, but in the walls and all along the floor of this vintners' crypt there were graves in which bottles and perhaps also the previous directors of the establishment were buried. Very, very rarely there would be an exhumation. The heavy stone slab over a grave would be raised and a bottle of wine carefully taken out and held up before a very select audience of whom only the most illustrious few might be allowed to sample it.

This wine would be a *Trockenbeerenauslese*, the origin of which was the result of a fortunate accident of ecclesiastical hegemony.

On the lands of the famous Johannisberg monastery a short way upstream of Rüdesheim, the grapes might formerly not be gathered until permission was received from the Abbot of Fulda, but the cathedral city of Fulda was separated by many leagues of forest from its Rheingau vineyards, and one year the message or permit was delayed. Perhaps the good abbot merely forgot to send the licence at the proper time, or maybe his messenger was held up by wolves, Rhine maidens and other natural causes. The actual reason for the delay is buried in medieval mists, and all that is certain is that the man arrived weeks later than usual. Meanwhile the good people of the Rheingau had not dared to harvest a single bunch of grapes on the abbatial hillside and so risk the temporal wrath of their spiritual overlord.

When at last the permission came, starlings, mildew, foxes, blight and hail had removed much of the crop. All that remained were some shrivelled grapes, dark and withered. This worthless-looking fruit was gathered and pressed, and from it came the first barrel of *Trockenbeerenauslese*, or dry-berry-selection. To the general surprise the wine was superb. Nowadays this speciality is made deliberately. In good vintage years the best trusses will be left to ripen in the autumn sun until the first frosts of early winter have begun to sparkle on the shaly slopes, and if the year is one of those rare superlative seasons for the Riesling grape, then this late wine will also be exceptional.

The directors of Adlerturm will consider the vintage of the year with all the seriousness of medieval judges. If the year is good enough for a *Trockenbeerenauslese* then three bottles of it will share with their forebears the strange fate of being solemnly buried alive. An expert taster writes a scientific epitaph, a detailed description of the savour, bouquet, and feel of the wine in such terms that long after he is dead another taster will be able from the surviving account of the wine to imagine in detail just what it was like in every way in the days of its first youth.

Down in the cellar a heavy tombstone will be carefully raised. Already there are other bottles interred in the grave, representatives of other great wines in years gone by. The three newcomers are carefully laid to rest, the stone reset and sealed. Thirty years will pass before a single bottle is exhumed for the ritual of a second tasting. Twenty years further ahead another bottle will be taken up. Not until a century after the burial will the last of the three be opened in the flickering light of the candles ranged down the gangway between the two rows of dark, red-rimmed casks of only slightly less noble wines. The latter-day taster has before him the notes of his three predecessors across the years, partly subjective but also highly biochemical and analytical, and he makes an elaborate comparison.

This century old wine from the shrivelled grapes of a forgotten generation may taste like vinegar. Certainly the Rüdesheimer of 1653 still in the possession of the City of Bremen is said to have such a taste that one should pity the very important drinking personages allowed the rare honour of sipping it. But as the techniques of vintner and cellarman improve, there is hope that the storage life may be extended, so there is much sound sense and a spirit of scientific enquiry behind the ritual disinterment in the Adlerturm cellars.

As only the rarest years are worthy of entombment, the un-buryings are very uncommon events, but every opening of a vault is a great moment for the taster and the men of the cellar. Only one bottle will be withdrawn, whereas close beside the tombstones I noticed that the carved end of a barrel recorded the filling of the twenty-nine millionth bottle to come from this one Rüdesheim firm alone. All those millions may have been good, tasty, branded wines, or just a simple honest Riesling fit for a pleasant evening of genial company; but they would certainly not have been in the same snob and summit class as the almost holy *Trockenbeerenauslese* shut away in the funereal vault beneath our feet.

As no vault of treasured wine was to be opened for a year or more, the *Thames Commodore* was straining at her mooring lines to remind us that she wanted to be off. Down past the water police jetty she skirted the ruins of what once had been a railway bridge and took a deep breath to blow a single long drawn out hoot followed by two short ones, to warn any passing ships that she intended to shoot out of the harbour entrance, spin on the eddy and point her nose upstream. The next number-board on the bank told her that she was now at kilometre 525, measured from the town bridge in Konstanz. At Rotterdam the number had been 1002, and although the upper reaches of the river were not navigable she still had a long journey ahead of her before she reached the limit of navigation at Km 149.

This was a summer voyage, and the Rhine is of course a river for summer visitors. Few see it in its winter-dress, when the vines are bare, the ground white with frost, and the villages of vintners quietly asleep beneath the haze of aromatic smoke as the super-annuated vine-stocks perform their last service in heating the great tiled stoves in a thousand parlours. Only the bargemen then frequent the river, and perhaps it was an inherent streak of eccentricity which made my wife and myself resolve on another occasion to join them and voyage up the stream at a time when all good yachtsmen are laid up at home – and missing a wealth of experience. It was just eight days before Christmas that we went aboard in the harbour at Bingen, a mile above the Mouse Tower.

I had taken the boat to Bingen single-handed in October, running her down the Main from Bavaria in the golden autumn days when, through the binoculars, I could watch the wine-maidens busily plucking the clusters of grapes and tipping them into the tall conical hods of wood which the older men carried on their backs. Then, there had been luncheon parties of vine-dressers on the terraced slopes, with ham and sausage and bottles of the last year's wine. Now the valley was changed. We arrived by the Rüdesheim ferry in such a snowstorm that even the hardy old watermen who handled the lines took shelter in the saloon warmed by the engine.

Bingen's harbour was deserted except for a laid-up steamer and a group of those water-authority muck-boats without which no German creek or inlet would be complete. At the further end the yacht club float lay detached from the shore, its drawbridge and barbed wire sparkling with ice, its pleasant summer restaurant closed and shuttered. Against the pontoon the *Thames Commodore* lay alone. She looked in good shape, though the snow on her deck gave her an appearance of white-haired old age. We opened her up, refilled the cooling systems of her motors, which I had fortunately been wise enough to drain, and like her old self she started immediately. Soon we were under-way, heading for Bingen town quay in a flurry of snow but with a good warm smell drifting back from the cowl of her stove.

The harbour of Bingen is used all the year round by a motor-ferry which carries the road traffic across the stream – for there is not a single bridge across the Rhine between Schierstein, just below Mainz, and Koblenz at the lower end of the long and winding gorge. Observing that the ship was not lying at her Bingen station I knew that she must be either at the further shore or making a crossing, and as the outer mole of the harbour was high enough to hide anything which might be about to come in, I thought it prudent to give the three long blasts and two short ones which the Rhine regulations demanded. The *Thames Commodore* cleared her throat and bellowed splendidly. As there was no answer I ran her to clip the point, just below the shoal which always extends downstream of such a disturber of the flow.

At that moment the ferry came round the corner on the wrong side, her masts a blaze of lights, the scores of motorists peering through their misty car windows. Probably her skipper had never known a ship put out of Bingen in the dark, and certainly not in mid-winter, and it unnerved him. We dodged his ship easily enough, but he put on his double-magnifying loud-speaker and shouted at us.

'One should give a signal when leaving the harbour!' he yelled in a megawatt voice.

Unfortunately I had not yet put back the batteries in our own shouting-down equipment. Otherwise I should have replied reasonably enough, 'Turn off your radio, open the window, and listen. And incidentally, one should also give a signal when entering the harbour. *Gute Nacht!*'

Bingen's river quay is one of the few places on the Rhine where one can make fast alongside for the night without being pounded to pieces. This is because the traffic is almost stilled at dusk, and the upcoming ships are in any case on the further side of the stream half a mile distant, their wash being swept away by the force of the current. Down-goers run close past the Bingen shore, but as they are about to anchor or are waiting for the signal from the Mouse Tower they are more drifting than running. Only the

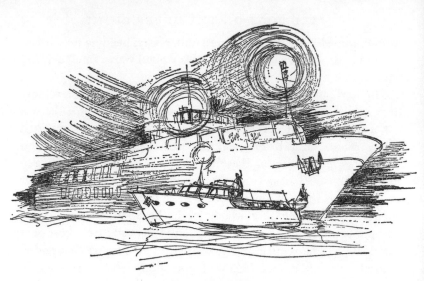

Bingen by night

mechanical chisels are active all through the night, but one becomes so accustomed to the sound of grabs and dredgers and pile drivers that one can sleep undisturbed through a noise of machinery which would make any sensible hotel guest pack up and leave.

The chisels were chiselling all round the clock, and maybe on Christmas Day also. All across the river they were hard at work, their anchor buoys winking, their boilers hissing, and the frosty air carrying a faint sound of mixed calls and orders blending with the tug-a-ti tug-a-ti of their small attendant tugs. They were preparing for the great day, still a few years ahead, when the famous rapids at the Binger Loch would be gone for ever – a sad day, I thought, for much of romance and thrill for shippers would disappear when the charges of dynamite were touched off which would finally demolish the formidable reefs and convert them into dust and shingle.

The *Loch* of Bingen has nothing to do with a loch of the Scots. *Loch* is merely the German for hole, and that is precisely what the Binger Loch is – a hole in an otherwise continuous barrier of reef which holds up the water so that it runs through the gap at a very impressive rate indeed. In its present form the Loch is a larger hole than it once used to be, and a monument on the right bank reminds any mariner who dares to let his glance wander from the water ahead that the gap was widened under an enterprising Kaiser and some of the dynamited stone was used for the memorial.

To blow up the whole reef would of course make navigation easier at that point, but it would also remove the rim which holds back the water in the reach immediately above. Clearing away the barrier would drop the water by six feet or more, and some effect would be measurable as far up the river as Mainz. That was why the steam chisels and grabs were working all night upon the rocky bed of the river, carving it away lump by lump until a broad channel would be chopped in the river floor, deep enough still to be navigable when the reef itself should be removed.

Our first winter morning dawned clear. The downfall of the previous night lay matted on our deck and traced a white trim to the mooring lines which held the *Thames Commodore* against the wall. A sound of heavy motors filled the air as the barges ahead of us set off up river, and when we had shovelled the snow overboard we followed, crossing the stream below the steam chisels to cut close inshore past Rüdesheim. The lower slopes lay white and bleak but the tops of the hills were hidden in the clouds. Somewhere above us and a little astern the huge, ponderous and warlike amazon Germania was shrouded in the drifting mist, but further ahead the famous Johannisberg monastery was just visible at the cloud base, watching proudly over the immense wealth of its vineyards. The broad reach – for here the river is nearly one mile wide – can never have looked more splendid.

Johannisberg stands well back as though to have the better view across the vineyard slope from which the Erntebringer and other famous vintages are culled. The building is mellowed and peaceful, but what began as a Benedictine monastery had many adventures before it was seized by Napoleon and given to his Marshal, Kellermann. In 1815 it passed to the victorious Allies and was given to the Emperor of Austria, who very sensibly passed it on to Count von Metternich upon the single condition that he was to hand over to the Austrian crown one tenth of the total wine production in every year. As one's eye sweeps over the wide expanse of some of the best vineyard country in the world one can see that the Emperor was no fool. The institution has immense cellars and it is almost unnecessary to add that Goethe had a drink in them – probably the day before or after he had several more at the first Festival of St Roch when the new Rochus Kapelle was opened on the hillside across the river to replace an earlier one destroyed by artillery in the Napoleonic turmoil.

Next upstream of the chapel of St Roch on the starboard hand is the hamlet of Kempten, an insignificant place which is said to have been the scene of a vital decision in the days when Charlemagne had a favourite residence there to which he could escape from his court of Ingelheim, further up the river. He happened to be there with his empress Hildegard and their three boys, Pepin, Carl and Ludwig, when the youngsters began to pester their parents about which of them was to take over the empire when their father died. Charlemagne grew angry with them, but his wife whispered in his ear that she had an idea for solving the problem. Knowing her to be a woman of considerable sense, the Emperor nodded his agreement to whatever she might propose.

Hildegard, the story goes, sent the boys up to the village to buy themselves each a cock for a cock-fight, and soon a three-cornered contest was being fought out in the yard before a crowd of village children and royal attendants. For more than an hour the birds flew at each other with sharp beaks and the deadly barbs attached to their legs, until at last only one survived.

The winning bird was that of Ludwig, the youngest of the brothers; and however fictional the tale of the Kempten cock-fight may be, it was indeed the youngest of the three sons who succeeded to the imperial title. However, he only did so because both his brothers had already died.

I have already mentioned that the observation that the slopes on the Rüdesheim side were warmer is attributed to Charlemagne when he was in residence on the further shore, at Ingelheim. His residence is reputed to have been no mean affair, and though no doubt its dimensions have been multiplied during the frequent retelling of its wonders, the palace is said to have been eight years in the building and to have had one hundred pillars of white marble which had been dragged over the Alps from the quarries at Ravenna – though only one fragment of a single column now remains. The building contained a wealth of mosaic and carving and must indeed have been the wonder of the Carolingian world, and it received its name because of a curious adventure which Charlemagne had during his first night there, when he was visited by an angel who brought the unusual message that the Holy Roman Emperor was to prove to the Almighty his unswerving loyalty by getting out of bed and indulging in a little burgling. And when the Emperor sat up in bed and objected that he really could not be expected to believe that God would wish him to do anything so improper, the angel told him sharply that his life depended upon it. Either he would go stealing or he would die; and as unfortunately there was not even standing room in Paradise at the moment, and little chance even of being wait-listed, death would not be advisable just yet.

So Charlemagne went out on a night prowl, and being fair-minded he decided to rob a certain Count Harderich, a notorious brigand and oppressor. He managed to break in unheeded but his movements roused the count's horse, which became restive in its stall. Wakened by the noise Harderich lit a lamp and searched the hall, while Charlemagne hid trembling behind a curtain, but finding nothing the count retired to bed again and started discussing with his wife the details of a plan they had hatched for attacking Charlemagne's new palace on the following night before it was properly defended, and murdering the Emperor in his bed.

Stealing Harderich's own horse the Emperor quickly returned home and when on the following day Harderich and his gang arrived at the Rhine they were met by Charlemagne and a powerful force. As soon as the count saw his own steed with Charlemagne in the saddle he realised that the plot had been overheard. To fight was useless, so Harderich gave himself up and threw himself upon the Emperor's mercy. Of this commodity there was little to be had, however. Charlemagne wisely had him hanged from the nearest oak-tree before returning home for dinner and formally naming his palace, Engelheim (or Ingelheim) in memory of the angel who had brought him the strange request which had indeed turned out to be a matter of life or death.

It was at Ingelheim, on a night when the snow lay thick upon the ground, that Charlemagne looked out of his chamber window and started violently at the sight that met his eyes. There in the courtyard below him was his own daughter Emma, stealing across the open space and carrying on her back a burden which the Emperor recognised to be none other than his secretary, Einhard, or Eginhard. In this way she hoped to avoid the tell-tale footsteps leading from her apartment.

Charlemagne was enraged, although, as Dr Ruland so succintly puts it 'the Great Emperor ought to have known what would be the consequence of allowing the young scholar to enjoy the society of his dark-eyed passionate daughter'. He had the lovers seized and conveyed to Dausenau on the River Lahn where they were imprisoned in the tower which still stands, even if it leans so much that it has had to be shortened for safety. It is pleasant to know that the Emperor so admired their faithfulness to each other in face of captivity that he eventually relented and let them marry. Einhard later wrote the life of Charlemagne, but somehow he omitted to record the incident on the snowy night at Ingelheim. It remained for another and later writer, the Chronicler of Lorsch, to set it down to delight future generations.

Across the stream from Ingelheim the snow was lying on the clustered roofs of Oestrich, and we could not chug past the place without recalling the dreadful tale of the nun who fell in love with a young nobleman,

> *who lowly kneeling swore*
> *to free her from her prison's fangs*
> *and love her evermore.*

Of course he soon tired of her and threw her over for another, and another, and many many more after that. But his jilted sweetheart was no soft conventual lily. She hired a band of professional murderers to pay him off. The details I must leave to Joseph Snowe:

> *They sought and slew him; many a blade*
> *in his black heart was buried;*
> *and his dark soul in sulphur-reek*
> *to hell's drear regions hurried.*
> *Wild wailed it on its downward way,*
> *whilst watched it fiends so fell;*
> *and then his gory corpse laid they*
> *with worms for aye to dwell.*

Even that was not the end, for the nun herself hurried by night
to the churchyard

> *and dragged her dripping lover's corpse*
> *without into the porch,*
> *then tore his base heart from its breast;*
> *and then, his scorn to pay,*
> *down flung it with a laugh unblest,*
> *and trode it into clay.*

One could hardly do such a thing without becoming doomed and
damned and converted into a ghost. Such, according to Snowe,
was indeed the poor girl's fate, and she certainly sounds like the
kind of spectre one would not wish to meet unless fortified with
some of the very best wine Oestrich can provide. For, according to
that excellent author,

> *Her hollow, hideous eyes then flash*
> *a fire full fierce but pale;*
> *like brimstone flame they glint and gleam*
> *through her thick white veil.*
> *Then on that mangled heart these eyes*
> *she sets with horrid mirth;*
> *then flings it thrice towards the skies,*
> *then casts it on the earth;*
> *and then those awful orbs she rolls*
> *which gleam with hell's own fire;*
> *and shakes her veil while blood-gouts fall,*
> *then treads that heart to mire.*

No, nuns were not always soft, self-effacing, forgiving creatures
who nursed a secret sorrow in silence.

III

*Steam on the Rhine – the Central Commission – the river to
Mainz – Schierstein and the old flame – riparian rivalries –
Mainz, city of the past – cartwheels of Willegis – troubadour
of the women – the Virgin's shoe – by fog to Worms*

VOYAGING up the wintry river and dodging the ice-floes
carried down from the quieter waters of the River Main the
thought occurred to me that since I first saw the Rhine more than
thirty years earlier a great change had come over the river. Steam
had become extinct.

After the centuries of horse-hauling from the bank the Industrial
Revolution brought steam to the Rhine, and with it the beginnings
of a new way of life for ships and shipmen alike. The first tugs were
slim and somewhat awkward-looking, and they were barely able
to creep against the stream, yet one can easily imagine the astonishment with which the people along the Rhine saw the first steamer
puffing upstream. She was English, too, a fore-runner of the
Thames Commodore. Steaming direct from London, the *Caledonia*
drew in to the quay at Cologne, just as our own little craft was to do
a century and a half later. In time the early steamboats and the
first prim, stately and not very effective tugs gave way to what I
think were undoubtedly the most handsome and awe-inspiring
vessels the Rhine has ever known, the great paddle-wheel tugs still
seen on the picture postcards and travel brochures of the Rhineland
even if they no longer plough the river. Many of these splendid
vessels were sunk during the Second World War, but they were
raised and took a magnificent curtain call before one by one they
were scrapped. Fourteen men comprised the crew of each of those
great tugs, and immense quantities of coal were consumed as they
thrust up the curling passage of the Rhine gorge with half a mile
of barges strung out behind them. Below Bingen ten men would
be stoking with all their might. The paddles threshed the water,

42

the smoke rose to drift away over the hilltops, and when at last the bow was thrusting beneath the bridge at Mainz the two tall funnels would lean gracefully backwards as though in salute to the landlubbers on the parapet above, and for a few seconds the vessel would almost disappear in the smoke and steam which issued at deck level.

They were giants, these tugs, more than two hundred and fifty feet of grace and power, the staff for the blue meeting flag stretched far out to starboard, the mast decked out with the regulation towage-barrel, the overhauling flag, and the insignia of the firm to which they belonged. I still remember how in the early 1930s and long before I had a boat of my own I would bicycle over to the Rhine after a day in the embryological laboratory at Freiburg and climb up to the top of the rock by Breisach cathedral to watch one of those wondrous vessels creeping up the stream and see the men on the bridge of boats that crossed to the French shore winding at their winches to draw enough of the bridge away to leave a passage for the queenly ship and her courtier tows.

My own voyages, thirty years later, were made just in time to see the last survivors of that great lineage. The first we met was in 1961, when we were voyaging down to Cologne aboard the old *Commodore*. As we turned the long easy bend towards Andernach there appeared down beyond the wharves what seemed to be a cloud sitting on the water, very much larger than a man's hand. Brown and white, twisting and wispy, the strange phenomenon seemed to hang in the gorge like a fog-bank and it was not until I looked at it through the binoculars that I saw the long bowsprit and the turmoil of water where the paddles were churning it like cream. Then came a gust of wind and the shroud was lifted to reveal the *Oskar Huber* in all her glory.

But it was the glory of a dying race. The diesel tug with a drip-feed that could do the work of all ten sweating stokers took over, and the Rhine saw such immense craft as the *Prinses Beatrix* and the *Unterwalden* dragging eight, ten, twelve even fifteen thousand tons of barges up the river without a single man to shovel coal. Soon, these mighty diesel tugs and the single motor vessels seemed to be set for a future extending to the horizon. Certainly the automotors would always remain, for they carried single loads to distant destinations in half a dozen countries, but before long the diesel tug itself was becoming old fashioned – and by tug I mean a special craft with a hook in the middle of its dorsal surface from which trail the long hawsers running to the separate lighters astern.

If the tugs did not endure for ever, that was partly a matter of sheer man-power. It was difficult to recruit sufficient crew, and the cost of employing steersmen and hands on each lighter in the tow-train was a serious disadvantage. The incentive to try a new system came from across the Atlantic, when the occupation of the Rhineland had brought the Americans to the river. For Americans tackle problems radically. In their honest, open way they expressed amazement that anyone should haul a tow-train of such length that the last ship in line was sometimes not even in sight. Every huge lighter had its crew, too. Why not shove 'em, huh? Back home we sure got tow-boats that could shove that lot as easy as a pretty nurse can push a goddam baby carriage. (For with curiously un-American lack of logic they called their peculiar vessels tow-boats, even though they did not tow at all, but shoved from the rear. The Germans and French call the same type of craft by the more natural names of *Schubschiff* (shove-ship) and *pousseur* (pusher).)

The French were sufficiently convinced to begin experiments. So were the Germans, who joined with the energetic Hollanders to build the *Wasserbüffel* (Water Buffalo) which in 1957 began to buffle its way up the river. Ten years later almost every major transport firm on the Rhine had its giant pushers, shoving the heavy dumb lighters which now needed only a lad or two to superintend the braces of the whole pack instead of a family on every barge.

Today these massive craft with their family of lighters packed tightly round them go sweeping down the gorge, their progress signalled at one flag-station after another so that the vessels moving upstream can take avoiding action. High overhead the ruins of the robber castles look down on them, and I think that if the ghost of a medieval toll-collector should haunt any of the sites he must be mortified to think of the money that might have been extorted if his armed men of long ago could have held up such a tonnage of shipping. But there are no tolls nowadays, and unlike many other rivers of the world the Rhine levies no dues upon the ships that use it. The stream is as free as any in the world.

The first blow for freedom of navigation was struck by a resolution of the Council of the Convention of revolutionary France in 1792. 'The courses of the rivers are the common and inalienable property of all those countries watered by their streams,' it declared, and went on to say that no riparian state could impede its neighbours from enjoying the same advantages as itself. However, this admirable principle could in fact only be applied to the Meuse and Scheldt which ran through France and the Low Countries, for as yet the French had no jurisdiction over most of the Rhine. And the resolution also specifically limited the proposed freedom to riparian states, and did not include other flags. Perhaps the intention was to freeze out the iniquitous English, the perpetual source of so much trouble.

With the collapse of Napoleon, the Treaty of Paris extended the same principle to the Rhine and left it to the Congress of Vienna to work out the details, which it did. The conference confirmed the basic freedom of navigation, removed all tolls except for certain regulated dues to pay for the upkeep of the channel, and abolished the staples of Mainz and Cologne and all the restrictive privileges of the ancient local guilds of shipmen. The treaty naturally ran into trouble with the Prussians over the abolishing of the German staples, but a more serious dispute arose with the Dutch about the meaning of the phrase 'from the source *jusqu' à la mer*'. The Vienna powers said that 'to the sea' meant to the sea – to the Hook of Holland entrance or its equivalent at that time; but the Dutch maintained that 'to the sea' meant to the first point at which the influence of the tide could be detected. It was sixteen years before a compromise was reached.

In 1868 the Treaty of Mannheim finally removed the last of the dues and proclaimed equality for all ships from Basle to the *open* sea, provided they belonged to riparian states. After her defeat by the Prussians in 1870 France ceased to be a riparian state of the Rhine, but the Treaty of Versailles restored Alsace and a water frontage to the French. It also extended the freedom of navigation to ships of all nationalities whatsoever, and not only those along the banks of the river itself. The same treaty confirmed the authority of the Central Commission for the Rhine, with its seat at Strasbourg, and added Belgium, Italy and Britain to the previous members, although none of these newcomers had actual physical contact with the river. In 1945 Italy was dropped and replaced by the United States, but twenty years later the Americans came to the conclusion that their interests in the Rhine were extremely nebulous, and they dropped out of their own accord.

Actually the Central Commission for the Rhine is by far the oldest of all the international institutions of Europe, for it was founded in 1815 at Vienna. It is a remarkable demonstration of the viability under even the most difficult circumstances of a body which has a clearly defined and practical job to do. Nearly fifteen hundred air-raids upon the Rhine and its harbours during the Second World War dealt the river some crippling blows. The water flowed as before, regulated not by armies but by the freeze and thaw of the Alpine uplands of Switzerland, but between the Siebengebirge and Emmerich nearly one thousand large lighters lay sunk in the stream, 185 tugs were wrecked, some six hundred other vessels lay sunken and rusting. Every bridge between Switzerland and Holland had been felled into the river, and before the waterway was clear for shipping more than 200 thousand tons of twisted girders and broken concrete spans and pillars had to be laboriously cut away under the difficult conditions of a swift current. Many thought the Rhine was closed for ever, the task of clearing it superhuman. But the Central Commission for the Rhine still existed, and slowly the seemingly impossible work was begun. Countries contributed all the lifting and cutting and dredging material they could lay their hands upon, and the piles of wreckage hauled from the river began to grow upon the banks, where some of them still remain. At Cologne the spans of the Hohenzollern bridge, felled at one end, were jacked up inch by inch and supported so that trains could once more cross the stream. Night and day the work of clearance went on, and without the long-established body with more than a century of experience behind it the Rhine might have remained as ruined as the nests of the tough medieval ship-robbers along the craggy sides of the gorge.

When first I discovered that Britain was a permanent member of the Central Commission for the Rhine it surprised me. More

than that, I wondered if it could really be true, and as I happened
at the time to be having a little trouble with the French about
whether the autonomous port of Strasbourg was or was not within
the area of free navigation, I went tiptoe to the telephone and
summoned the immediate aid not of London's Noble Fire Brigade
but of the Foreign Office in Whitehall.

'I want' I said boldly, 'I want to speak to the British permanent
representative on the Central Commission for the Rhine.'

Of course I expected the girl at the switchboard to say 'What?' Or
perhaps 'Could you spell that, please?' But no. Without a flutter
in her voice she merely responded with a 'Hold the line. Trying
to connect you', and a moment later I was speaking to a most
charming brigadier who was filed away somewhere in Whitehall to
fulfil the letter of this one article of the Treaty of Versailles. He
was obviously delighted to be rung up at all, and the thought
crossed my mind that he might have been sitting dutifully at his
desk for nearly forty years without a single enquiry coming his
way until I was put through to him. Even though he could not
help me with the intricacies of French customs regulations, which
indeed are beyond the understanding even of Senior Wranglers,
he was very charming and we had a long conversation about boats,
and how I had reached Strasbourg not by the Rhine at all but
through the French canals, and how pleasant a place Strasbourg
must be in the summer, as indeed it is, and how he would like to
have a boat himself. The conversation did nothing to solve my
problem but it left me with the conviction that Britain at least
took her international responsibilities seriously, provided they
were not too exacting.

From Bingen to Mainz is an easy haul up a broad river which
flows gently and magnificently past the edge of the Rheingau.
Geisenheim, Oestrich, Hattenheim, the villages renowned for their
wines spill along the shore with only a sloping wall of stone between
themselves and erosion. Timbered houses lean against fragments
of town walls surviving from the days of war, suspicion and
brigandage, and here and there a pleasant baroque church reminds
one of the great upsurge of hope and striving which followed in
the wake of the dying middle ages. But the houses are grey, too,
and towards Mainz they become even greyer. It is not a matter of

old age, but of the continual peppering with dust, dropping from
the plumes of smoke which drift down the valley from the tall
chimneys of the cement factories.

It is a pity that the phagocytes of the human blood can make a
meal of calcium carbonate and enjoy it. At least, I seem to remember being told that that was the case, but of course my informant
thirty years ago may well have been a P.R.O. for some powerful
cement combine, disguised as a physiologist. If cement dust
caused silicosis to all within its range, then the state of affairs
would be much better. Cement manufacturers would not be
allowed to cover square miles of country with their horrid powder.
Medical officers of health would be roused to action, and the
nonsense would have to stop. But with things as they are, there
seems nothing to prevent one so polluting the atmosphere with
the grey shroud of dirt-laden smoke and steam that nobody for
miles down wind can open a window, grow an evergreen, serve
their supper without washing the crockery before the meal as well
as after, or sit by the river bank and bask in what would have been
sunshine if the cement men had not put up a pillar of cloud to
shut it out.

Ten years earlier I had left the old *Commodore* at anchor
throughout the winter in the backwater behind the Petersau, or
Peter's Ait, a short way below Mainz and on the Wiesbaden side
of the river. We arrived there under escort of the water police,
who had ingeniously extracted us from a tentative agreement with
a boatyard further upstream, which, they said, it was not their
duty as impartial officials of law and order to criticise in any way
whatsoever although, had they been just ordinary mortals, they
would at once have designated it as a nest of unprincipled scoun-
drels who would strip a boat of anything of value and then swear
in unison that the things had never been aboard at all. Much wiser,
they said, (or, more correctly, they stressed that if they had not
been impartial police officers they might have been sorely tempted
to say it was much wiser) to leave the boat lying off another yard,
at the side of the shallow backwater by Biebrich. And in case Herr
Rumpelstiltschen of the first yard might feel aggrieved and
inclined to tear up the ground with his paws and fling stones at
the *Commodore* as she left the foot of his slipway to head for the

other, they would nonchalantly appear at the right moment and put their smart ship between us and him.

Thus it was that we arrived in the Petersau backwater below the railway bridge of Mainz-Kastel. The following months proved that the creek was indeed not infested with thieves and the boat-yard was reliable, but we had drawn in to the anchorage in the failing light of an evening when a slight breeze was breathing pleasantly from the north-west, and so we suspected nothing. The moment we had left our beloved boat the wind slunk round the other way and from late September until the following March the dirt of the cement works at Kastel was blown straight into her ventilators, round the edges of her windows and in through every available orifice. Once inside, the dust explored the whole boat from end to end, penetrating the medicine chest, settling in my shirts and filling even the teapot in its cupboard with a layer of solid finely laid concrete. As for the outside of the vessel, my first impression was that she had been commandeered by the German Navy and re-painted in battleship grey.

Our winter run to Mainz was only the work of a short morning, and two hours up from Bingen we were already turning the long bend to starboard to cut behind the Rettbergsau. To our left lay Schierstein with a good harbour, the entrance spanned by a very handsome new footbridge. There is a sad tale about Schierstein which seems incongruous now that the place is one of factories and cement-works and a smooth new road-bridge leaping the Rhine, but of course Schierstein was not always thus, and once it was much like any other little towns of the Rheingau, a place of vintners and vines and of beautiful maidens. And among these, none was so fair as Irmtraudchen, the pretty daughter of a Rhine fisherman. Indeed all the young men of the place courted her but she would have none of them. Secretly she was in love with the handsome young knight of Frauenstein, and every evening at dusk she would meet him and lie on the bank of the Rhine, close by the water's edge, or under the shelter of the vines.

Junkers were, I fear, always junkers, and it was not long before the results of his passion were such that the young nobleman dropped her and came no more. In vain she visited their familiar haunts, and when at last she realised that she was abandoned by her lover she flung herself into the river. But – and this is where the story departs from the usual line of Rhineland tragedies – her spirit rose from the waves as a little flame which followed the knight wherever he went. Even when he invited his friends to a carousal at Frauenstein his old flame hovered behind him. And so it continued until it drove him to death from sheer worry and fright.

The junker's dying wish was to be buried in his armour, which he no doubt considered reasonably flame-proof. But the determined flame came that same night and chased his spirit, armour and all, through the vineyards and down to the water. After which I suppose the poor girl extinguished herself, for she has not been seen among the vines since that last exultant occasion.

At Schierstein the great palace of the Archduchess of Luxembourg is almost in sight, standing magnificently pink and ochre along the river front at Biebrich, which otherwise is rather a dull place. One may wonder how the House of Luxembourg comes to be installed at Biebrich on the Rhine, but this territory used to be Nassau, and the Luxembourgers were a branch of the Nassau family whose ruined hilltop castle above the River Lahn is of course a holy place for Netherlanders on holiday, for it is all that remains of the ancestral home of William the Silent. That Biebrich and the water in front of it was very definitely Nassauisch was demonstrated very clearly by the trouble that once occurred between Nassau and the owners of the opposite shore.

At Biebrich and down through Schierstein the Rhine is still very much broader than it is in most of its reaches, and so across most of this greater width it is correspondingly shallow. Before the modern course was laid out and dredged the shipmen had often to complain of the sandbanks upon which they ran aground. Obviously it would have been sensible to dam off part of the stream so that the increased flow in the remainder would keep the channel scoured, but this would have meant that one or other of the riparian states would lose its frontage on navigable water. Hesse-Darmstadt wanted the channel along their (left) bank. Nassau wished it diverted to the Biebrich side. Eventually the Hesse-Darmstadt authorities grew tired of argument, and one evening they sent down the river sixty barges laden with stones, which were all dumped in the Rhine off Biebrich.

Such high-handedness was not allowed to pass unchallenged. Nassau took its rival to court and the result was that the Hesse-Darmstadters had to spend a lot of time and money in removing the stones and taking them away, all sixty barge-loads of them.

Unless one happened to live in the palace I doubt if one could easily consider Biebrich romantic. Yet one man at least found the view inspiring when, a century ago, he stood on the balcony of his two-roomed lodging, the small rent of which he could barely afford, looking up the river toward where the golden-domed city of Mainz glowed in the early evening light. Before it the Rhine flowed majestic, throwing up to him the colours of the sunlit clouds. As he stood there a new melody took shape within his head, and at last he stepped indoors to put it on paper and score it for the orchestra. It was to be the overture to the *Meistersinger von Nürnberg*.

Before midday we had fought eight duels with Rhine-ships, slowly but successfully overhauling each in turn so that we could put in to the commercial harbour at Mainz to lunch on deck in the crisp frosty air and under a pale wintry sun which managed from time to time to send an oblique finger of pinkish silver through the thin gauze of cloud above. Mainz harbour is a good place for such a pause. The water is sheltered from the wash of ships, there are good solid quay walls, and no distractions. Besides, the pigeons will come wheeling down from the warehouse roofs and offer to clean up the crumbs, and there is sure to be a barge dog at hand to help with any spare bones from the chops. It is very different from the splendid hotels which receive the summer visitors, and I personally prefer it. But then I am not very attached to Mainz.

Not that this is the fault of the burgomaster and echevins. It is merely the sad case that the once golden city has progressively fallen upon times more and more evil. Gone are the Archbishop-Electors, good and bad. Vanished are the days of Gutenberg the printer or – further back in time – of Boniface. Restored to a shadow of their former glory the vast romanesque churches of the once great ecclesiastical city stand looking a little bit lost among the steel framed blocks of a newer age. For the plain truth is that Mainz has been sacked too often to have retained very much character. Once on a Sunday morning I wandered through its

c

streets to find a church. There were plenty, all nicely patched and rejuvenated, and yet the one I entered was renewed only in its fabric and its hymnboards and its lighting. A grey-faced sorrowful man preached a grey and sorrowful sermon to a grey congregation muffled in dark winter coats which looked as though they dated from before the Second World War. It was a depressing occasion and in fact the only church experience in post-war Germany which I have not found extremely stimulating. Nevertheless I suspect it was a true reflection of Mainz, a city with an impeccable and romantic past and an extremely dull present.

As for the past, Mainz has its tale about the good Willegis, who rose from being the son of a carter to become Archbishop of Mainz. His enemies of nobler birth tried to make his life unbearable by rudely painting cartwheels on the palace walls, but Willegis did not object. On the contrary, he had his own painters paint more cartwheels on the walls and ceilings of his apartments, that he might always remember his humble origin and never be tempted to pride. Finally he adopted the cartwheel as his insignia, and to this day it forms the arms of the City of Mainz. One can see the wheel far and wide in the Palatinate and along the Rhine, a sure indication of how far the sway of the Archbishops of that city once extended.

Then there was Heinrich von Meissen, the troubadour who received his nickname of *Frauenlob* because he sang so wonderfully about women. Nothing delighted the vanity of the ladies of Rhineland castles more than to have Heinrich sing his verses in their halls, for it was his custom to glorify womankind as something superior to mere men. As a result his death was an occasion when women from far and near flocked to Mainz to attend the funeral, and after the twelve greatest beauties of the city had carried his coffin into the cathedral the remainder wept their tears over it, strewed the coffin with flowers, and poured such a quantity of vintage wine into the vault that it overflowed and flooded the cloisters. But best of all the stories of the Mainz that has vanished is – at least in its medieval flavour – that of the impecunious fiddler.

Reading these tales from long ago one is often struck by the fact that in the hard days before the dawn of a scientific approach to the phenomena of the world, people would believe any tale, however unlikely. But there were limits to credulity, as the poor fiddler discovered when he was arrested in the market at Mainz when trying to sell a slipper of pure gold which was easily recognizable as being from the foot of the image of the Virgin in Mainz cathedral. Hauled before the justices and charged with sacrilege – perhaps the most serious offence of any in the middle ages – he told a story which was at least original. He was only a poor fiddler, he said, a sort of street corner musician, and he always felt a little out of place in the ordinary public services in the cathedral. Yet with his money spent and no future ahead of him he had gone into the cathedral and prayed mightily before the statue of the Virgin, singing his prayers as well as he might to the accompaniment of simple airs of his own composition, which he played on his old violin. The cathedral had happened to be quite empty at the time, or he would hardly have dared behave in such a way. None had seen or heard him. None that is, except the statue of the Virgin, for just as he was rising from his knees at the end of his performance she lifted one foot and lobbed the golden shoe right into his smock. She had given it him, and wanting to change the shoe into more negotiable coinage he had naturally gone straight to the market and had offered the piece of footwear for sale to a goldsmith.

The court was not impressed. We are all agreed are we not? Quite so. Immediate execution in public, up in the produce market outside the cathedral which he has dared to violate with his miserable larceny. A wholesome example to others.

It did not take long to build a scaffold, for in cities such as Mainz there was often use for one. Just as he was about to be taken up the steps the fiddler asked that before he was hanged, or decapitated or more probably burned alive, he could be taken into the cathedral to say a final prayer before the statue of the Virgin who had treated him so magnanimously. It was not in any way out of order for a condemned person to wish to say his last prayers, but no doubt the judges were also pleased that the poor fellow should make a request which would inevitably show how untrue his tale had been. They took him under guard into the cathedral, and in case there should be any nonsense the city executioner was stationed behind him as he knelt and played his violin.

As the fiddler came to an end the guards were about to seize him and lead him back to the scaffold, when to their horror they saw the statue move. Raising its right foot it took unerring aim and flicked its second golden shoe right into the old man's arms. The onlookers shouted pious praises, the guards and executioner burst out of the cathedral with the news, and soon the poor old fiddler was being carried in triumph through the city. I hope he was allowed to sell the shoes and get a good price for them, but of that there seems to be no record.

It is difficult for a boatman to chug up the river past the water-front of Mainz and the confluence of the River Main on the opposite shore without being overcome by a wave of sadness. For magnificent though the Main may be where it flows through the Bavarian forests and the land of the great baroque abbeys and cathedral cities, it was once the route to the Danube and the mysterious lands around the Black Sea. The Ludwig's Canal was too small to carry useful traffic and in 1950 it was finally closed, although it had for long been unusable. Only at its western end is the ancient waterway still navigable for more than a minnow. I have actually taken the *Thames Commodore* through Lock 1 and hung her at anchor in the centre of Bamberg city before an astonished multitude of burghers, one of whom was so anxious to shake hands with the skipper of the first ship for many years to visit the city that in his exuberance he stepped off the deck into the River Regnitz. But having sounded them I decided that the town hall rapids were more than I could attempt in the ship herself, so it was in our dinghy that my wife and I rowed vigorously up to the canal cut and past the deserted wharves towards Lock 2, which to our great surprise was still workable and equipped with a resident keeper who must, I think, have had the least exacting job in all the Bundesrepublik. We locked through for the sum of one mark – about all the waterway had taken that year, I suspected – and rowed up a mile or so of the wooded reach of clear and fast-flowing river until we were tired of struggling against the current and drifted back towards the city.

However, the closure of the Ludwig's Canal was not to be

permanent. It was the herald of better things to come, for in its place the *Grosschiffahrtstrasse* Rhine-Main-Danube was to be built to carry huge Europa-ships right over the divide. More than that, in 1969 this splendid link was to be complete. I had intended that the *Thames Commodore* should be near the head of the queue of ships to enter the magnificent new waterway, but unfortunately the project itself had to be slowed down. The construction of the ship-lifts on the descent to the Danube was proving extremely costly, and as there were limits to what even West German finances would stand the date for completion was put forward twelve years to 1981. And twelve years is a long time in the life of a ship, and still more in that of her not-so-young skipper.

So, as we forged past the deserted snow-decked steamer berths at Mainz we kept to the right at the confluence and did not enter the black water of the Main, darkly stained by the effluents of Frankfurt and Hoechst. We steered up past the range of vineyard hills of Nierstein and Oppenheim on the next stage of the haul upstream to Switzerland, still a long way off.

I have never actually seen the toads' well which must exist somewhere among the vines on the hillside behind Oppenheim if the best known wine of that little place should be called Oppen-heimer Krötenbrunnen, but I have at least seen from the river the church in which there is a window famous for the excellence of its glass. It is said that the master glazier had a wager with his apprentice that he would make the finest window in all the church. Each man set to work on his respective window, but when both were nearly completed it was plain for all to see that the master was outclassed by his pupil. Both were good, certainly; but the work of the young lad was finer than any yet seen.

Unfortunately the local people were not reticent in expressing their opinion, even before the work was finished, and the natural result was so to anger the master craftsman that he pushed his apprentice off the scaffolding to his death.

When steaming up the Rhine with only a few short hours before dark would fall it seemed prudent to have a chosen destination to be reached in daylight, and after examining the map for possible ports I had decided to make Gernsheim harbour for the night. I had never been to Gernsheim, and having now seen it at arm's

length I have no particular wish to visit a place which I suspect
has no attractions beyond a collection of extremely pungent
chimneys of chemical works. Yet on the chart at least the harbour
looked a reasonable sort of place to lie. However, the Rhine had
now put on a little more speed, with the result that dark had in fact
fallen before we reached the place, yet enough light from the
factory sparkle was reflected on the aromatic water to show that at
such a low level of the Rhine the port was too far dried out for
even the empty barges to pull in to the quays. A pair of huge Ruhr
lighters filled the still navigable middle of the channel, and as we
had no wish to lie alongside them and have a grab of coal dust
passing overhead twice every minute we decided to continue in
search of a better berth.

The Rhine after dark is not everybody's choice for a pleasant
trip, for it is less easy to be certain of one's exact position to the
nearest forty feet – a matter of vital importance in a river so well
provided with shoals. However, we had now caught up a further
bunch of traffic, and the stern lights of the ships running ahead
gave us a reasonable guide to the channel. Soon, however, a faint
mist came down, a veil which did not shorten in too drastically the
visibility ahead, but which somehow managed to hide the bankside
markers, so that we had no idea of just where we were. Only when
we passed under a set of power cables which leaked electricity like
Thurber's aunt's house and turned the dial of our echo-sounder
into something like a moving picture of a firework display, could
I identify the place glowing in the mist to starboard as Rhein-
dürkheim.

An hour or more ahead we came up behind a half-tow, a large
motorised Rhine-ship being towed by another equally sizeable
vessel about three hundred feet long, half barge and half tug. The
Thames Commodore had put on her utmost to pass the pair, when
quite suddenly the stern lights of another pair of ships ahead went
dim. A moment later one of them vanished, then the other. It was
as though they had run over the edge of some giant gulf and had
been swallowed up. I was still wondering what had hit them when
we plunged straight into the same thick fog-bank which had
enveloped them. Undoubtedly they must have stopped dead in
their tracks, I thought, only a hundred yards ahead or even less.

We would leave the half-tow to run them down and cut a quick pirouette to starboard to remove ourselves from any chance of being the jam in the sandwich.

In fact the fog bank proved to be thick and stationary enough to contain a dozen or two of ships lying at anchor. But the fact that they could only hang fore-and-aft in such a stream told us in which direction to probe cautiously ahead, and eventually I sighted a pile beside a factory unloader. Making fast, we had gone below to make supper and settle down for the night when I dimly heard a prolonged clanking. It was the unmistakable noise of a train crossing the river on a girder bridge, and examining the chart I concluded that we must be within a mile of the harbour of Worms. Going on deck again I started up the engines and hovered in the freezing fog near the edge of the river until I heard another train approaching. Dimly the lights of the carriage windows caterpillared above the river, but it was enough to give me a run-up course on the bridge. Just as we were passing under the right hand span the fog parted. It was not for long, but it gave us the chance to make a quick run at full speed for the port.

Soon the murk closed in again, thick and freezing – but by then we were already picking our way on foot across the hoar-frosted railway sidings towards a glass of wine in the city of Reformation.

IV

The Worm of Worms – Luther at the Diet – Milk of our Lady – the Rheingold – Ludwigshafen's chemistry – Mannheim – the Flying Baronet – Speyer and the sanctuary bowl – Karlsruhe – lure of the Black Forest

THE joke about the Diet of Worms is as old as the teaching of history in English private schools. Yet the fact remains that Worms is an odd name, particularly for such an august and episcopal city as that which bears it. However, the name seems to have puzzled local chroniclers long before Martin Luther, and from them we have the assurance that the city was in fact named after a giant worm or dragon which had fled to the Rhine from some middle-eastern desert, a creature with a wormy tail, two feet, sharp teeth, a flame-thrower in its gullet, and an altogether rather unnerving appearance and manner. It ate humans as readily as cattle, and all efforts to appease the creature's wrath failed. Once a year the dragon had to be bought off with the sacrifice of a human. This was of course quite usual, and I have never yet sailed across the trail of a dragon of which this was not true. The Tarasque of the Rhone, the creature of the Drachenfels in the seven Hills near Bonn, the fearful Roggenbuk of the Trave estuary below Lübeck, each of these had to be propitiated in just the same manner. An annual meal of hominid was, it seems, the regular requirement of dragon metabolism.

At Worms (though the place as yet did not bear that name) the persons to be devoured were chosen by lot, but after a while the Council refused to conduct the lottery any more, and the people feared that the delay would lead the animal to attack them wholesale. However, they had a worthy and self-sacrificing young queen who promptly decided to set a good example by putting herself and all her court officials down for the draw.

When the queen's number came up a young man stepped

forward and said he would try to save her on condition that he might marry her if he succeeded. To this she quickly agreed, and the young man went off to prepare for the encounter. In fact he was no fearless St George but one of three brothers who were cutlers, experts in fashioning and sharpening blades. The three men had together built a special suit of armour of a new design, entirely set with sharp projecting knife-blades, hedgehog fashion. In this ingenious casing the young man was thrown by his brothers to the dragon, which foolishly swallowed him whole and died in the greatest agony. When it had ceased to squirm and twitch he climbed out unharmed to marry the queen, and everyone lived happily ever after. As for the 'worm', it was commemorated for ever in the new name of the city.

I am not sure exactly when this took place but it must have been before dragons became extinct. The famous Diet was held very much later, and it was on an April day in the watershed year 1521 that Martin Luther reached the gates of Worms under Imperial escort. Swiftly the news spread through the streets, and many of the citizens rushed out to meet him and to escort him enthusiastically to the Johanniterhof, where he was to reside. There was no doubt at all which side the people were upon in the great debate which was breaking over the city. They had seen too much of the materialism of the church dignitaries and the political scheming of rich clerics.

The Emperor and his brother, Six Electors, 24 dukes, 8 margraves, 30 prelates and a host of earls and counts and diplomatic representatives made up the magnificent Establishment audience before whom Luther was called upon to recant and to withdraw his writings. But no, he could not. After explaining that everything he had written came from his conscience and through a profound study of the Bible, he would give them, he said, an answer 'devoid of either horns or teeth' – in other words it would not indict or malign any person. So he let them know that he could not and would not withdraw one word, because it was neither safe nor right to do anything against one's conscience. 'Here I stand' he concluded. 'I can do naught else. God help me! Amen'.

One further day was spent in fruitless attempts to reason with the obstinate reformer. He was then given twenty-one days in which to recant, without punishment. Slowly the time of grace passed, but Luther had nothing more to say. On the day after his span for reflection was up, he was conveyed to the Wartburg. The Reichstag having declared against him, a ban of excommunication was pronounced and the public executioner burned his writings in the open air at the market place. Inevitably the great split begun further up the Rhine by Geyler of Kaysersberg and enlarged by Luther was not breached by these actions but widened still further, and it was to be more than four centuries before the first faint stirrings of a spirit of reconciliation made themselves felt.

As for the city which had been chosen as the venue for that momentous meeting, it was from then onwards to be continually rent by a split in its loyalty. Backed by the mass of the townspeople the city council declared uncompromisingly for Luther and reform. Yet the city itself actually belonged to the Emperor, and to the powerful Holy Roman Empire which had consigned Luther to damnation. Worms had to pay nominal homage to the catholic bishop who ruled over its church, but in its heart and conscience the city had declared irrevocably for Luther, and to this day Worms is predominantly Protestant.

Once a place of ecclesiastical glory, Worms was almost annihilated by the bombardments of the Second World War. Much was lost for ever but the cathedral has been restored from a ruin, and the Reformation Memorial still stands under the trees near a piece of town wall which may well go back to Roman times. The monument is huge – it was put up in the period when Germany was sprouting giant memorials without hesitation – and whether or not one likes the scatter of earnest and more than life-sized reforming theologians surrounding the central figure on his pedestal it would be impossible to conceive of Worms without it. Probably no event in history was, in the long run, more far-reaching in its results than the meeting of the Diet at Worms. As a Roman Catholic priest once said to me, 'You protestants have no idea what we in the Roman church owe to Luther. He saw the evil in it and spoke out. He reformed *us* as well as that part of the church which split off for ever.' And this, I think, was true.

It was a freezing night when my wife and I climbed the cold steel ladder from the foot of the quay wall and shuffled through the lying snow to pick our way over the railway sidings and between the silos and warehouses toward the glow of light over the town itself, not so very far away. We had only walked for a minute or two when we came upon fields of vines, the stakes standing white and frosty between the wrinkled stems cut back for wintering. There must have been twenty acres or more, and set among them the huge shape of a splendid church with two towers and a thin central spire above the nave. In the crisp white light thrown up from the snow it looked the sort of building some early bishop might have seen in a vision, shining with a cold unearthly light.

Suddenly I realised that this must be the famous church with the baroque altar and the statue of our Lady to which pilgrims had once come in their thousands. Our Lady – *Unsere Liebe Frau* – and these vineyards stretching up from the harbour to the edge of the old town itself were of course those from which Liebfraumilch (Milk of Our Lady) was once produced. But that was long ago, when no grape was worthy of that destination unless it grew within the area of shadow cast by the church of *Unsere Liebe Frau* during the course of the year – a patch which of course would be much larger than one might at first imagine, for at sunrise and sunset the shadow stretches as far towards the horizon as intervening buildings will allow. Liebfraumilch has now changed, the name having been extended to cover any wine in the whole of Rhein-Hessen sour enough to have been sugared before bottling. This is not a very attractive description but it comes from the German wine trade itself, and no German vintner would ever attempt to fool the German public about the appellation. Not that some brands of Liebfraumilch may not actually be quite pleasant; but in Britain the old romantic association still lingers on, and many a grocer genuinely thinks (particularly if he only drinks beer) that he is doing his customers a real favour by securing for them a wine in which, if he only knew it, many Germans would not so much as wash their dogs.

We fuelled from a tanker in Worms harbour, and while the diesel was running into the *Thames Commodore*'s tanks I set to work to sweep the night's fresh snow-fall off her deck and superstructure, snow being a good cleaner and sweeping it an excellent way of getting warm on a winter's morn. Then we sounded our way down

Worms bridge. Hagen with the Nibelungs treasure

the harbour, blew three long and one short, floated gently over the entrance bar of silt and mud, and put the wheel hard over while giving her all the power her Perkins horses could muster so that her bow would be forced round to head upstream before the Rhine itself could push her round the other way.

Beyond the outer harbour wall and just below the bridge with its tall-arched gateway a figure was standing in the bow of a boat which in turn was placed solidly on a stone pedestal which in fact was that of a former medieval crane for unloading Rhine cargoes. The man wore a tunic and had a mighty sword hung from his belt, and in his upraised arms he held a shield, using it as a tray to carry a pile of objects which he appeared to be ready to cast into the river. Knowing that this was Worms and the countryside to port was the land of the Nibelungen it was not difficult to guess that this mighty fellow was the tough but evil-natured Hagen, and the objects on the shield the famous treasure hoard of the Nibelungen, whose land had once been conquered by the mighty Siegfried of Xanten.

Siegfried gave the treasure as a wedding gift to the fair Kriem-hilde when he married her, but our hero was slain by the crafty

Hagen, who waited until Siegfried was stooping to drink at a spring and swiftly ran him through with a spear which he deftly thrust into him at the one spot on his back where a falling leaf had caused a defect in his outer garment of invulnerability. Kriemhilde was inconsolable, and it was after she had refused for three years to speak at all that her brother Gunther sent for the Nibelungen hoard to cheer her up. Twelve truck-loads of riches were loaded on a barge which set off up river and eventually docked at Worms, near to where we had done so ourselves on a night of cold and fog.

Kriemhilde was indeed somewhat cheered, but being a worthy girl of responsible outlook she began to distribute the riches to the poor and needy. This very naturally made her extremely popular, and her husband's murderer went down even further in the estimation of the common people. Hagen soon realised that her charity must be stopped, and with the connivance of one of her brothers the key was stolen, the whole remaining hoard quickly laden on a ship and at some point unknown to the Wormsers flung overboard. And there I assume it still lies, and if anyone should be surprised that none of it has ever been recovered by dredgers that is merely because the Rhine Maidens who were told to guard it are so good at their job. They are not above moving an anchor buoy out of position, so that when the dredgermen return to work after the week-end their bucket chain will miss the gold once again.

Actually, the *Rheingold* is not just a legend and a Wagnerian opera, nor even a crack Bundesbahn express. The Rhine gravel is in fact to some extent auriferous, and the Celts used to extract gold from the shoals anywhere between Basle and Mainz. It was in that period that the stories of the Nibelungen first began to take shape; and that Rhine gold was a real enough article is shown by the fact that Bishop Remi of Strasbourg in the year 777 assigned to a convent in Alsace the right to extract the gold in one particular reach of the river. This monopoly was of real value; certainly it was in the upper reaches of river, the gravel stretches of Baden and Alsace, that most of the gold was found, and the metal itself was of high quality, being of 22.4 carats, not far short of the 24 carats of complete purity.

Throughout the centuries and right up to modern times men have been fired with the idea of getting rich by merely securing the

Rhine gold for themselves, but commercially the project was never very successful. Cost analysis has shown that one needs to work at the pan for nine hours to extract gold to the value of rather under two pounds sterling, and at modern wage-rates this is hardly attractive. Still more frustrating is the fact that the actual water of the Rhine carries 0.003 milligrams of gold per cubic metre and empties it into the sea. A little arithmetic shows that this means that about two and a half hundredweights of gold are voided annually through the Hook of Holland, but lest any reader should decide to embark at once with an extraction outfit I should add that the concentration of gold in the Rhine is only one tenth of what it is in the oceans, where about eight million tons of the precious metal are in solution, magnificently and tantalisingly unattainable. Even the two-and-a-half hundredweights passing down the river is more than the gold-panners of the Rhine ever extracted in a year's work.

If nobody nowadays pans the Rhine sandbanks this is partly because dredging has carried away the shoals, but more on account of the very much more profitable industries which have grown up along the banks. One can become rich more easily from the black gold of Duisburg's coal than from the microscopic grains of yellow metal in the gravel banks, and although there is supposed still to be gold to the value of about 15 million pound sterling lying as grains in beds of auriferous sand between Basle and Strasbourg alone, the long process of digging and extracting it would certainly cost very much more than the value of the metal itself.

Scenically the upstream voyage has nothing to offer above Mainz. Except where the banks break out into a rash of refinery jetties or loading wharves the course goes ever onward between banks lined with grey masonry, broken here and there to admit a tributary, a loop of the old pre-regulation Rhine, or for the entrance to a busy gravel pit. The bank carries a service track for the work-men who here and there are seen facing up the stonework, and then comes a thicket of poplars which may at times be reduced to a single line but is more likely to extend for anything up to a mile and cover the swamp area of the former unbridled river. There is not much else that can be done with this riverside wilderness, for the ground is nothing more than disinherited shoals of gravel, but at least the copses are a wonderful place for the hunter. Fish abound, there are duck in every creek and gully, deer and even wild boar roam the riverside jungle. It is a curiously wild world that sometimes extends right to the edge of the towns, and it is only inhabited where a pub stands on the bank at a ferry-crossing, or where once there used to be a bridge of boats. One can tire of poplars, and it is a relief when along the upper reaches the sky is clear and a distant view breaks through of the hills of Baden, or the Vosges in Alsace, or even of the mighty snow-clad peaks of Switzerland.

But these views are still some days ahead, and at the moment we have before us a two hour push up a river which would be decidedly dull were it not for the great amount of traffic spanking down the Rhine from the next major port ahead, the twin industrial towns of Mannheim and Ludwigshafen which face each other across the river at the upper end of a long, straight reach. Ludwigshafen is on the starboard hand, and as the upstream channel is along that shore we have plenty of opportunity to observe the long range of wharves and silos of the B.A.S.F. I was familiar enough with the initials, for the *Thames Commodore* used tapes made by the Badische Anilin und Soda Fabrik on her recorder, and if it had puzzled me that either aniline or soda could be transmuted into triple play, it now astonished me even more to see that the factory with its marshalled ranks of dye-stained tanker-wagons and its nostalgic laboratory odours was not in fact in Baden at all, for that state lay on the opposite side of the river and embraced the territory of Mannheim. However, it seems that the Badische works were once genuinely Badisch, but outgrowing their site on the right bank they had no choice but to jump over the river and extend into the land of another state. A clue to what that state must have been is contained in the name of Ludwigshafen itself. The Ludwig was Ludwig I of Bavaria, and the territory was Bavarian–Hessian.

Charlemagne once decreed that the workshops for women on his various estates should be equipped with supplies of certain textiles for weaving, teasels for teasing, and woad and madder for dyeing the cloth. The madder plant was still a mainstay of the dye industry as late as the nineteenth century, and the revolutionary government in France sponsored plantations of it in Alsace, on the left bank of the Rhine. The dye came mainly from the skin of the roots, which contained a substance (now known to be ruberythric acid) which could be hydrolysed to form sugar, and the actual dye itself, alizarin. So much in demand was this colour that 70,000 tons of it were used in Europe alone in the year 1868, when something happened. The something was that a pair of German chemists, lured by the rich prize of stealing this old-fashioned trade for the laboratory, succeeded in elaborating a series of reactions to produce alizarin synthetically. The only drawback was that the process involved using bromine, the cost of which was prohibitive.

It was just then that the B.A.S.F. happened to have a large quantity of anthraquinone, an apparently useless by-product of one of their factory processes. One of their employees, a calico-printer named Heinrich Caro, wondered what would happen if he mixed it with oxalic and sulphuric acids. It was just one of those strange musings to which men of scientific bent seem unusually prone, but Caro decided to try the reaction. He mixed the three materials together and heated them.

No, the roof is not going to be blown off the B.A.S.F. factory (though this occurred in 1921 when more than five hundred were killed). Very much to Caro's disappointment nothing occurred at all, except that the oxalic acid decomposed. He was still frowning over the undramatic nature of the results when a messenger brought him an urgent note to go to another part of the works. He left his room so quickly that he forgot to turn out the flame under his chemical cookery, and when he later returned he found a charred mess in the bottom of the dish. But there was also a bright pinkish crust. Accidentally Caro had produced the dye of madder by a simple process which involved little more than strong heat.

Caro raced ahead to take out a patent for he knew that in England, Perkin was also hot on the scent. The race was such a close one that Perkin had his patent granted on 26 June, but Caro just beat him to the post by twenty-four hours. Caro's patent was taken over by B.A.S.F. but they generously rewarded Perkin by granting him a monopoly licence to make the dye in England. As for the men who farmed the thousands of acres of the madder plant *Rubia tinctorum*, they were ruined overnight. The factory dye was far cheaper and the growers had to turn over to maize or tobacco.

B.A.S.F.'s other great achievement also came about as the result of chance. The firm had spent a million pounds in trying to synthesize indigotin, the dye found in the woad and indigo plants, when one day the mercury thermometer used to control an experiment broke. To the astonishment of the chemists the mercury acted as a catalyst and indigotin was produced. The way to make cheap blue dyes and large profits lay wide open. In India alone one fifth of a million acres of land which had been entirely given over to indigo-growing were put out of commission, but Ludwigshafen flourished more than ever.

Across the river Mannheim lies in the angle of the Rhine and the Neckar, a dramatic stream which curls through the Odenwald and is navigable right up to Stuttgart. Once a humble fishing village, Mannheim only became notable when the Elector Karl Philip moved his official residence to it from the much more splendid situation on the cliff above Heidelberg. He must, I think, have been a man who liked sunshine, for the glorious castle of red sandstone at Heidelberg is set on a north-facing slope and may well have been chilly at the best of times. Besides there was no room to expand. Better the wide unobstructed plain beside the Rhine at Mannheim, where one could build a palace worthy of one's position, and plan the town around it. There was also plenty of space for a park, with a view of the river and its ships. And very magnificent those ships might be. Schelling described (in 1796) how he stood on the Rhine bridge to watch one ship after another arrive, all with their different ensigns from Cologne, Mainz and other places. Finest of all were the so-called *Jagdschiffe*, one of which he inspected closely at the landing-stage. These craft were those on which the Electors of Mainz and Trier and other spiritual and temporal lords of the neighbourhood undertook their pleasure voyages. Seen from outside they were so magnificent that when the sun shone upon them they sparkled in the distance and from near-at-hand were almost too brilliant to behold. Inside they had several rooms splendidly furnished and so designed that at one moment they formed one great state apartment, at another a series of separate rooms of modest size.

Mannheim's palace is huge, and with its expensive decor it became what Voltaire described as 'the most pleasant of residences for visitors of rank and merit', but to achieve this took no less than forty years, at the end of which the days of Electors were numbered. However, there was just time for the young Mozart to play there with the court orchestra in the great Hall of Knights, and in the State Theatre Schiller's *Die Rauber* was first performed in 1782.

The Elector also laid out a town where hardly any existed. The design was simply a cross within a horse-shoe, the open end of which was crossed by the Palace. The entire town was put down as geometrical blocks in numbered and lettered rows, so that even now it is as easy to track down an address in Mannheim as to find one's way about New York. But in spite of the magnificence of the Electoral installations it is the port of Mannheim which must appeal to the boatman, for in size it is second only to Duisburg. With the Ludwigshafen quays across the Rhine and its own wharves on the Neckar and the basins joining the two rivers, Mannheim has thirty miles of actual loading quays, scores of acres of warehouses and whole flocks of cranes among which the two giants are appropriately named Hercules and Goliath, the latter lifting one hundred tons at a time without having to pause for breath.

Mannheim was always something of a centre of invention and industry, as it still is. There in 1885 Carl Benz built the first motorcar, and before him the Freiherr Karl Friedrich Drais von Sauerbronn had constructed his 'Draisine'. If people asked him what it was, he explained that it was a *Laufmaschine* or runningmachine, and he would be very willing to demonstrate it.

Drais was a forestry inspector, and a titled one at that. Yet his heart was in his home workshop, where he was perpetually making gadgets. He built a kind of typewriter, designed a new stove, a steam-cooking saucepan, apparatus for distilling brandy – and his Draisine. On this he sped about his work in the forests by kicking the ground first on one side, then on the other. The *Fliegender Freiherr* or flying baronet was a source of amusement to many, and certainly of embarrassment to his employers in Karlsruhe, and when Drais asked for leave of absence to develop his runningmachine it was willingly given.

So, astride his Draisine, the Freiherr appeared in fashionable Vienna where he was a great success. People of fashion came to watch – and laugh. The forestry commission in Baden however was not amused, and they sternly warned him that although what he did during his leave of absence was his own business he must nevertheless do nothing out of keeping with the dignity of his high office, and certainly he must never wear his forestry inspector's uniform when fooling about with his invention. In fact Drais, like so many inventors, was to die disappointed and unrecognised. Although he demonstrated his running-wheels to the Tsar Alexander and the Emperor Franz II of Austria when they came through Karlsruhe, nobody took the bicycle seriously. Admittedly it had no pedals, but it was the first of a long lineage of useful machines that was to spread round the world.

'I cannot stay in Mannheim any longer. The people, circumstances, earth and heaven are all against me. I have no soul here, no one at all who can sense the emptiness of my heart, no girl-friend, no friend at all. The local horizon lies heavy and oppressive upon me like the guilt of a murder.' That was Schiller, not the skipper of the *Thames Commodore*. Yet I hope the Mannheimers – among whom I certainly have some friends (though, like Schiller, no girl-friends) – will forgive me if I also think that we should stay in Mannheim no longer, but keep in the middle of the stream and aim up behind the Swiss tow-train ahead of us, curving round to starboard past the park of the electoral residence and putting the speed up to nine knots to be sure of making Speyer before sunset. Speyer is twenty kilometres distant, but although the current is beginning to stiffen we should be in sight of the cathedral within two hours.

Between Mannheim and Speyer there is nothing whatsoever to break the lines of poplars. There is no port, no village of one-time fishing houses, nothing but the long, curving, grey-walled river with the ships crossing from side to side as the groynes deflect the channel from shore to shore. It was a bleak scene in winter, and I was not sorry when an afternoon of steering in the freezing wind was over and we could slide into the old harbour of Speyer – for of the places which lie on the German Rhine itself Speyer is certainly the most charming of any upstream of the castled gorge.

Speyer was dressed overall for Christmas. Its noble buildings along the Maximilianstrasse flaunted silver bells surrounded by wreaths of fir and spruce, and garlands of green hung between the

lamp-posts. At one end of the street the splendid gateway was
floodlit up above in red and carried on its body a giant stained glass
window of Father Christmas, a more saintly figure than usual in
spite of his red robe and snowy beard, and at the further extremity
the cathedral tolled its heavy bells for an advent service, much as it
had done for more than seven centuries. Down in the old harbour
there was little movement, for half a mile upstream a new port had
been excavated for the tankers and grainships, the colliers and
gravel-carriers of the Rhine trade. Our only companions were a
little Lahn-ship serving as a pile-driver, and the never-resting
launches of the water authority and the police. Christmas week
was not the most popular time for yachting.

Speyer is extremely ancient. It even has a Jew's Bath, which is
known to have been in use more than six hundred years ago, and
may well be older. It was part of the lay-out of a whole synagogue
complex, and it consists of a bathing-place excavated down to
below the level of the Rhine in the ground, with a stone staircase
leading down into the water. This was to fulfil the Old Testament
injunction that women had to be purified after menstruation by
washing in running water. Of course it all depends on what one
means by 'running', but at Speyer the almost imperceptible flow
of the ground water was evidently taken to be adequate for the
hygienic principle involved. Complete with washing facilities and
changing rooms it reminds one of the smaller bathing places in
Bath, and in its medieval elegance it is certainly a reminder that the
Jewish community of Speyer must have been important, and therefore that the city was a rich one. And so it was. Its cathedral was for
centuries the largest in Germany, and it was started by the Emperor
Konrad II in thanksgiving for his coronation in 1027.

Konrad wished to provide a burial place for the Emperors of his
own (the Salian) dynasty, and the cathedral he envisaged was not
only to be glorious as the imperial line itself but larger and finer
than any other building in all Europe. There may have been a
variety of reasons for selecting the river bend at Speyer as the site
for his dream, but certainly he would have been influenced by the
fact that a church had already stood on that hill for four hundred
years, a church built by the Merovingian King Dagobert.

So vast was Speyer's cathedral that it was only finished in the

Speyer

time of Konrad's grandson, but while it was still incomplete its
founder was himself buried there. In fact he died in Utrecht and
his body was placed on a barge and hauled all the way up river by
men plodding along the shore. In every church then in existence
the bells tolled as the funeral boat crept up the river. How long the
journey took I do not know, but it must have been a matter of
weeks.

The cathedral became a royal burial place just as Konrad had

hoped. Three Emperors and two Empresses were interred in the
lower layer, and their graves were plastered over and only came to
light in 1900. They had had a remarkable escape. '*Brûlez le
Palatinat*' was the order given by Louis XIV, and so fearfully did
his soldiery carry it out that even the Sun King's own chaplain
long refused to give him absolution for his manifold sins and
wickedness. At Speyer the French not only plundered the houses
but broke into the cathedral and tore open the graves of the
Emperors and their families, but because the men never realised
that there was more than one layer of tombs the earliest Emperors
escaped. Yet it must have been a gruesome scene as the soldiers –
if we can believe Victor Hugo – rummaged through the coffins,
snatched any jewels or objects of gold, seized the rings from the
bony fingers, and when nothing was left but dust and bone and
shreds of royal shrouds, swept the remains into a hole in the floor.
'Drunken corporals rolled the skulls of nine emperors into a hole,
with their feet' he wrote. A guide to Speyer goes further and speaks
of the soldiery 'playing ninepins with the heads of Barbarossa's
wife and children, of Henry V and Rudolf of Habsburg.'

Worse than the lack of respect and the greed shown by the
soldiery was their blind fury of destructiveness. Orders were given
to destroy the entire cathedral, and with the firing of the building
the first four arches of the nave fell in, to lie derelict for nearly a
century. They had been completed just in time for the French to
storm the town again, and once in possession, to attempt in good
atheistic ardour to raze the cathedral to the ground. Fortunately
the walls were too solid, and the Revolutionaries had to be content
with declaring it a quarry and instituting a system of penalties for
any citizens who should try to obtain stone elsewhere. Yet the
difficulty of taking down a cathedral is that one has to begin at the
top, and not everyone is willing to climb so many spiral steps to
fetch down a stone. The cathedral suffered little damage, and was
spared any further destruction by the defeat of the French at
Waterloo. After its sufferings during the destruction of most of
Speyer in the Second World War it has been magnificently
restored, and by its sheer vast emptiness gives at once a sense of
awe and reverence which the bones of emperors could never
provide. Its bells were pealing as though to hurry Christmas on its

way, and their softly serious tones poured over the roofs of the town to the harbour where we lay.

In front of the west portal is a curiosity in the form of a vast sandstone bowl known as the Domnapf. Long ago it was the custom that this should be filled with wine at the installation of a new bishop, and the townspeople set about drinking the health of the new prelate until the dish was empty. More curious still, it was an asylum, corresponding to the more usual sanctuary at the steps of the altar. If a person fleeing from justice could reach the bowl and climb up into it he was to go free, and I have never docked in Speyer without climbing the steps in front of the cathedral and peeping over the edge of the bowl in the hopes of seeing some wanted man sitting happy if rather hungry in the bottom of it. Maybe in these days of rationalisation the Domnapf no longer has the same saving grace that it used to have, and in thinking of those times gone by I have sometimes wondered what would happen if a fleeing criminal should arrive at the installation of a bishop. No doubt the eventuality was catered for, and I suspect that if he were drowned in the wine the man would have been given a posthumous free pardon.

The haul from Speyer to Karlsruhe was a longer one, and as the current still increased it cut our progress to only about eight kilometre marks in the hour. The snow had at last decided to let us alone for a while, but after four or five hours of standing at the wheel in several degrees of frost I was almost beginning to wonder whether our idea of boating to the Black Forest for Christmas was such a clever one after all. However, the State Opera Company was performing *Don Carlos* that evening, and even a return of sleet in the afternoon did not deflect us from our purpose of making Karlsruhe in good time. It was still light when we passed under the bridges below the town and headed up for the entrance to the port.

Karlsruhe means Charles' Rest. 'Here where the Margrave Carl once rested in the shade of the Hardt forest and the town arose which recalls his name, on the spot where he found his final peace this monument which encloses his ashes is dedicated to him.' So runs the inscription on the red pyramid of sandstone, not very large, but nevertheless slightly incongruous where it stands in the centre of the city, at the edge of the Forum. The Margrave seems to have been tired of life, or at least bored with his residence at Durlach. He rode off into the forest and lay under a tree where he had such a sound sleep and pleasant dreams that he was convinced that he had found the place where he would spend the rest of his days. Thus the great palace of Karlsruhe was built, and with it the town with the allees radiating from the focal point of the residence to disappear into a horizon bounded by the forested hills behind.

A doctor of philosophy with humanistic tendencies is said to have made an agreement with his son that he would let him know what truth there might be in all this talk of judgment and eternity. All the son had to do was to loiter near the pyramid between eleven o'clock and midnight for two or three nights after the doctor's own funeral. If his father did not appear before him, he could safely assume that life after death was indeed just a lot of wishful thinking.

So the doctor died, and the son dutifully came to the pyramid as arranged. Naturally he was expecting to see either nothing at all or his own father in more or less ordinary shape and form, so he was decidedly surprised when a black dove addressed him from the pyramid.

'Forswear thy error, my son! There is indeed such a thing as eternity, and a purgatory also.' (The dove was Roman Catholic, we may presume).

Shattered in the non-faith he had received from his father throughout his youth the son thereupon went home, and shortly afterwards became ill. However, he had time to summon a priest and undergo a belated and repentant conversion before he died.

Modern Karlsruhe is hardly a place of rest, except that the term might properly enough be applied to the steamer jetty three days before Christmas. There was activity enough in other parts of the huge inland port with its long fingers of artificial basins, but down at the end of the mile of central cut nothing moved. Not even the solitary fisherman, and from the temperature I would not have been surprised if he had long been frozen solid. Like ourselves he had probably chosen that particular situation for a good reason. I knew that the outlet of a cooler from a generator was situated at the end of the cul-de-sac, and it would raise the temperature of the water just enough to prevent our being frozen in if a wave of really severe cold should settle on Karlsruhe overnight.

I have never shared the Margrave's delight in this particular town, except that the gallery in part of the palace contains some Grünewalds, and no pictures have ever given me more of a vision than have Grünewald's panels on the famous polyptich in the Unterlinden museum in Colmar. But it is a good opera-stop, and one of the great delights of boating on the German Rhine out of the high season is the ease with which one can step ashore to a first class opera-house. The first time we went down the Rhine we went to twelve in two weeks, and these ranged from *Parsifal* at Frankfurt to *Die Fledermaus* at Koblenz and *Die Nachtigal* and *Das Kind und der Zauberspuk* at Cologne. If anyone were to wish a special reason for chugging up more than 500 miles of Rhine, then surely the splendid opera-houses provide it. Unless one happens to dislike opera altogether, in which case one must fall back upon the wine.

At Karlsruhe the Rhine begins to close the hills of the Black Forest, and when the weather is clear one can already gaze up to the dark woodlands a little to the south of the city. To the captain of the *Thames Commodore* the Black Forest is more than a view; it is an area which he has known and loved for forty years. So the first looming of the northern edge of the vast tract of mountain country is enough to make him feel almost as though he is at last making port after a fearful storm.

I was first introduced to the Black Forest in family holidays, but at the age of sixteen I was either too old or too young, or perhaps too insensitive to feel the magic of the great woodland in all its incredible wonder. Looking back I am inclined to think that if anyone was unpleasant when we went away as a family, that person was probably me. My parents would have us up and dressed in time to finish breakfast and catch the six o'clock bus from Furt-wangen to the Simonswäldertal. From down in that valley we set out on foot to climb the Kandel, and all morning I gurned and growled and grumbled as we walked, just because I had been brought out of bed two hours too early. Scrambling out of my bunk in the *Thames Commodore* forty years later, ready to enjoy every fleeting second of the beauty of an early morning start along a river when at four o'clock the sun is giving notice of its present coming and the cows are already munching, sleek and glossy, their noses dipped in the six inch layer of mist which covers the buttercups like a silvery bedspread, it often surprises me that I can really have been quite so boorish at an age when I might at least have been energetic. But certain it is that I was much more concerned with my sleep and my adolescence than with that Schwarzwald which was many years later to become one of my very personal loves.

At the same time, those first visits when my father fished so happily in the trout streams by Furtwangen and in the Simonswald must in an indirect way have laid a foundation. Two years later it was decided that I should go for a while to a German university before going up to Cambridge. The idea was a sensible one, for if (as people seemed so easily to assume) I was to become a great scientist it would obviously be a great advantage if I could not only speak German fluently but understand German scientific language as easily as its English counterpart. My school German had been excellently taught and I already spoke moderately well and without an English accent, so it was decided to plunge me straight into a German University to read for what at home we would have called the Part I Zoological Tripos. Since as a family we had already taken holidays in the Black Forest, Freiburg seemed an obvious choice. It had a good Zoological Department under the Nobel Prize-winner Hans Spemann, and the university itself seemed very willing to accept me. (Germany was at that time short of foreign currency, so from their point of view I was a sort of invisible export.)

I was accepted by post in the last weeks of 1932, but before my arrival in the following April the fateful date of 30 January 1933 had come and gone. That was the chill day of the *Machtübernahme* or power take-over. The Reichstag had been burned, and Hitler was in. By the end of July I was out. Looking back it is strange to realise that I was actually present at the famous rectorial address of Martin Heidegger, the Vice-Chancellor of the University. His speech has since become a landmark in existentialist philosophy and yet all I noticed at the time was that the aula was rather over-crowded for such a hot day. I was glad to be standing near an open window. I wondered how much longer this funny little man was going to go on droning. (Actually he shouted; but these were Nazi times, when shouting was so much the fashion that unless you were yelling the audience had a tendency to drop off to sleep.) I doubt if any of the students listened attentively, and it may just have been some accident of later exhumation which invested the speech with such an aura of importance – but that I must leave to the philosophers. So far as I have later been able to understand Heidegger's thesis at all it was just this – that man only lives his noble self at the present in the manner he faces the future, and that this future contains nothing but death and extinction. It was unfortunately to prove only too true for so many of my cheerful fellow-students gathered in the aula of the Albert Ludwig's University that the future was not only lethal but extremely short, so in this respect Heidegger may have been right. But such a philosophy is not likely to give one added confidence when steering up the Rhine between shoals and two-thousand tonners flogging down to Rotterdam, so there perhaps we can leave it.

Yet if student days under the umbrella of the Third Reich were sometimes very strange they could be stimulating also, particularly when just occasionally I penetrated deep into the Black Forest, into a peace which in those days of hating seemed unbelievable.

And that was why, as we chugged up the long cut from the Rhine towards the Karlsruhe docks my eyes kept searching for a parting in the clouds through which perhaps I might just glimpse that heaven of tall, silent pines.

V

Thirty years back – the West Way – from Pforzheim to the Murg valley – end of the Red-Cloaks – Hornisgrinde – Mummelsee mermen – rafts of the Kinzig – source of the Danube – the bathroom of the Golden Raven – night of the snow

MY NEXT encounter with the Black Forest came thirty years later and was the result of my daughter's impending marriage. It is a curious fact that as a wedding approaches even the most level-headed women who have consistently proved themselves to be balanced and intelligent will become so immersed in the detail of invitations, and flowers, and bridesmaids, and trousseau, that the rest of the world ceases to exist for them. I would not have it otherwise, for there is something delicious about those months of preparation. It may even have been the stimulus of that extreme happiness permeating the house that led me to decide it was time I tried my hand a second time at a book on something ultimately more important even than boating on canals. It may astonish canal enthusiasts and those who travel stowed away as readers in the *Thames Commodore*'s bilges that I should really believe that any such thing could exist, but I do. The older I get, the more convinced I become that the one subject of prime importance is – theology. Not the theology of the theological college which closes its study of Church History at the Council of Trent, but the vital, ever-present meanings and relationships in the comings and goings between the individual and his surroundings, which of course includes other individuals as well as things transcendent. Man, universe, 'ground-of-our-being', God, the same search for an understanding of that mysterious environment has occupied a part of mankind for millennia. I have always found that boating is a stimulus to such thoughts. When hanging for twenty minutes in the current while a slow barge comes through the lock, or when

78

steering for hour after hour along a seaway by night or up the snow-
clad Rhine, there is nothing to do but to sing, compose poetry, or
think theologically. I am not a good singer, and as I have no great
desire to try my hand at poetry I fall back upon philosophical
musings.

Yet to write seriously in a pre-wedding environment is not easy.
I doubt if it is even possible. To sing, certainly: to compose odes,
perhaps. But to try to marshal ones thoughts about the meaning
of pain in evolution and its relationship to a God of love – no. It
was not long before my wife realised that the wedding preparations
and the continual ring of my telephone as photographers and cake-
makers canvassed their services were making me mentally barren.
She packed my bag and about midnight she drove me out to
London airport. I boarded the first flight – which happened to be
going to Basle. From the terminus I caught the first train, which
was already straining for the green light, ready to head northwards.
At the first stop I got out. It was Freiburg, the same Freiburg I had
known before a vicious war swept over it.

I walked out into the street. The air smelled just as it had thirty
years before. The two large hotels across the street had vanished
and a variety of new blocks had taken their place. To my left some
taxis were drawn up against the kerb. They were Opel Kapitäns
and Mercedes. That first time the leading car in the rank had been
a Horch and as the driver took me out towards my lodgings on the
edge of the city I had asked him whether he thought the appoint-
ment of Hitler as Chancellor was a very terrible event.

'A terrible event? Him? The Führer?' He drew up at the kerb
and turned round, not in anger but to launch upon an impassioned
speech of praise.

'There is no man like him. There will be work, bread, peace,
everything. He alone can do it. Look!' He opened his overcoat and
displayed furtively a magnificent belt from which hung a sheath
containing a silver handled dagger. He drew out the knife and I
shrank back.

But he meant no harm: he merely wanted to show me the
inscription. It had been presented to him by order of the Führer
himself for his unflinching allegiance and devotion to duty.
Curious, I asked him what he had done to earn it. Political murder,

I presumed; but it turned out that his particular duty had merely been to carry dispatches from the divisional Nazi office by motor bike at an average speed of over sixty miles an hour.

'I have sworn eternal devotion to him,' he declared, replacing his treasure in its sheath. 'To the death, if need be. I have signed my oath with this very dagger, dipped in my own blood.' He had pulled up his sleeve. 'See, that is where I drew the blood to write with.'

This time I did not take a taxi. I wanted to go further afield, so I turned to the bus-station. The first post was to leave at seven. It was going to St. Märgen, a village I did not know, and it took me with it. I arrived in time to have breakfast at the Hotel Hirschen (the Stag).

To be in the forest was not like being on a boat except in one particular – that a day spent walking through that quiet land of rolling woodland could unlock the spirit and release the imagination as surely as a calm night voyage between the skerries or a day of storm among the sands of the German Bight, or a run up the soft and silent Meuse. I stayed three weeks and then I took the train home, the manuscript of *Heaven's Alive* in my case. I had written it in the evenings, but by day I had been out walking, thinking and falling in love with the Black Forest as I went.

During those weeks I discovered that the forest had a number of *Höhenwege* or Heights Trails which crossed it from end to end. Three of these ran from Pforzheim in the north to the Swiss frontier. The *Westweg* set a course parallel to the Rhine along the crests of the western heights, where all the highest land of the Black Forest is situated, and for more than a year it kept haunting me. 'Only 280 kms to Basle', it seemed to urge. 'If you've never tried a long walk, now is the time to begin. Better to start at fifty than at sixty.'

> *O Schwarzwald, O Heimat, wie bist du so schön!*
> *Wie locken das Herz deine schwarzdunkeln Höh'n*
> *zum fröhlichen Wandern in Hochsommerzeit.*
>
> *O, Black Forest country how lovely thou art!*
> *How green thy dark mountains enticing my heart*
> *To wander among them in midsummer days.*

The man who wrote those lines had the sense of the forest right enough. Enticing my heart – that was it. At last the seduction of the dark hills could be resisted no longer, and once again I took the night flight to Basle. This time I knew where I was going, and at eight o'clock I was finishing breakfast in the Pforzheim station buffet. Just to ensure that there would be no idling I had given a firm booking for the return flight from Basle ten days later. That meant an average of 28 kilometres a day, but I thought I could probably do it. When boating in France or Germany I had often walked surprising distances fetching food, seeking milk, running ahead to prepare a lock, scrambling up a hillside for the view, or tracking down a hamlet in the hope of an evening glass of wine for the crew.

After breakfast I walked out into the hall of the station, and somewhat like Christian Morgenstern's hen I walked up and down.* Admittedly I did not cry 'Where, where is the stationmaster?' Instead I examined the walls and windows, stared at the backs of the seats, looked everywhere. An Inspector watched me with obvious anxiety, and eventually came over.

'*Suchen Sie was?*'

'*Ja*', I said. '*Ich suche eine rote Raute.*' I was looking for a red lozenge.

'A lozenge?'

'Yes. A red one.'

I could see the thoughts racing through his mind: – This type of animal can be dangerous. Do not attempt to feed it. Avoid all sudden movements. With a faint and somewhat worried smile he walked away from me backwards until he had put several yards between us. Then he suddenly spun round and bolted.

I went out into the street, determined to make known my intentions more clearly. A taxi-driver was sitting in his car.

'Do you know where I can find the West Way?'

'The West Way? Never heard of it. Probably one of the new streets up where they're building the big estate.'

---

* In der Bahnhofshalle, nicht für es gebaut,
  Geht ein Huhn hin und her.
  'Wo, wo ist der Herr Stationsvorsteher?'
                    Christian Morgenstern, *Galgenlieder*

I said No, the West Way was old, probably a century at least, I was not sure. It was a footpath, a track which ran all the way from Pforzheim to Basle, and it was marked with red lozenges on a white background. But he had never heard of that either, and he could only recommend me to walk south (the direction of Basle) and ask somebody in the town centre.

I did as he suggested and at last I found a young postman. Like a London policeman he would surely be omniscient, I thought. But no, he said he was a Pforzheimer born and bred yet he had never been into the Black Forest, not even on his motor-cycle. He spoke of it as though it were in Central Africa, although in fact the forest began not two miles from where he stood. He was amazed to hear that it contained marked trails.

Next I tried a grocer who was selling from his van. He put his fingers in his mouth, whistled loudly, and several women came running to his assistance. Yes indeed, one of them confirmed, indeed there were such paths. Another said she had seen some sort of red mark up by the water-tower.

And there in fact I found the first of the red lozenges, just as she had said, and as I followed the lane I came upon others. Here and there the trees with the marks had been cut down or bulldozed away to make room for a new house, but on the whole the encouraging little diamonds were clear enough for all the 170 miles of the walk to Basle.

The first two hours were somewhat uninteresting, for the woodland was not very elevated and there were no real hills, but about three o'clock I came to the scattered little village of Dobel, where men were decking out the threshing hall with fir branches for a harvest home supper and dance that very night. I was tempted to stay, but as I had only put thirteen miles astern I decided to go on. I had to average eighteen if I was to catch my plane at Basle on the tenth day.

'I'll walk another hour,' I decided. 'Then I'll find a pleasant inn and lie up.'

I walked another hour and saw many millions of trees. I walked a second hour, then a third. I neither saw nor heard a soul in this remote northern part of the forest and it was long past six when I at last came to a hut. The windows were shuttered, the door bolted. About seven o'clock I was beginning to feel tired in the legs, when I came upon a road. There was a car under the trees, and a man was trying to stow in it his wife and grown-up daughter, three chairs, a dinner-table, a variety of pots and pans and a cooking range. He told me I only had to go another quarter of an hour and I would come to the Hohloh tower. If I dropped down to the left from the tower, twenty minutes would bring me to Kaltenbronn.

'There is a Kurhaus there', he said. 'You can't miss it.'

I was alarmed. 'A cure-house? But I'm not ill.' I tried to explain. All the same, with twenty-five miles already behind me I was so weary that I would willingly have rolled my eyes, hung out my tongue and counterfeited the symptoms of any reasonable disease in order to be admitted for a night's lodging.

The man smiled. 'You don't need to be ill,' he explained. 'Kaltenbronn is what they call a *Höhenluftkurort* (a Height and Air Cure Place). It happens once to have been a hunting lodge of the Archduke, and now it is an inn. You need have no worries.'

A better and more comfortable inn I have never discovered. I slept splendidly, and when I awoke I noticed that the rain was falling with determination. But this did not worry me, for having lived all our lives in England my wife and I always maintain that if one makes plans dependant upon the weather one has no option but to stay at home and indoors until overtaken by death at a ripe old age. Either the radio forecast is bad and at the same time wrong; or favourable – but also incorrect. So either in the wireless bulletin or in fact it is sure to be raining. Much better – and voyaging on the *Thames Commodore* has confirmed the theory – is not to listen, nor even to look up anxiously into the sky, but merely to carry on with what one intended. The *Sauwetter* (weather for sows, as the Germans so nicely put it) will then realise that one is not to be intimidated, and take itself off elsewhere.

From the Hohloh tower the path dropped steeply to cross the River Murg at Forbach. The Murg is one of the few rivers that intersect the western hills of the Black Forest and it is – well, murgish. It is also reddish in its water, not as one might suppose from the red sandstone through which it flows, but for quite a different reason. The fact seems to be that long ago the Murg

D

On the Westweg

valley was from time to time raided by giants who came from the direction of Ruhestein and were known as the Rotmäntel, (Red-Cloaks) because that was their garb. They were wild men, heathen, and not only large but fierce. They would fling knives at innocent hard-working farmers, and as the knife was on a long chain a Red-Cloak had only to flick the chain and back came the knife. Some however had guns – a fact which dates them reasonably well – and they would suddenly appear in the valley on a mission of robbery and murder. Only one man could understand their language and that was the landlord of the Linden (Lime Tree) who could speak Latin.

One Sunday some hundred of the Red-Cloaks descended upon the villages in the Murg valley, and every man who could bear arms sallied out to surround them and shoot them down. Unfortunately it turned out that the Rotmäntel had made themselves invulnerable, but one of the Murg men outwizarded them with a charm so that the protection failed. All were mown down except their leader, Schlotki, who still remained invulnerable.

The men of the Murg shot at him, threw spears and knives and rocks, but not a wound did he receive. In desperation they rushed him, bowled him into the river, covered him over with logs and worked day and night to cover the pile with earth and rocks.

Beaten, Schlotki tried to bribe his captors to free him, but they wisely refused. In desperation he at last told them the secret of his safety and they were able to undo the magic and kill him. As he bled to death the Murg was stained crimson, and today the water is still tinted with the traces of blood washed from the moraine of debris under which his body still lies buried.

Nowadays the Murg valley forms a succession of reservoirs, with dams holding up a head of water to work the turbines of generator-stations. Formerly its wealth lay more in lumbering, the tracts of forest being leased to the guild of Murg shippers, or more properly raftsmen. Several families amassed great wealth from rafting timber. One of the richest was a certain Jakob Kast, who lived about the end of the sixteenth century and had so much money that he decided to roof his house not with straw or wooden shingles, but with silver pieces. But before he could carry out his intention he had a dream in which an angel appeared to him and suggested that instead of tempting the Almighty he would do well to think of the many who were poor.

Kast abandoned his idea and used the silver pieces to found alms-houses instead. But even after all his good works he still had so much silver unspent that his legatees had to come and carry it away by the bushel.

From Forbach the path climbed steeply up the side of the valley and after three hours I was standing high on the ridge of the Badener Höhe. Deep and beautiful forest lay all around, but now and again I could see through a gap in the trees and down across the side valleys toward Baden-Baden and Bühl. In the misty distance lay the copses of the Rhine stretches I knew so well and beyond them the ghosts of the northern Vosges, far behind Strasbourg. Gradually the clouds parted and the sun rose hot and bright. Only down in the Rhine itself did the thin steamy veil remain unmoved, hiding the great river in mystery. It was so still, so peaceful that one could not believe that this great rift valley between the two sets of forest hills had been fought over time and

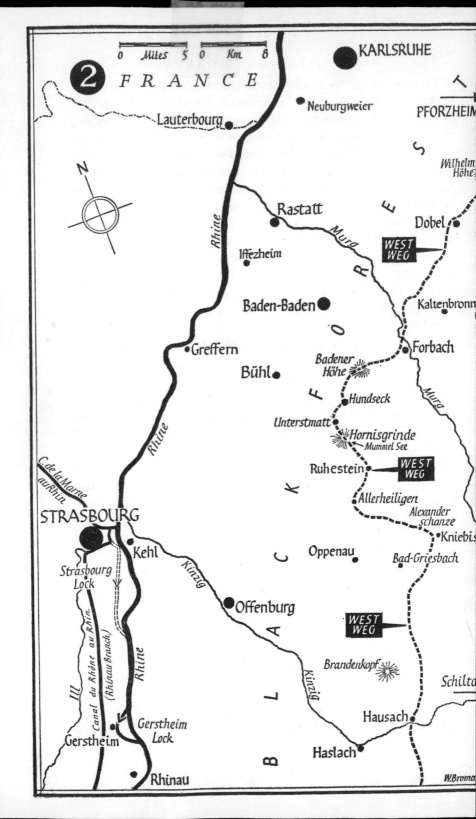

time again, that Attila and Louis XIV and Napoleon and the Kaiser and Hitler had all sent their troops to ravage the countryside and burn the villages down in the plain. Only in one war – the Franco–Prussian of 1870 – was the tragedy somewhat lightened by comedy when the French were routed (in the German version of the tale) by a ruse that was almost medieval in its simplicity.

The fact that one can glimpse the tower of Strasbourg's great cathedral from these hills of Baden means of course that the same hills of Baden can be glimpsed from Strasbourg cathedral. During the Franco–Prussian war a poet named Seubert, who happened to be a Prussian army captain, was sent to the Black Forest at the head of a single company of infantry and instructed to 'make a noise' with the dual purpose of reassuring the local people and frightening the French. His first action was to take his men to the hilltop behind Neuenburg (now two locks below Basle) and scatter them over a wide area after dark to hack up fir-branches and light campfires. The illusion created was such that all but one division of the French army marching up from Belfort to the relief of General MacMahon was diverted to the Rhine bank to be ready to repel a German crossing in force. The fires could also be seen by the Swiss and reporters in Basle sent dispatches to their papers saying a vast army was on the move. The mayor of Sélestat in Alsace telegraphed the wildest reports to Paris, and soon the French Government was convinced that the Prussians had forced crossings of the Rhine at Kembs and Marckolsheim and 150,000 men were advancing across Alsace. General Douay promptly decided to retreat to Belfort with its strong fortifications, and losing the last vestiges of common sense he sent messages ahead that the local people would be wise to hide or bury their valuables. Naturally this was taken as a clear sign that the enemy was on its way, and the poor villagers loaded all their possessions on carts, setting off as a sad trail of refugees, their wives and children with them. This in turn caused panic in the towns ahead. People drove their cattle into the hills and fled, mingling with a French army that was on the run from nothing at all. Only at the Belfort Gap did they stop, having left twenty miles of deserted country behind them.

Further north on the Baden heights, Seubert had every available brass instrument blown and drum beaten. Fires were lit at night and villagers assembled to walk perpetually across the line of vision of the sentries on the roof of Strasbourg cathedral as a real stage army. In this way the imaginative poet completely demoralised the French under General MacMahon and prevented the invasion of the Black Forest – a campaign which would have been a push-over as all other troops had in fact been withdrawn from the area.

I spent my second night at Untertsmatt, and by nine o'clock next morning I was on the summit of the Hornisgrinde, the one high mountain in all the northern Black Forest and one which I had more than once seen above the cloud layer when steaming down the river. Every good Black Forest child knows that on this high, bald mountain top there exists a whole flock of spirits and spooks, ghosts, imps and witches, all busy about their own particular sinister tasks. What fascinated me was how modern and forward-looking these creatures had become, moving with the times and adapting to the ideas of a sceptical generation. Even a century ago it was probably good enough to creep about in half-human, half-animal shape, or simply to pop up as a giant or a dwarf, or to appear as the 'Moospfaff' evidently did, slouching along the West Way with bowed legs, wearing a huge floppy hat and bleating like a goat. Such things were expected, but nowadays they would be unconvincing. The old repertoire of spooky tricks has had to go. On the Hornisgrinde I found that all the spirits I met were now of standard size and wore modern clothing. Some were dressed in imitation of French soldiers, others were driving over the moorland in Jeeps. Even the witches had got rid of their old cauldron and erected in its place a great steel skeleton complete with aerials and insulators, all set about with little shields bearing the letters S.D.R., so that one might almost have believed that they were real humans, technicians of the Süddeutscher Rundfunk.

Down the other side of the Hornisgrinde I came to the dark, mysterious lake of the Mummelsee. It is said that in the year A.D. 33 (or maybe 36), at the same moment that the veil of the Temple was rent in twain and there was darkness over the face of all the earth, the Mummelsee overflowed its banks and all the rivers of the Black Forest rose in sympathy or in horror at the death of Christ. On this morning of late summer I found the water smooth and

unruffled, and if I had any regret it was that the endearing freshwater mermaids of the Mummelsee had gone and I no longer had
the chance to be presented with a bundle of straw which would
turn into solid gold before evening. Yet I suspect that the nymph
of the romantic Glaswaldsee further along the path was still living
in that lovely sheet of water, for it is now a nature reserve. And
what could be truer to nature than that a nymph should live in so
wild a spot?

The Mummelsee mermen and mermaids were famous. One of
them had trouble with his straying cattle – for they kept cattle
under water just as most people keep them on land. A cow once
escaped and began to get mixed up with a land herd, and the
village herdsmen had to help recover it. The Mummel merman
who was dressed in rat skins and apparently had legs rather than a
fishy tail as the marine sort usually have, rewarded them with
some pebbles. If ever they wanted a hot medicinal bath they had
merely to drop one of the stones on the ground, he said. Some time
later one of the men bounced a pebble down a hillside, and at each
spot the earth cracked open, and out came a hot spring. Later the
group of openings was exploited by the local land-owner and
developed into Baden-Baden, probably the most distinguished
bathing establishment the world has ever known.

Then there was the curious event at the village of Seebach, where
the lads and lasses used to meet in the evenings in the spinning
parlour. One evening they were joined by a trio of lovely maidens
in white, girls they did not recognise. These had brought their own
spinning wheels with them, and demurely asking if they might
join the industrious party they were made welcome. They stayed
until nearly midnight, spinning and chatting and becoming
extremely attractive to the young men of the village, who were
very sad indeed that these three beauties had, for some strange
reason, to leave before the rest. One young man in particular had
fallen head over heels in love with one of the pretty visitors, and
anxious to have her company for rather longer he decided one
evening to put the clock back a whole hour.

It was only when the girls were collecting themselves to depart
that the young fellow gaily told them of his simple prank. To the
astonishment of their companions the girls gave wild cries of

distress and rushed out into the night. Next morning three patches were seen on the surface of the Mummelsee, not oil-slicks but stains of bloody crimson. From that time onward there might sometimes be heard a watery wailing and weeping from far below the surface, particularly in the evenings at the hour when the girls had formerly come to spin in the village. The girls were of course, freshwater mermaids, and everyone knows that these creatures have to be home – like all other young females of good reputation – by midnight. Evidently their crusty old father deep down in the Mummelsee had beaten them for their late return, and he never again allowed them to visit the alluring land of their distant human relatives.

I once read that a young man walking all alone through the Black Forest came to the Mummelsee and found a mermaid sitting on the shore. Bewitched by her astonishing beauty he lay on the ground beside her and spent several happy hours in talking with her, and telling her how lovely she was. Eventually she plopped into the water and disappeared. As I followed the path along the edge of the lake I wondered whether it would happen to me also, and whether any of my friends would believe me if I sent them a postcard of the lake with a mark to show just where we had met. However, no mermaid came to sit by me on the strand. Perhaps it was just because I was no longer young.

From the Mummelsee the faithful red lozenges led me through one of the loveliest stretches of all the forest, high over the heathy moor near the Kniebis. This wild and rather inhospitable area is nowadays safe enough, but a traveller who walked the ridge 150 years before me was found – or partly found – eaten by wolves. The people were then poor, because the land was not good for farming and the forests belonged to the nobility. They eked out a miserable existence as resin-thieves, slashing the trunks of the trees and raiding them by candle-light, often dodging the ducal guards who would fire upon them at sight. The resin was rendered down in their cottages to produce turpentine and axle-grease, and was eventually sold from barrows in the markets, or hawked from door to door in the valley villages.

Though the heath itself was deserted the main road was near at hand, yet always far enough away so that I heard little and smelt

even less of the holiday motor-traffic sweeping ceaselessly across
the tops. After a while I discovered how to know that the pathway
was going to cross a road, for then I would meet not just the bright
orange slugs stretched out in patches of shady damp, but other
and larger creatures which had brought their orange mattresses by
car and were now lying at full length, snoozing in the sunshine.
Otherwise I met few people, and such rare walkers as I encountered
were not young people full of *Lebenslust* but grandfathers like
myself. I discovered from the visitors' book at the Alexanderschanze
that more than two hundred others had preceded me down the
West Way that summer, most of them lone walkers, but almost all
had made the trail early in the year and before the summer heat.

I too stayed the night at the Alexanderschanze. A *Schanze* is a
redoubt or earthwork, and the Alexanderschanze is only one of
several scattered about the western ridge. The Schwedenschanze
of course dates from the Thirty Years War, when the villainous
Swedes so improbably spread down the map of Europe, laying
waste anything Catholic that moved, but the Alexanderschanze
was thrown up in 1734 and was originally named Fort Alexander –
the particular Alexander being a Duke of Württemberg.

Before leaving the Alexanderschanze I bought a bun and a
piece of chocolate, for on this one day there would be no possibility
of finding lunch at an inn. In fact from there to the next inn at
Hausach is a pitch of twenty-two miles without a house, farm, cafe,
or any other establishment on the way. Three springs of cold water
lie near the path, and that is certainly something; but I found the
countryside so rich in wild strawberries, raspberries and bilberries
that even the most fastidious gourmet should have been satisfied.

At the end of a hot afternoon I reached the end of this longest
leg of the trail and dropped straight down over the meadows to
Hausach, which lay hot and steamy in the Kinzig valley. A
century earlier the little river would have been a scene of great
activity, for the swift Kinzig was then still a busy route of rafting,
and it was a dismal day in 1894 when the raftsmen of Schiltach
floated down the valley on a raft decked out with greenery hung
with black bunting, their poles and axes wound round also with
funereal black ribbons. Sadly they floated through the villages,
the people watching them in silence from the bridges. Some who

watched were in tears, for all knew that this was the end of an era. The last raft was now passing down and out of sight, and with it went a whole way of life. For rafting had gone on for centuries.

With a swift stream and good water the men might make the Rhine in two days, but even if the level was low and the journey took a week the pay was the same, except that at the outset of the voyage a flagon of wine was filled by the Guild of Raftsmen and as often as it needed refilling during the voyage this was done at the expense of the Masters. It was the business of the youngest aboard a raft to keep the flagon filled; and rafting could be thirsty work, especially in cases of grounding, when only the combined brawn of all the men would free the craft. Arrived at the Rhine, the raftsmen were treated to a meal in one of the local inns, and then the journey home began, on foot across the forest.

The Martinmas raft-run was traditionally the last of the year, and after the final meal at the Rhine each man received a wreath to place around his hat. Then the party was conveyed home at the expense of the Masters, calling on the way at each inn they had visited on their voyages, there to receive a free drink of wine. So the hilarious journey proceeded, a preparation for the long winter months of felling and lumbering in the snow-covered forests to prepare the timber for the rafts of another year.

I found Hausach well provided with inns, but as I went from one to the other I always received the same answer – No, they were very sorry (even if it did not always appear so) but there was not a bed to be had. In fact all the hotels, large and small, had sold their accommodation block-wise to the great international companies which organise the world for travellers, and every bed was reserved for the groups of package tourists arriving from Ostend and Cologne on their way to Austria, Switzerland and Bavaria. This was a nice enough trouble-free system for the landlords, but not quite so attractive to the solitary West Way wanderer whose feet were very well aware that they had put twenty-three miles under them that day and only wanted to stretch out in a hot bath.

I was making my way dismally back down the street to see if I could find a bus or train to the next village up the Kinzig valley, when a man came running out of one of the inns to say he had a

bed free after all. This was a fine piece of understatement, for I
soon discovered that I was the only guest in all the hotel. The great
organised party had duly left Ostend that morning to speed all the
way to Hausach and a telegram had just now arrived to tell the
landlord of their fate. The bus had broken down a few hundred
miles short of its destination.

I ate what I could of a dinner which had been prepared for
twenty-eight and then retired to bed, where I slept so soundly that
I heartlessly never even dreamed of the load of jolly travellers who
should have arrived to dine in Hausach and now were tossing
sleepless and disconsolate in beds in Luxembourg – if they were
fortunate enough to find beds at all in the high summer season.

Leaving Hausach I followed the red lozenges up past the castle
ruin to the western ridge, where for hours as I walked the narrow
track I saw no man or mermaid living and moving and having its
being, nothing but tits, jays, two squirrels, a small deer and two
United States jets. But on a tree-trunk just beneath one of the
lozenge-shields there was a notebook in a little box, put there by
the Schwarzwaldverein (Black Forest Association). I sat under the
tree and turned over the pages, astonished that most of the West
Way wanderers appeared to be poets, even if not of any great skill.
But one traveller had simply taken the pencil and written a single
sentence.

'My God, how glorious is your world!' More concisely than that
I could never have distilled the essence of the Black Forest.

At this time there had been no rain for several weeks, and the
woodland rills contained not a drop of water for the traveller, but
about mid-day I came upon eight boys playing in the wood, and
noticing that they were apparently camped in a hut I deduced that
there must therefore be water in the neighbourhood. I asked a
bright, fair-haired sun-tanned laddie of perhaps twelve years
whether there was a spring.

'Sure.' he said, 'Down that path.' He pointed along a track which
meandered through the meadow grass. 'The spring is down there,
at the edge of the wood behind Bruchsal.'

'Bruchsal?' I knew that Bruchsal must be at least sixty miles
away, a little too far to deviate for the sake of a sip of water. 'How
far is it to the spring?'

'About two hundred yards,' the boy said. 'Come on, I'll show you.'

I ran down the path with him, and two others came with us. Perhaps they were just curious to see what kind of being had suddenly materialised in their remote world. Sure enough, a hundred paces down the hillside, and at the edge of the wood a spring of cold, clear, and wonderfully fresh water was gushing from a pipe into a trough made from a hollowed log. I drank, and the boys filled a bucket for their cooking. Still uncertain as to where precisely their camp was situated I laid out my map on the ground.

'Just where are we? Show me where your site is,' I said.

All three stared at the map with as much comprehension as if it had been a newspaper in Japanese. The conventions of geographers evidently meant nothing to them at all.

'What is this place, this part of the forest called?' I tried to encourage them.

'Bruchsal', said the blond one. 'The wood is the wood beyond Bruchsal.'

'No, stupid,' one of the boys corrected. 'This isn't Bruchsal. It's Karlsruhe.' He obviously meant it.

And then I understood. These lads came from some large city, perhaps Essen, or Bottrop, or Wuppertal or Gelsenkirchen, some vast and hideous sea of bricks and smoke. The Black Forest must have been as remote to them as the moon. Their school or youth committee had sent them off on holiday 'to the great forest beyond Bruchsal' as the teacher had probably explained. Maybe they had changed trains at Karlsruhe and had had a first glimpse there of the distant hills. To them it was a matter of no importance what their camp location might be called, for once away from their home town, place-names lost all significance.

'Do you like being here in Karlsruhe?'

Yes, they did. All three found it wonderful, and to my surprise not one of them said that he found it too quiet, too lonely.

Merrily they climbed back with me to the path, and I went on my way. The landscape was beginning to change now, and occasionally I came upon meadows and cultivated strips stretching further and further into the forest. Now and again the trees parted to give me a view down to farming hamlets tightly clustered among their fields in the broad sunlit valleys. Another long rise, and I unexpectedly came round the edge of a wood to find myself on one of the great European watersheds. The moisture in the grass to my right would flow away to reach the Rhine and the North Sea, but every drop of water to my left would trickle away toward the Danube, and so be on course for the Black Sea. Just outside the pines stood a little chapel, and near it a simple inn. Behind this building the Danube flowed cold and clear from a hole in the ground. I took off my shoes and socks to cool my feet after the day's walk.

Like the Thames, the Danube has more than one source, the local people being of course convinced that theirs is the only genuine one. Naturally I accept the Martinskapelle spring as being the real true blue Danube, but I have a sound reason too, for it lies within sight of the actual watershed between the two great rivers. Others may prefer the castle fountain at Donaueschingen.

This second source has a tale about it which concerns a visitor from Schwaben (Swabia). The Schwabs are notorious for their slowness of wit, and a music-hall dullard is even nowadays often portrayed as a man from Schwaben, so it can only have been a bumpkin from that area who came to Donaueschingen in 1813 and surprised the inhabitants by climbing into the fountain basin to sit by the overflow pipe and put his hand over it. After he had been there for some time another visitor asked him what he was doing.

'I'm playing a trick on the Viennese', was the serious reply. 'They'll laugh on the other side of their faces when they find the Danube runs dry for a whole quarter of an hour!'

I now faced my seventh day of walking and as the lozenges would pass within a few miles of St Märgen I decided to make a detour and visit it in summer instead of snow. Thus it was that I came to the Brend Tower and saw further down the slope the Gasthaus zum Goldenen Raben (the Golden Raven). Until that moment I had forgotten the dreadful incident of the bathroom, but now it all came back.

I had gone to the inn in my student days for a ski-ing holiday and I had invited two Cambridge friends to join me. One morning I decided that it would be quite safe to leave them on the gentle slopes near the inn while I made a quick run across country to see my friends in Freiburg. Even though neither of them spoke more than two words of German (*Ja* and *Nein*) I was sure they could not get into trouble.

That however was where I was wrong. I was only away one night, but when I got back I found the village joiner in his shirt sleeves repairing the door of the bathroom.

'What has happened?' I asked him.

'It is the Englishmen', he replied ominously.

I hurried away to find them in the snow. 'What have you been up to with the bathroom door?' I enquired sternly.

'We? Nothing. It was Herr Ehrath,' Jack assured me. (Herr Ehrath was the innkeeper).

Little by little I discovered the truth. On the previous day they had come in from ski-ing and had decided to have a bath. Fearing however that there might not be enough hot water for two baths Nigel had suggested tossing for it. Jack however had had a better idea; they would fill the bath and both get in at once.

They started their joint bath soon after four o'clock, just before it began to get dark. There was an electric light on the ceiling but there was no switch on the wall. They noticed however a cord hanging down the wall alongside the bath, and beside it a notice: '*Bedienung 2 × läuten*'. They discussed for some minutes the meaning of this piece of algebra and Jack (who was studying logic) said that it clearly meant 'Pull twice and the light goes on.'

Nigel pulled twice. Nothing happened. He pulled twice more. Still nothing happened. Jack took over and tugged for all he was worth but no ray of illumination came to pierce the gathering gloom. He was still pulling intermittently when there was a sound of running feet followed by a knock at the door.

'*Ja?*' It was the chambermaid's voice.

Nigel leaned quietly forward. 'If we don't make a sound she'll probably go away', he whispered. So they sat motionless in the bath, careful not to make the slightest drip or splash.

But the maid did not go away. On the contrary, she knocked repeatedly. Had somebody rung? Was there anything wrong? The bathers sat still as Mummelsee mermen in the water as she went on knocking, calling and speaking to them in a tongue they could not understand. At last she stopped, and they heard her footsteps fading away down the passage.

'I told you so', said Nigel proudly. 'She thinks she's made a mistake.'

His diagnosis of the chambermaid's thoughts proved inaccurate, however. The next thing the pair heard was the heavy tread of Herr Ehrath, with the lighter steps of the maid as an undertone. Further behind came the tramp of a whole platoon if not a regiment. The entire staff was soon congregated in the passage, and so were the hotel guests. Herr Ehrath had the situation under control, however.

'*Ist jemand da?* Is anybody there?' He hammered on the door with his fists. No answer.

Herr Ehrath then said something else, and I asked him afterwards what it was. He had merely declared that he would count three before bursting the door in. Then, clearing a space and explaining to the assembled crowd that somebody had met with an accident in the bath and that only instant action could save them from drowning he opened the door of a bedroom on the other side of the passage, backed over to the window, and charged.

But the woodwork of the local joiner was very well put together and the door failed to spring open even under Herr Ehrath's bison assault. The walls shook however, and a largish piece of the plastering came away and fell with a splash into the water. Herr Ehrath rubbed his bruised shoulder and backed up for another attack. Meanwhile there was a hasty consultation in whispers inside the bathroom, and as usual Jack's logic proved a useful training.

'The next time somebody knocks or speaks, we'll answer,' he suggested. 'And so that we don't give any wrong answers I'll always say "*Ja*" and you can say "*Nein*". Then one of us is sure to be right.'

Nigel had just nodded his assent when Herr Ehrath's massive weight struck the door again like a tank. There was a sharp rending noise and the panels split but they did not part. Some plaster struck Nigel on the head.

'*Ja! Nein!*'

The relief outside was immense. The hotelier, panting with his exertions, spoke loudly.

'*Ist jemand drinnen?* Is anybody in there?'

'*Ja! Nein!*'

'It is one of the Englishmen?'

'Yes. No.'

'Herr Neitschel?'

'No. Yes.'

'Herr Tschack?'

'Yes. No.'

There was a moment's silence followed by consultation. It was by no means certain who was in the bath; Nigel or Jack, or neither. The guests could be heard offering their advice, then a lady knocked gently.

'Are you injured?' she asked in concern.

'No. Yes. Yes. No.'

At this stage the nine-year-old daughter of one of the guests took over. She pushed to the front and whispered through the key-hole in French.

'*Que faites-vous là?*'

'*Nous nous baignons,*' came the reply.

'*Ah! Il n'y pas d'accident?*'

'*Non.*'

'*C'est bon, alors?*'

'*Oui. C'est très bon.*'

The girl announced her findings in German and the crowd melted away disappointed. Herr Ehrath phoned for the joiner, whose last act before he left the bathroom in a somewhat restored condition was to screw a small plate on the wall.

'The light finds itself *outside* the door,' it read. But the information was only given in German.

Standing up among the meadows and looking down toward the inn I remembered another incident too. We had only been a week at the Golden Raven when the three feet of snow began to shrink. A warm wind blew ceaselessly across from the west and by the Saturday morning we could only reach some very patchy ski-ing grounds by carrying our equipment over a meadow of sodden green grass. On north slopes some poor snow remained but elsewhere it had thawed off completely.

If we were depressed we were certainly not the only ones to be dispirited, and it was a gloomy crowd of guests and local people that filled the shuttered saloon that evening. By next morning ski-ing would be finished, and we all knew it. Herr Ehrath strove to keep up our spirits, and he even brought out a British rifle which he had collected during the First World War, hoping to cheer us up by showing us how it worked.

Seated at the corner of a table was a weather-beaten old man in a grey felt cloak and corduroy breeches. This curious individual arrived each evening at about six o'clock and began to drink away a bottle of Schnaps. He had a remarkable blunderbuss that always stood in the corner beside him. About once an hour he would look at his watch and exclaim seriously if rather thickly 'After midnight he will come. He will run across the meadow.' Then he would have some more Schnaps, and wait; and each night the landlord would advance upon the huntsman shortly after midnight with the words 'He will be here.'

The one of whom they spoke was a fox, and when the landlord had spoken the old hunter would rise unsteadily and perform a curious old-fashioned loading operation down the muzzle of his gun. Then he would hold the muzzle to his eye and peer into the darkness of the barrel. I thought it a wonder he never shot himself as he lurched about with the weapon, but Herr Ehrath asked me one evening if I had not noticed that the man lacked several fingers. He was repeatedly shooting himself, it seemed. Only a week or two previously the huntsman had called in as usual for a final drink after shooting at a fox, and on his way home afterwards he had noticed a trail of blood on the moonlit snow. Clearly he must have wounded the fox after all, so he carefully followed the traces of blood across the fields. To his surprise the trail led round in a curve towards the inn, passed straight through the door, and ran directly to the chair where he had been sitting. It was not his experience that foxes usually frequented public houses, so he asked Herr Ehrath if he had seen the creature. It was then that the innkeeper noticed that the huntsman had shot himself in the foot when the gun had gone off by a mistake, but owing to the heavy dosage of Schnaps he had apparently not perceived it himself. He was quite unaware that he was following the trail of his own blood.

The huntsman's midnight departure was usually the signal for apprehensive silence. Each night we waited tensely for the bang, but still more anxiously to hear him fumble at the door again, a sure sign that he had missed not only the fox but himself as well. On this night of the great thaw he rose as usual, loaded the gun, and staggered to the door, but as he opened it he let out a terrific cry.

'Snow!'

There was a couple of feet of new snow already, and it was falling so fast that one could almost see it piling up. All of us rushed out into the moonlight, gathered armfuls and flung it in the air. We shouted like children, and soon we were engaged in a snowball battle of unparalleled energy, a struggle which slowly moved from the snows outside to the warm comfort of the saloon itself. Even the huntsman slung his gun on his shoulder and joined in.

One of the guests was a rather portly business man, a jovial fellow from Stuttgart. Compacting a solid ball of snow he stood in the doorway, took deliberate aim at Herr Ehrath as he stood polishing a glass at the end of the room, and then flung with all his might. He scored a bull's eye, but not on his intended target. He aimed too high and the shot passed well above the landlord's head to strike straight between the eyes the portrait of Adolf the Great which glowered down upon us disapprovingly from over the further doorway. As the snow squashed out to cover the whole of the Führer's nose and temples there was a roar of delight which lasted for only an instant before being frozen into an embarrassed silence. It was just then that the huntsman appeared round the door, brandishing his blunderbuss. Sensing the strained atmosphere he looked first at the others and then in the direction in which all their eyes were turned. When he saw the Führer's face obliterated by the snowball he let out a roar of approval, and in front of the horrified gathering raised his gun to his shoulders, swaying unsteadily from side to side.

'I'll finish the f . . . for good and all,' he exclaimed. He came to something like a steady stance and took aim.

The man who had flung the unlucky snowball happened to be a party member, and this sacrilege was more than he could prudently endure. He snatched at the blunderbuss and wrenched it away.

The huntsman was bewildered by the pained silence around him, and after looking blearily first at one then at another, he shrugged his shoulders and turned to stagger out into the snow, leaving his gun behind.

As the door closed after him there was a very slight easing of the tension. The snow was beginning to melt on the Führer's face and he appeared to be weeping at the shortcomings of mere humanity. Certainly the sight of him did little to restore the gaiety of a few minutes before.

Herr Ehrath picked up a dishcloth, looked at it and put it down again. Then he drew out a very fine silk handkerchief, and climbing up on a chair he mopped off the snow with all the delicacy of a midwife cleaning up a newborn child's tender skin. Full of emotion we watched him. Somebody, I felt, should pronounce the blessing, and in a way that was just what Herr Ehrath did. He laid the cloth down gently and swept his hand over the congregation with a curious reverence.

'*So*,' he said soberly. '*So, so. So!*'

Herr Ehrath paused, like a priest waiting for the congregation to say 'Amen'. Just for an instant I caught his eye, and as our glances met I saw a flicker tremble on his lips, and I quickly looked away. It had been a matter of touch and go whether or not he could carry off his scene. I knew instinctively that if the guests had not been present Herr Ehrath himself would have seized the huntsman's gun and blown the picture to pieces.

VI

The Frontier at Neuburgweier – Lauterbourg – the great Christmas race – Iffezheim creek – Thames Commodore *arrives at Strasbourg – Freiburg in the thirties – the birthday speech – Stiegler and the meteorite*

ABOARD the *Thames Commodore* we headed upstream on a course more or less parallel to the heights I had walked, and soon we were travelling at little more than walking pace. For the first few miles we were still covering nine kilometres in the hour, but I knew that further ahead our rate of progress would be considerably cut, for apart from the passage of the Binger Loch no stretch of the navigable Rhine is as swift as that from Lauterbourg to Strasbourg.

A run of only forty minutes brought us up to the creek at Neuburgweier, an inlet with the jetties where the customs cutters of the Bundesrepublik floated like contented ducks. From here onward the Rhine ceased to be a wholly German river and to starboard we should now have Alsace, to port Baden-Württemberg as before. It was the duty of the smart customs launches to surge up and down the river, checking papers, looking important and providing a pleasant occupation for the genial young men who manned them. We were barely in sight of the customs post before a fast launch larger than ourselves was sweeping down on the current to swing round, close us, wish us a right good day, a hearty welcome, a merry Christmas, a happy New Year and pleasant boating. After which its loud hailer pleasantly requested us to draw in to the creek.

When we had pulled in and made fast to a jetty the customs men came aboard, more out of curiosity and courtesy than for any official reason. Besides, one of them wanted to take the rare chance of exercising the English he had learned when a prisoner in Evesham nearly a quarter of a century earlier. He had worked on a fruit farm, spraying and pruning, picking and packing, and once again it was the familiar story of friendships formed and retained over the years, at least to the extent of sending holiday postcards and Christmas greetings even twenty years after.

The British seem to have had an extraordinary streak of kindliness towards the youngsters captured among the dis-organised remains of a disintegrating German Army. On the Moselle and the Lahn, in Holstein and Saxony and the Rhineland we had known men come aboard just to tell us of the kindness they had received from individuals in Britain, and we had never heard talk of harshness or cruelty. Yet among those who had been taken to the United States – a country of generous-minded people if ever there was one – we had never met any who did not look back on the time of captivity with almost as much loathing as those who had been in Russia and were lucky enough to survive. I never discovered why this was so, but often it seemed that the farmers and villagers in England, and even the camp guards, had gone out of their way to treat the prisoners as though they were their own sons. I was glad that they had, for it was much more likely to help to bridge the gulf caused by the Hitler years than merely to mete out retribution or hatred.

All down the river bank below the customs post the Rhine-ships lay ranged along the shore, two, three and four abreast, a Christmas tree at the stem or stern, a wreath of spruce tied with scarlet ribbon hanging from the deckhead. Here and there a deck-hand was painting bright stripes or triangle sectors on the anchor buoys, but there was no movement of the ships themselves. This, the water police explained, was because the Rhine was at such a low level that there could only be one way working in the shoaled sections further head. The morning was reserved for down-comers, and no upstream craft might go further than Lauterbourg until the look-out on the harbour mole took down the stop signal of red and white stripes. Only then could the up-going race begin.

I decided to move up to Lauterbourg harbour and wait there instead. Once many years earlier I had been through the little town by car, and the memory came back to me of a jolly place of half-timbered houses ranged along either side of the River Lauter. I remembered that we had looked inside the church, and as it was then also the Christmas season there had been a tall fir tree topped by a golden star of Bethlehem, and at its foot a nativity scene ranged on an artificial hillside. There were shepherds and of course the holy family, and some good solid Alsatian oxen looking in through the window. Curiously enough, they were accompanied by an elephant, and later we were to see this beast in many an Alsatian crib. Perhaps he had come with the wise men from the east, carrying their baggage and their gifts.

But I also remembered Lauterbourg for its reliquary hanging on the wall, a jumble of bits and pieces of ossified humanity, not so gruesome as the chamber of horrors of the crypt at Toulouse but at least demanding an equal show of credibility, for down in the corner was a tiny splinter of bone hardly larger than a tin-tack, and under it the unblushing announcement: *Les Onze Mille Vierges de Cologne*. For here we were in the territory of the eleven thousand English maidens, and before reaching Basle we would be sure to encounter larger and more enduring traces of their extraordinary adventure.

At Lauterbourg there were perhaps seventy or more Rhine-ships waiting at the bank or at anchor until the last of the downward craft should have come by. However, the town was too distant for a visit, and as the harbour proved a very run-down and dismal sheet of water which had begun life as a gravel pit we waited just inside the entrance as the procession of *avalants* came sweeping past no more than one boat's length apart, the Dutchmen among them racing home unladen to make port for Christmas with a cabin cargo of German toys and French perfume, a Swiss watch for a friend, and a reasonable gallonage of the wines of Baden and Alsace.

Perhaps the watchman miscounted, but shortly after two-thirty he took in the stop sign, and every ship within sight sprang into activity, each captain striving to get his ship into the lead so that he would be well placed to race for the first lock above Strasbourg on the following afternoon. So close did they run that we had difficulty in slipping out of the harbour, and when we took our chance we found ourselves racing five abreast – to the dismay of the few lagging downward craft which were still approaching the sharp bend at full speed.

In the great Christmas race the Rhine craft were passing each other with only a few feet between them, but I was quite ready to be elbowed out of the way by their powerful bows. I never like to have a two thousand tonner going at full speed a mere two or three yards behind the *Thames Commodore*'s stern, particularly when it is a ship so high at the bow that her steersman can only see the top of our mast and just ahead of us there happens to be a heavily laden vessel which suddenly slows up because her captain is worried about the shallows where the channel changes from one side of the river to the other. And worried for good reason, too. Some of the barges were laden to 1.70 metres and over the shallower patches our depth-sounder showed that there was considerably less than 2.0 metres of water in the river. In case we should have thought that the gauge was inaccurate there was the not very reassuring sight of a ship's boy on the heavy craft ahead of us twirling his striped sounding pole and striking the bottom very close under his ship, raising his fingers to indicate the depth he had measured.

Three fingers – that meant a reading of three tenths of a metre more than the load-line of the ship. Three, then two. The lad sounded, raised his hand again. Two fingers, twenty centimetres, only eight inches of water beneath the great fat barge. The wash lessened as the skipper cut his speed, and I eased back our throttle too. If the ship should go aground I did not wish to run her down from the rear and spoil her paint just before Christmas.

The ship eased off a little more to cut across the middle of the river towards the deep-scoured channel on the bend ahead. The deck-hand twirled his pole.

'*Eins!*' He held up one finger and shook it. Only four inches between the hull and the gravel bottom. I hoped there were no deep-bellied fish just there. The barge-skipper eased right off and leaned out to beckon us past, but I hung back. If a Rhine-ship grounds she usually does so at the stern, and in a moment the stream will snatch the bow and swing her right round.

'*Eins!*'

The ship was drifting now, edging over on the current. Soon she would be clear, or else aground.

'*Eins, Zwei!*' and a little later, '*Drei!*' Three fingers raised, and with a chuff of compressed air the heavy motor started again and the vessel lumbered up the stream in good, deep water.

I decided to make Greffern for the night, this being the only harbour between Lauterbourg and Kehl. Dark was closing in as we came up to it, but there was still light enough to see that the entrance cut was dried right out. At the same time the crisp air swiftly began to distil a mist, and as I do not like navigating the Rhine in fog I decided to push through the next hole in the bank, wherever it might lead. Eventually our searchlight picked up a break in the flood wall, which I presumed to be the front door of a gravel pit, but cautiously sliding through the entrance we were surprised to find ourselves in a long, curving creek. There was plenty of water, and a quarter of a mile up we were surprised to come upon the pontoons and the closed clubhouse and restaurant of the Baden-Baden Yacht Club. It was an excellent place to spend the night, and after making fast we walked along the frozen road in a fog which deadened even the woodland sounds around us. Not that there would have been much noise to blanket, for we had walked for an hour between the deserted orchards and fields of plucked maize before we came to a lighted window in the first house of a village which proved to be Iffezheim.

Iffezheim was once a place where the aristocracy visiting Baden-Baden to wash away their rheumatism would repair to watch the racing. In the fog it was difficult to imagine that this somewhat run-down village could ever have attracted anyone for any purpose whatsoever, but at least we found a pleasant inn where we could close our eyes over a glass of wine and try to imagine the place full of ambassadors and counts, duchesses, society beauties, Turgenieff and Mark Twain. As for Baden-Baden we never saw it, nor even the ruins of Hohenbaden on the hills above. And this was a matter for regret, because the guide book assured us in impeccable English that 'often raw and gruesome, often glorified by the radiance of heavenly kindness, wonderful legends flutter round the old walls of rock in manifold forms, speaking witnesses of creative popular fancy, venerable poetry, an adornment of the ancient place where so many generations bloomed up and sank back into the tide of the past.'

That night it snowed yet again, and it was a bleak riverscape up which we doggedly chugged next morning from one shoal-shadow to the next. I was not sorry that we only had six hours chugging before we were leaving the dull and oil-stained basins of Kehl to port and sidling out at last into the still water of Strasbourg's outer harbour. This was to be the end of our run for Christmas week and there could never be a better place to arrive in midwinter than the Quai des Pêcheurs on the River Ill, right in the heart of one of Europe's most beautiful water cities. As though to welcome us a Christmas tree came sweeping down on the current, probably thrown in at the close of trade by a stall-holder in the market further ahead. I heaved a line over it, roped it alongside and erected it at the *Thames Commodore*'s masthead. It was her first winter voyage, and for a few days we were to leave her while we went up to St Märgen for Christmas.

Our journey took us to Freiburg, and the moment we reached the station I again had that same nostalgic feeling from more than thirty years back. The air was crisp as it had been in that fateful year of 1933. There was the same smell of wood smoke faintly pervading the station itself, mixed with cigars and an aroma of clothes damp from thawing snow. Again I remembered Stahl and his Horch taxi, the dagger with which he had scratched his arm to sign his name in haemoglobin. And then I remembered Borstmann.

The household where I was to lodge as a student consisted of Frau Geheimrat Hofrat Professor Doktor Wettstein, three of her daughters, her son Karl who was a post-graduate medical, two servant girls, an aged family nanny, several foreign students, and Borstmann. It is curious that I never discovered his first name, but then Borstmann was the sort of fellow who seemed to do without one. Borstmann came from Prussia. He was studying social history and when he spoke it sounded like a revolver.

Stahl delivered me to the big house in the Schwaighofstrasse early in the evening. The date was April 20, and in my insular ignorance I had no idea whose birthday it was that caused the streets to be decked out with flags. Innocently I thought the decorations were to do with Easter.

I had hardly carried in my bag when it was explained to me that the evening meal would be at seven on that particular and special

evening, so that we might be finished by eight. I noticed an erect
and keen young man who seemed very keyed up. He continually
looked at his watch, and all through the meal he would break in to
urge his fellow guests not to dally over their food. This was my
first sight of Borstmann, and I did not greatly take to him.

Borstmann was stiff and hygienic – he told me he took four cold
baths a day – and his tightly curled blond hair was shaved so close
around his ears that he bristled. His eyes were pale bluish-green
and they never seemed to blink. They fascinated me and sometimes
I could almost believe he was equipped not with eyes at all but
with a pair of death-rays.

Over the dessert, Borstmann continually interrupted the
friendly and humorous flow of the Frau Geheimrat's conversation
as she tried to discover from me why it was not correct to ask
people if they fumed, and what we wore for smart occasions in
England if the *Smoking* was not dinner jacket and black tie but
really meant fuming. He repeatedly fixed his hostess with a look
of imperative urgency and reminded her that we must not be late.

'There will be no time for coffee', he announced abruptly when
the maid came in to clear the plates. But there he was wrong, for
the coffee was brought at the Frau Geheimrat's request – though
in a spirit of compromise we drank it hurriedly.

After dinner we all moved through to the sewing-room, where
apart from a sewing machine and a few chairs and an elderly
aspidistra the only furniture was a radio. The Frau Geheimrat
asked one of the other students to turn it on.

'He will be speaking any moment now', she said to me by way of
explanation.

'He, Frau Geheimrat? Who?' My question seemed natural
enough, but Borstmann let out a sound like a machine gun.

'*Who?* Who do you think?' His voice vibrated with contempt for
anyone who could ask such a stupid question.

I thought very hard. A footballer perhaps, it might be. Some
radio comic, or a film star. I had only been in the country for a few
hours and I had no idea as yet who the celebrities were. I said as
much to Borstmann. 'If you know, you can tell me,' I added
encouragingly. 'I give up.'

Borstmann's heels clicked with a sound like a pistol shot, and he raised his right arm swiftly as though to brush a cobweb from the chandelier. Then he let out a bellow which would have electrified a parade ground.

'*The Führer!*'

'Oh', I said 'Of course, you mean . . . er . . . yes? I'm so sorry.'

It was just then that one of the daughters of the house explained that with the very greatest regrets she must deprive herself of the joy of staying to listen. Carefully avoiding Borstmann's glare she went on to say that she was half way through the *Critique of Pure Reason*, and was so gripped by it that she simply had to read further. I knew little of Kant, but sufficient at least to guess that we were in for a remarkable evening if anyone could seriously flee for refuge to the *Critique*. Unless, of course, only such high grade erudition would count as a reasonable excuse for deserting the audience.

The rest of us ranged ourselves around the room, and the radio was moved to the centre as though it were part of some strange fertility rite. The ladies took the stools and chairs, and I sat on the floor in a corner. A student from Berne slipped out of the room and eventually returned with an armful of bottles of beer.

'You'll need this', he said as he handed me a litre.

Borstmann regarded him very disapprovingly.

'To drink the Führer's health', the Swiss boy added smoothly. I began to understand how the Confederation had managed for centuries to avoid being embroiled in wars.

Suddenly, and with the din of what seemed to be a massed gathering of all the brass bands of the world, the wireless crashed into sound. Borstmann leapt to his feet and stood rigidly to attention. The rest of us rose more slowly, and the bands blared out a curious jogging tune.

'The Horst Wessel song' Petit the Swiss explained in a whisper.

We stood in silence until the bands had finished a verse and an army of voices then joined in. I noted something about comrades shot by red front and reaction marching in our ranks, and later a passage which told how millions already gazed hopefully on the hooked cross and the day for work and bread was dawning. We sat down at last, and then came The Voice.

Guttural but flowing, and with just a trace of the country

bumpkin about it, the voice of Adolf the Great began to pour from the loudspeaker and rebound off the walls. The Frau Geheimrat sank back on the sofa and took out her embroidery. One by one the guests relaxed, and I stretched out with my back against the wall. Petit flipped open the stopper of his beer, and encouraged by his example, I did the same. Only Borstmann remained erect, frozen in a strange stance of worship like a statue from the Louvre. I had to fight a desire to pinch him to see if he was real.

Just what the Führer said I do not remember – in any case I was not paying very much attention. But even thirty years later I could recall the way in which his rising crescendos carried his voice up through a couple of octaves to an impassioned assertion that there was indeed no such thing as a 'German Question'. And as climax followed climax I noticed that others in the room had fallen beneath his spell and were motionless, hypnotized by something in the sound – perhaps, though it did not then occur to me, by the sound of sheer evil, unabashed and only thinly disguised. The Frau Geheimrat laid down her needle and even the Swiss left half his glass of beer untouched. I myself found the *Führer* hypnotic, but in a different way. His voice did not galvanise me into a highly charged emotional state, nor did it mesmerise me in a statuesque posture such as that in which Borstmann was fixed motionless. The effect upon me was nothing other than soporific. Now and again a rising wave of invective would bring me back to semi-consciousness, but the total effect of a sleepless night in the train, a litre of brown ale and ten minutes of Adolf the Great was to make my head droop upon my shoulder. By the time he came to the glorious future of the Saar Territory I must have been very sound asleep indeed.

What finally woke me was the sudden cessation of his voice. The room was in absolute silence, but I noticed traces of tears on the Frau Geheimrat's face and I could see that she had been deeply moved. I also saw that Borstmann was still poised as I had last seen him, but his death ray eyes were now turned straight towards myself. I tried to smile at him politely.

'Has he finished? It must have been rather a short speech', I said.

If possible Borstmann's frame stiffened even more. He raised his arm, not to salute but to look at his watch. 'The *Führer* has spoken

for fifty-four minutes precisely', he announced. Then his arm shot
out as though he would have skewered me to the floor. 'You were
asleep!'

'I must have dropped off', I said, 'I'm not really very interested
in politics.'

'*Politik!*' I thought Borstmann was going to choke. 'You call
that *Politik*? The *Führer* . . . politics?'

'Well, I just thought he would have been talking politics and . . .
and that sort of thing, you know,' I said, feeling somewhat
uncomfortable. 'Have I missed anything important?'

Although Borstmann was obviously incensed, the emotion
which gripped him most strongly was one of genuine and helpless
astonishment that any human could quietly go off into a doze
whilst his own idol was filling the ether. He began to stutter
something, but unable to find suitable words to express his
amazement and contempt he executed an abrupt right turn,
saluted the ceiling, and left the room. One by one the others
followed, embarrassed. The Swiss collected the empty beer
bottles and gave me a non-committal smile. Soon I was alone
except for my hostess and the eldest of her daughters.

The Frau Geheimrat rose, and I did the same. She gave me a
kindly look but I could see that she was distressed at what I had
done.

'You do not understand' she said. 'You *cannot* understand. It is
a new Germany . . . a new world . . . a new age. Things have changed,
and the old order has gone. A new spirit is born.' She broke off
and left the room.

As soon as the door was closed, Dorothea began to shake with
suppressed laughter. Then, seeing my bewildered expression she
shook her head.

'No,' she said. 'No, I was not laughing at you. It was . . . just the
relief after all these weeks.' Suddenly she became very serious.
'What *is* it? Why does it take people that way, good ordinary
people like my mother and the others? That Borstmann, of course
he has nothing up here.' She tapped her forehead. 'But the rest,
they are not stupid – and yet this . . . this Führer has them in his
hand. Why? Why do they lose their reason the moment he speaks?
You heard what he said – no, of course you did not hear much,

because you were asleep. But I can tell you that he said nothing, not one single thing apart from lies and hate. I too was listening, and it seemed as though I had to fight to prevent myself being drawn out of myself. And then I saw you were asleep. You actually snored, you know.'

'I'm sorry' I said.

'No! Please don't say that. It is now eleven weeks since the Nazis seized power, and since then we have all been mad. Mad, quite mad. But tonight on the Führer's birthday, to see that there *are* still people in the world who can go to sleep when he speaks – that is the only happy thing that has happened in this house.' She paused for a moment and sighed. 'My mother talks of a new age. But what sort of an age? Not an age fit for humans to live in unless . . .'

'Unless?'

'Unless they are like Borstmann', Dorothea said simply.

Throughout that first summer of the Third Reich the more permanent guests at the Frau Geheimrat's were supplemented by birds of passage who came for a few weeks to improve their German. Most of them were English. There was a quiet young man from Caius who read the financial columns of The Times every day after breakfast, there was Grace – not a girl, but a young man from a strictly episcopalian family – who refused to hail Hitler, to join in the Horst Wessel Song, or even to stand up during Deutschland über Alles, yet who miraculously spent four weeks in Freiburg without becoming involved in even the slightest misunderstanding. There was a French girl too, who was anti-German to such a degree that she attacked Petit the Swiss with her bare hands when he mentioned German rearmament, and an Italian lady who was rather fond of the bottle.

To help keep all these people amused and to satisfy their desire to indulge in as much German conversation as possible, the Frau Geheimrat hired an assistant, an impecunious German student of rather unhealthy complexion but with no doubts as to his own excellence. He was given his supper and two marks, in return for which he was to make conversation from after lunch till late at night.

This young man certainly earned his money from the point of view of talking, but it hardly amounted to making conversation because nobody else had much chance to speak. Stiegler ran like a long-playing record, tirelessly and monotonously, and when we quietly slid out of the door to escape he pursued us without pausing for breath. On one occasion Grace and myself and Petit the Swiss were so desperate that we ran out of the house and boarded a passing tram, but Stiegler just managed to scramble into the trailer. At the end of the line we were forced to get out, and he was there waiting for us.

As Stiegler had to talk he of course had to talk about something, and I think he sat up all night reading a popular encyclopaedia in order to tank himself up to capacity for the next day. He was a science student, but he would bore away by the hour on music or economics, country customs or geology, regardless of whether anyone was listening or not. He was omniscient, or so he assumed. We often discussed how we could get rid of him, but we never succeeded in thinking up a satisfactory strategy. His humiliation, when it came, was utter and final, yet it happened quite accidentally. He fell into a snare which was laid for another.

From time to time the hot sunshine of the South German summer would be interrupted by terrific downpours of rain. The approach of these storms could always be forecast without difficulty, for after a week or so of bright clear weather there would come a morning of absolute stillness. Not a leaf moved, and the air was heavy with moisture and apprehension. Jackets and ties were stripped, windows were thrown open and the doors wedged ajar with books. Borstmann stayed almost continually in the cold bath.

In the late afternoon a breeze would spring up, and from high on the Schlossberg to the east of the town one could see clouds forming upon the Vosges, twenty or thirty miles away on the French side of the Rhine. Suddenly the Vosges would disappear, dissolved in sheets of rain, and I learned by experience that it needed only some forty minutes before the deluge would have raced across the plain to strike Freiburg. The storm never came from any other direction, nor did it ever arrive except in the wake of these portents.

Late one evening a storm was due, but it did not arrive until after dark. As usual there was plenty of lightning, but this time it was exceptionally violent and the sky was continually lighted up by the vivid flashes as the trees outside swayed and shivered in the downpour. The sight was so spectacular that several of us gathered behind the windows of the dining-room to watch the show. Besides myself there was Petit the Swiss, a cautious young man named Leonard who was going into the Foreign Office, Grace, and Thornborough – an Oxford Classicist who was so completely unscientific and dead-civilisation minded that thunder and lightning still held something of primeval terror for him. His face shone very white in the intermittent flashing as he twisted the edge of the curtain between his fingers, and every peal made him start as though he had actually seen Jove fling his arrows. In fact this was the first continental storm he had experienced, and it was an exceptional one. I think all of us were soberly impressed by the immense power of nature, but Thornborough seemed almost supernaturally affected. He was just clearing his throat to say something when there was a blinding flash and a noise that was not just a sharp crack but a kind of immense rending sound followed by a metallic thump. The whole house shuddered. Later it turned out that the noise was due in part to a nearby tram being struck as it rattled its way toward Günterstal.

With the shock, all Thornborough's classical folk-lore surged within him, and in a voice that was almost a scream he yelled the one word 'Thunderbolt!'

'What do you mean?' enquired Petit the Swiss, startled.

'A thunderbolt. Didn't you feel the house shake? Thank heaven we're still alive. We might all have been killed. It would have just been fate, I suppose.'

He always took an essentially Greek view of our tenuous existence on Earth. 'It's out there, somewhere, the thunderbolt. It must have missed us by inches almost. I heard it strike the ground.'

Having heard his scream the Frau Geheimrat was now rattling at the door and we let her in. Stiegler slipped in at her heels.

'Is it that somebody is damaged?' Frau Geheimrat looked at us with affectionate worry all over her face, but we quickly reassured her. Nobody was damaged, we said.

Thornborough however was excited about the thunderbolt and he attempted to explain the matter to the Frau Geheimrat. Stiegler intervened at once.

'Herr Zornbra means a *Meteorstein*, Frau Geheimrat. I think it unlikely. Meteorites are known to fall, but there is no reason to suppose that one should fall in the same moment as a flash of lightning.'

Yet Thornborough could not abandon his belief in the divine dart and he continued to speculate about where the bolt from the blue had struck the ground, until one by one the guests drifted off to bed. Even Stiegler left early.

Meanwhile the storm had vanished, and the stars shone clearly in the deep cool sky. Only Leonard and I remained up, sitting alone in the hall. I noticed he was not reading as intently as usual, and I thought he was worried.

'It would be queer if there really was a thunderbolt in the garden,' he said slowly, at last.

Until that moment I had not given serious consideration to the possibilities opened up by Thornborough's allegation, but Leonard's remark touched off a train of thought.

I leaned over and whispered. 'Come to my room. I want to show you something.'

Leonard followed me upstairs, and sitting on my table we spoke in whispers. I pointed to a large specimen in the middle of my desk.

'Will that do?' I asked.

The stone in question was one which I had extracted a week or two previously from the remains of an extinct volcanic crater in the Kaiserstuhl hills. It glistened with metal and sulphides, and had obviously been subjected to tremendous heat. Here and there on its surface tiny but clear crystal domes overlay bubbles caused by the vapourising of some of its constituents in the volcanic furnace.

Leonard stared, then he smiled. 'It looks right to me. Of course I'm no authority, you know.'

We decided that the stone had only one fault, and that was its chunkiness. Leonard agreed with me that a meteorite should probably be more or less round like a cricket ball, and to make it convincing we would need to shape it up. The stone however was a very hard one, and it would be quite impossible to sculpt it on the premises without arousing the whole house, so at Leonard's suggestion I stuffed my geological hammer in my trousers and he concealed the rock under his jacket, to move to a more suitable

E

site. Like thieves we stole down the stairs in our socks and quietly let ourselves out of the front door.

The trimming was carried out in a wood on the edge of the town. Leonard was worried that the ringing of the hammer might attract somebody and it would be difficult to explain why we were hammering away at a stone after midnight, but we remained undisturbed. The work took some time, but we were back at the house by two, with the stone shaped up to an almost smooth sphere.

By good fortune the only bedrooms that overlooked the garden belonged to Leonard and myself, so we were able to get to work without fear of waking the household. The lawn was some ten yards square, and we chose a spot roughly in the centre. Leonard had a sharp knife with which we cut the turf, and with various implements from the kitchen we slowly excavated a broad hole nearly a foot deep. Next we collected the ashtrays from the hall and sifted out the fine grey dust of cigarettes and penny cigars, carefully removing any other tell-tale specks before we tipped the ash into the hole and rubbed it round the sides. Our *Meteorstein* was carefully placed in position and rammed down tightly, and as a final artistic touch we used a whole box of matches in burning the grass on the immediate edge of the hole and scorching it for a few inches all round. Satisfied with our work we crept stealthily up to our beds.

We had chosen the centre of the lawn because it was there that dear old Luisa the Nanny hung out the washing every morning and we thought that this simple soul would be the best person to make the discovery. But as we watched from the shadows inside Leonard's room we saw her come and go repeatedly over the very obvious hole without apparently noticing it. In the middle of the morning Thornborough, our intended victim, ensconced himself in a deck-chair within a few feet of the thunderbolt, but he seemed entirely preoccupied with a volume of Greek verse.

I had just settled down to read some zoology when Leonard whispered to me from his spying-point.

'Stiegler!'

The man had evidently seen Thornborough peacefully studying in the sunshine and with conscientious anxiety to give the maximum service for money he was advancing upon him from the

French windows to indulge in one of his one-sided conversations. The hole lay between him and Thornborough, and he simply could not miss it. Nor did he. He stopped suddenly, peering downward, then fell on his hands and knees. He began to grapple frantically in the hole, digging with his claws like a dachshund.

'The *Meteorstein*!' he exclaimed excitedly. 'Look Zornbra, you were right, I knew it! Look!'

Thornborough looked up from his book, but he seemed to be only mildly interested. 'I thought there was a thunderbolt', he mused. 'Do you know, I've never seen one before.' And with that he returned to his reading, anxious not to become further involved with Stiegler.

Within a few minutes Stiegler had summoned the whole household including Leonard and myself. We squatted in a circle upon the grass, staring awestruck at the thunderbolt which Stiegler had laid reverently besides its hole. Occasionally somebody leaned forward to examine it more closely, but the moment they raised a hand to touch it the Frau Geheimrat uttered a shocked gasp and the hand was quickly withdrawn.

'To think', she said proudly, 'that of all the gardens in this road, yes of all the gardens in Freiburg, in Baden, in the whole of the Reich – to think that mine should have been the one. The stone might have landed next door.'

'Yes', said Leonard, 'it might have, but it didn't.'

'No Leonard, it did not! It was my garden, my lawn that was chosen. Yes, selected above all others by some mysterious power.'

We all congratulated the Frau Geheimrat on the great honour.

'As a mark of the occasion,' she said, 'we will have a special tea, here on the lawn, around the hole.' She gave instructions, and in due course a magnificent spread was carried out, with strawberries and cream and wine. We drank her health, and most solemnly we drank to the meteorite.

After a while Leonard leaned over and whispered.

'He's gone.'

'Gone? Who?'

'Stiegler.'

It certainly struck me as curious that Stiegler should have failed to take such an unparalleled opportunity for boring us with astrophysics and geology, but we soon guessed the explanation. He was not well up in thunderbolts and he had cycled off to the library to prime himself on the subject.

There was no supper that night. A running buffet was served beside the stone for the neighbours who dropped in at the Frau Geheimrat's invitation to see the wonder which had so nearly descended in their gardens but had finally chosen hers. Some were interested and shared the Frau Geheimrat's excitement. Others however were clearly envious and cool in their attitude, but the Frau Geheimrat appeared not to notice. All her attention was fixed upon the stone, and she murmured incessantly her gratitude that her lawn alone had been chosen by divine lot.

I began to be seriously worried. 'Sooner or later the myth will be exploded,' I whispered to Leonard. 'It will break her heart to discover the thing is a fake.'

Leonard agreed, and he thought that we should begin to soften the blow by spreading doubts about the genuineness of the exhibit. He stood up and declared his conviction that a meteorite of such size should surely have been embedded much deeper in the ground. I quickly said I thought so too, and added that I considered the stone to be of quite the wrong consistency. But every objection we could think of was smoothly countered by the Frau Geheimrat with a demand for an explanation as to how else the stone could have got there. Was not the ground scorched, too, and the hole filled with fine grey ash?

We had to admit that the evidence was overwhelming, but I insisted I was still unconvinced. 'Perhaps somebody put it there as a joke,' I suggested tentatively.

It was at this moment that Stiegler returned and pushed his way to the front, crammed to the brim with new knowledge. He heard my suggestion, and took his cue.

'I know something of meteorites,' he said modestly. 'There can be no question but that this is genuine.'

Immeasurably relieved, the Frau Geheimrat glanced round the circle. 'Herr Stiegler will tell us all about meteorites,' she said with a smile towards her ally. 'It will be very interesting I am sure.'

Stepping into the circle, Stiegler asked permission to touch the sacred stone, and Frau Wettstein agreed. Holding it up he began where the encyclopaedia began, and launched out. We heard all about the rotation of the Earth, of the fragments of rock lying in space, of the tremendous speed at which they hurtled towards the Earth, of the incredible temperature generated by atmospheric friction. The audience listened spell-bound as he warmed to his subject, and there was absolute quiet except for his voice. Altogether he spoke for just under an hour and a half and the visitors shook him by the hand as they left, expressing their gratitude for the chance to hear the whole matter explained in such clear detail. Stiegler purred in the glow of admiration.

The next day brought a surprise. Stiegler came importantly into the garden after lunch and held up his hand for silence.

'I have 'phoned to an illustrated paper in Munich,' he declared. 'The photographers will be here tomorrow afternoon, and I have agreed to explain the whole matter to them. A reporter is coming also.'

The Frau Geheimrat was beside herself with excitement. 'My *Meteorstein*! In the papers! And it might have been in Frau Kersten's garden or Frau Hess's, but no – it is in mine! It will be famous!'

Just before supper her son Karl returned from a specialist course in a regional hospital. Snatching away his bag the family and guests almost dragged him across the hall and out into the garden. His mother embraced him wildly. 'Look, Karl, in our garden of all the world, a meteorite!'

Karl looked at the object which Stiegler thrust under his nose. Then he laughed. There was a shocked silence.

'You don't really, honestly believe that that stone has fallen from the skies?' Karl looked at the audience good-humouredly, then shook his head and laughed again.

Stiegler jumped on the incipient heresy and began his address anew. But Karl's laughter could not be stopped, and finally Stiegler faltered.

'You think it is not a meteorite,' he broke off angrily. 'But I know. I have knowledge of these matters.'

Karl smiled. 'That may be,' he said. 'But I've seen this stone before. It's been on Roger's desk for some time. He uses it as a paper-weight.'

Leonard and I were watching Stiegler. He went very white, then

looked round and advanced rather nervously across the grass until
he stood in front of me.

'Is this . . . true?'

'Yes,' I said. 'I told you somebody had probably planted it as a
joke but you wouldn't believe it.'

He seemed uncertain how to carry off the situation. 'And you
knew all the time?'

'Yes, we put the stone there. Leonard and I,' I explained.

'You and Leonard! And you sat there these two days . . .'

It was Thornborough's delighted laughter that rang out,
followed at once by that of Petit the Swiss. The ripple of merriment
spread over the whole circle.

'Herr Stiegler, you had better cable the newspaper not to come,'
advised the Frau Geheimrat, unintentionally adding yet another
humiliation.

Stiegler disappeared through the French windows. But he had
not gone merely to telephone the paper. He walked out through
the front door and we never saw him again. In a curious way I was
sorry that he had brought such a disaster upon himself, but I was
very much more concerned about the effect that the disillusion-
ment would have upon the Frau Geheimrat. I could see that it was
a cruel blow to her pride that she had been robbed of her unique
present from outer space, particularly after Stiegler had depicted
its history so graphically. For several days she seemed downcast
and we were all of us careful not to mention the thunderbolt. Then
came an evening when she and I were alone together, and I felt
that she was trying to summon up the courage to say something.
At last she put down her embroidery.

'Tell me, Roger,' she said gently. 'The *Meteorstein* – you know
that Karl said it was not a real one, and that it was a stone from
your room.'

'Yes,' I said. 'It was . . .'

She held up her hand.

'But he only said that because of Herr Stiegler, didn't he?'

'Because of Stiegler?'

'Yes. And you only pretended you had put it there, to get rid of
Herr Stiegler.'

'I . . .'

But she had not finished.

'It will be a secret between us, just between you and me. Tell me – it really was a real *Meteorstein*, wasn't it?'

Her lips were trembling, and I realised just a little of what it would mean to her if her hopes were dashed. I must have hesitated for a moment, for she laid a hand affectionately on my arm. 'Please tell me,' she begged. 'As a secret between us two. I shall not even tell Karl.'

I had not the heart to snatch away from her ruthlessly this last hope to which she clung so desperately. I lied, deliberately and I think convincingly. And it was a lie I have never for one moment regretted.

'As a secret, I'll tell you,' I agreed. 'Yes, the meteorite was genuine. A real thunderbolt, right there in your lawn.'

VII

Borstmann and the brass band – Hans Spemann – the tale of the Schwabentor – relics for St Peter – a French Alarm – the Balzerherrgott – Oma Waldvogel – spirits of the Feldsee – no welcome at Todtmoos – the farm at Schwarzenberg

I HAD of course been sent to the Albert Ludwig's University in Freiburg to study. Albrecht VI, Archduke of Austria, was the founder, and when he endowed it he expressed the hope that he was 'digging a well of life, from which the waters of wisdom might be inexhaustibly drawn and carried to the uttermost ends of the earth'. Stiegler's presence in the Schwaighofstrasse did much to contribute to this drawing of waters of wisdom, for he was the greatest incentive to work that could have been devised. Immediately dinner was over Petit the Swiss would hurry off to the main station to watch the trains go by – he was hoping to become a great brain of the Swiss Federal Railways – and the rest of us would retire to our respective bed-sitters, from which Stiegler was excluded. There we would sit all evening, Thornborough with his Greek poets, Leonard with German literature, Grace dutifully writing home and myself trying to grasp the embryonic development of the hemichordates well enough to orate upon the subject at the next laboratory seminar. None of us dared to unlock the doors of our cells until we heard Stiegler close the front door behind him. But with the advent of the thunderbolt and Stiegler's subsequent self-effacement, a reaction set in and a more casual mood began to prevail. The only cloud in our private summer sky was SS-Man Borstmann. It was not just his arrogance and his curly hair, his clicking heels and steely eye, his cold douches and his air of heroism as he went about his little official jobs, but his Prussian manners. At the end of a meal he would leap up and elbow others aside in order to be able to open the door for the ladies with a flourish and a heel-click, but he would make quite certain that he overtook them again in the hall to reach the best armchair ahead of them.

One evening Leonard, who had been reading the handbook of diplomatic procedure issued to Foreign Office trainees, asked me to step into his room.

'That fellow Borstmann', he said. 'I suppose he's quite a good sort really.'

'Hm.' I said not very warmly. 'Perhaps you're right.'

There was a pause. 'Mind you,' Leonard conceded at last. 'I'm not saying he's a particular friend of mine.'

'No?'

'But he's a clean sort of fellow,' Leonard added. 'Of course he ought to be with all those baths. And he's quite intelligent too. I thought all SS-men were pretty dim.'

'And you don't think Borstmann's dim?'

'Well, not in quite the same way, if you know what I mean. Mind you, I don't think that he's overbright.'

'No, I suppose not.'

There was another pause. Leonard seemed to be considering. 'I don't know, but I have an idea that you're not very fond of Borstmann,' he said.

'Well,' I replied, 'to be honest I prefer some of the others. Petit, for instance.'

'Oh, so do I, certainly.'

'And Thornborough,' I added.

'Of course. He's easy to get on with.'

'I put Borstmann about last on the list in that respect.'

Leonard seemed to consider. 'I think perhaps you're right.'

'You've some doubt about it, then?'

'Er . . . no, not since Stiegler went away.'

'Nor have I.'

I understood why Leonard had been selected for the diplomatic service. (Later it was proved to have been a good choice, for he did well as ambassador in a very tricky country.) I tried to discuss the matter in hand in Leonard's officially correct fashion.

'Borstmann is a curious fellow,' I said. 'I can't help wondering if he isn't just a little bit of an ass, really.'

Leonard took his time to reply. 'I think perhaps I agree,' he said slowly.

'I don't really like him much at all,' I confessed.

'That's strange,' said Leonard, 'nor do I.' He rummaged in a drawer, produced a bag of toffees and offered me one.

I thanked him. 'Borstmann has rather unusual manners, don't you think?'

'Oh yes. I think that's quite true.'

'You know, Leonard, I almost find him irritating.'

Leonard nodded. 'Yes, I know what you mean. He can be quite upsetting at times.'

'I think he's really a bit stuck up.'

'I suppose he is, yes.'

'In fact if you really want to know, I think he's the nastiest cold-blooded reptile that ever crept.'

Leonard looked up for a moment, then glanced out of the window as though pondering carefully before answering.

'I'm glad you think so,' he said casually. 'That's been my feeling all along. I think we must do something about it.'

'You mean, get rid of him?'

'Yes. Of course one can't murder him or anything of that sort. We shall have to think of something else.'

But Borstmann had heard about the humiliation of Stiegler, and we had a shrewd idea that he was on the watch for a trap. We turned the problem over and over but we could not immediately think of anything which would overthrow him.

'In a case like this,' said Leonard, leaning back in his chair and putting his fingers together like a specialist, 'In a case like this, the current practice in diplomacy is to soften up the subject with repeated pin-pricks. Not actual pricks, of course, but minor attacks of a mild yet irritating form which prey upon the nerves.'

'Such as?'

'Well, I happen to have purchased this gramophone record.' He opened his desk and lifted out carefully a 12″ disc.

Leonard went on to explain that Borstmann leapt to his feet and stood at attention whenever the Horst Wessel song boomed out of the radio, and we might well take advantage of this habit. And so we did.

In the hall there stood a radiogram. Every evening when Borstmann was due to return to the house one of us was ready with the
machine ready to run and Leonard's 12″ disc of the Horst Wessel
song played fortissimo by the massed bands of the SS. The first
evening Leonard released the brake as soon as Borstmann opened
the door, and the strains froze him into stiff attention on the mat.
Clearly he thought that it was good for us to hear such a piece, for
when the music was over he actually complimented Leonard on
buying the record.

The next night we let him reach about half way up the first flight
of stairs before we struck him to a halt, and the third evening we
froze him on the gallery just outside his bedroom door. By this time
Borstmann's suspicions were aroused, but his loyalty to the
Führer was such that nothing would have induced him to move
during the playing of the sacred song. Instead, he tried to beat us
by stealth or by speed. Sometimes he would burst in through the
front door and take the whole flight of stairs four at a time in an
effort to reach his room before the needle had hissed its way round
the silent introductory grooves, and once he came in by the back
door and through the kitchen.

After a few days we varied the system by introducing other quite
harmless records instead, and this unnerved him considerably. He
had to run, in case it should be the Horst Wessel song, yet if it was
merely a yodel he looked extremely foolish; and since he never
could admit that we were amusing ourselves at his expense he
always had to have a reason for his lightning ascent of the stairs.

'*Mein Gott!*' he would exclaim, brushing the Frau Geheimrat
out of the way as he met her on a bend of the flight. 'I must hurry
for my bath.'

We kept up this game for a week or two, and Borstmann carried
it off very ably. Nevertheless the strain was beginning to tell, and
Leonard and I thought we noticed a slight deterioration in his
temper.

One night Borstmann left the house very quietly at about ten
o'clock, and Leonard decided from the evidence – the stealth, the
special dose of hair oil, and the clean trousers – that he was meeting
a young lady. This meant that he would probably be returning
very late.

We went down to the hall and checked on all the other guests. Thornborough and Grace were working in their rooms, Karl was in and two of the daughters were similarly accounted for. Petit was still out, and so was the Italian lady, but everybody else was on the premises. At half-past eleven Petit returned. We knew that we could count on his turning up soon after the night express to Berlin had left the station. He was anxious to tell us all about it, but we gave him a rather cool reception so as to get him off to bed. Shortly after midnight the Italian lady returned alone and somewhat drunk, and we eased her up the stairs before we settled down over our books, to wait.

As expected, we heard the Frau Geheimrat open her door. She leaned over the balcony, an imposing figure in her flowing dressing-gown.

'Not in bed yet?'

'No, Frau Geheimrat. We both have important work . . .'

She sighed in a kindly manner. 'You poor things. You must be tired. Would it not be better in the morning?'

'No, Frau Geheimrat, we must finish our task tonight.'

'Then you will turn out the lights?'

'Of course, Frau Geheimrat. And we shall not be long.'

'Goodnight, then. And do not become too fatigued.'

We bade her goodnight, and she retired to her room. The house was ours.

I tiptoed upstairs to bring down the clothes-line which we had procured for the occasion, and taking off our shoes and socks we got to work to set the stage for Borstmann's return. We moved the radiogram over to the end of the hall near the front door, and put the massed bands of the SS in position, setting the dial to 'repeat'. Leonard, beneath whose hesitant manner lurked an excellent brain, produced from his pocket a little packet of needles marked 'Extra loud. For public performances and outdoor work.' He had walked into the town for it that morning.

Much trial and error was necessary before we had the apparatus perfect. On the inside lever handle of the front door we placed a loop of string, from which hung two heavy dictionaries. When the outside handle was turned, this loop would slide off, and the books would fall and jerk violently another string which passed over the

back of an armchair to the brake release on the radiogram. We
braced lines across the top, bottom and centre of the front door so
that it could open a few inches but not sufficiently to admit an
SS-man, and with fine inspiration Leonard climbed around on the
furniture and removed the lamps from every light fitting in the hall
and up the stairs. Then, satisfied that all should be well, we retired
quietly to our rooms.

I stayed awake until nearly two o'clock waiting for Borstmann's
return, but eventually sleep overcame me until a quarter past three,
when the massed bands of the SS struck up. Leonard's needle was
magnificent; the tubas might have been in my bedroom.

Almost at once there were sounds of movement. Doors opened
and closed around the gallery overlooking the hall and urgent
whispers could be dimly heard in the intervals between the phrases
of the tune. Then came the voice of Frau Geheimrat loudly raised
against the blare of brass.

'Who is it? What is it that is happening?'

I was anxious not to miss the entertainment so I slipped on my
dressing-gown and joined the gathering crowd. At the same
moment I saw Leonard emerge from his room. He had turned off
his light, but enough faint illumination came from the floor above
to reveal faces peering over the stair well into the darkness below.
Having failed to turn on the lights, no one seemed at all inclined
to venture down below. They were all quite at a loss to know what
was happening, for the booming of the band was accompanied by
queer scrabbling noises from the corner by the front door.

There was still no answer to the Frau Geheimrat's call so she
repeated it in a shrill demanding cry. 'Who is it that is down there?'

'It's me – Borstmann.' He sounded out of breath, and I thought
his voice lacked its usual bounce and confidence.

'You, Herr Borstmann? Then you will stop making that noise!
You have awoken the whole household.'

No answer came however, except that the bands struck up a
fresh verse, and the scuffling noise near the door grew louder.

'Are you out of your senses?' Her voice was shrill with anger,
tinged with alarm. 'Stop that horrible din!'

But still the music played.

'I cannot, Frau Geheimrat,' came Borstmann's voice rather

feebly through the music, followed by a rattling as he tried to squeeze through the door. He must have got his ears jammed for he gave a queer kind of yelp followed by some language that we had never heard him use before.

It was too much for the Frau Geheimrat. 'He's drunk, he's drunk,' she exclaimed in horror. 'To think that one of my own guests should make this drunken din and wake us all from our beds! It is too much for my nerves.' And with that she retreated to her room and slammed the door.

By now the domestics had joined the rest, and altogether there were fifteen people peering over the balcony into the gloom below. The record came to an end and started for the second time.

'For heaven's sake, man,' cried Thornborough into the void, 'for heaven's sake take your accursed brass band away. We don't want to hear it all night.'

Borstmann, being an SS-man, had a ceremonial dagger about his person, and he now had the sense to pull it out and slash furiously at the cords which barred his progress. Bursting through the door he fell over the chair and swore again. One of the domestics screamed.

'It's shocking,' said Grace. 'In front of ladies too.'

Thornborough had slipped back into his room and he now reappeared with a bicycle lamp which he shone into the gloom beneath. Its thin beam revealed the terrifying spectacle of a dishevelled Borstmann scrambling to his feet, in his hand a dagger.

The housemaid and cook-girl shrieked, and in the dim light thrown back from Thornborough's beam I saw Luisa the Nanny crossing herself. Petit the Swiss let out a cry of horror at the sight of a man apparently intent on murder. It was Karl who took charge of the situation.

'All the ladies should retire to their rooms,' he instructed, and they did so rapidly. Karl then took the lamp from Thornborough and advanced to the head of the stairs as the SS massed bands struck up another verse. Keeping the lamp trained on the creature below, Karl spoke authoritatively.

'Borstmann,' he ordered, 'put down that knife.'

The SS-man obeyed.

'Now, turn off the gramophone.' He did so, meekly.

'Upstairs to your room, and not another sound. Stand back, everybody, he's drunk.'

With surprisingly sober step Borstmann marched up the stairs, head erect. I fancied there was rather an unpleasant look in his eye, but he said nothing as he turned up the side passage towards his room.

What he had to say he said in the morning. He was waiting in the hall when Leonard and I came down to breakfast together. Six people had already reproved him for his unseemly and inebriate behaviour, we discovered.

'It was you!' He darted his steely eyes at each of us in turn. Then, as we did not deny it, 'An SS-man would never do such a thing.'

'No,' said Leonard cautiously, 'probably not.'

Borstmann seemed at a loss how to proceed. We waited for it, standing on the bottom stair, and at last it came.

'I do not wish to be friends with you any longer,' he hissed. He clicked his heels, turned round sentry-fashion and departed.

Yet SS-man Borstmann was made of sterner stuff than Stiegler, and he accepted his defeat with stiff resignation. He did not quit and run, but whenever he encountered us he marched past with head erect and eyes averted. And since the whole household sympathised very little with him and were obviously amused at the figure he had cut in the hall that sad night, he had to ostracize the entire company. The only person with whom he tried to establish good relations was the Frau Geheimrat, but here he was on delicate ground. Just as she had never accepted the artificial nature of the meteorite, so she refused to admit the idea that Borstmann's behaviour could be accounted for on any other basis than that he had been revoltingly and violently drunk. Just as he raised his eyebrows at us, so she raised hers at him, and if he fawned upon her like a cat she responded as one whose favourite pets were dogs.

Borstmann stayed on at the Schwaighofstrasse, and he was still there when I left some months later. I never saw him again. Twelve years afterwards, when food was very short in the New Germany arising from the ashes of the Reich, I heard that the eighty-five year old Luisa the Nanny had survived the bombardment of the little town of St Georgen in the Black Forest. I sent her a parcel of food, and she wrote to tell me the news of all the members of the Frau Geheimrat's scattered family.

'I do not know if you can remember Herr Borstmann,' she added as a postscript. 'He was in Stalingrad and did not return.'

And that, I thought, was how he would have wished it.

All this now seemed so very long ago, and the nightmare days of rampant evil under Hitler were long dead and buried. And rightly so, for whatever the historical reasons for his meteoric rise, I have never been one of those who could believe that the Nazi period was a natural product of some special German character. In Britain we have known politicians who could easily and willingly have headed a dictatorship of terror, and given an ingenious psychopath to act as figurehead over a bunch of unscrupulous characters I doubt if we could have easily escaped having a Nazi regime of our own. Students revelling in violence, ton-up lads who like to strut about in black and silver, a few Soho killer-gangs – all the raw material is there to make SA, SS and Gestapo in Britain as easily as in Germany. Of course there would be martyrs, men and women who would rather be murdered than serve such a system; but so there were in Germany, and if only the name of Dietrich Bonnhofer is well known in Britain we should not forget that he was one of a very great number. And from the earliest Hitler days there were those who knew exactly where it must lead.

My last evening in the summer of 1933 I was invited to Hans Spemann's house on a hill at the southern edge of the city. He lived in the Mercystrasse, which owed its curious name to the Bavarian general Mercy, who for three days withstood upon that same hill the attacks of Turenne and Condé in the violent battle of Freiburg. The same slopes figured in desperate fighting in the Wars of Succession, both Spanish and Austrian, but now they formed a pleasant residential suburb, gay with blossom in springtime.

Professor Spemann was one of the greatest biologists Germany had known – it was many years since he had won the Nobel Prize – and yet he was the humblest and most sensitive of men with a slow and rather halting voice which almost suggested one who was not very quick in understanding. We sat for a while and talked of his work and of various technicalities of embryological genetics, and we drank a glass of wine from the slope of a neighbouring hill. Yet all the while there was a tinge of sadness in his eyes. At about eleven o'clock he slowly rose to his feet, and I stood up also. But it was not the signal for me to go. He wanted to tell me something very vital indeed.

'So, Pink, you are leaving us,' he began in his quiet and deliberate voice – he could speak my name perfectly well, but he preferred the nickname which he had given me in his laboratory. He led me over to the window and we looked out together across the dark trees and the silent roofs to where the lights of the city sparkled in the distance under the warm night air. Dimly the spire of the cathedral stood out against the starlit sky, and beyond it and a little to the left we could even make out the lights of the Katharin-enstrasse where his laboratory lay. The scene was intensely beautiful, and yet hanging over it there was an intangible sense of tragedy. Spemann was silent again for a few minutes, then he leaned over and quite suddenly pulled the heavy curtain deliberately across the window to shut out the view.

'Already it is too late,' he said simply. 'I can do nothing. You can do nothing. In ten years all that we have seen out there, lying so peacefully at the foot of the hills, will be destroyed. Nobody can prevent it now.'

Spemann sat down at his desk and looked straight at me with his large, sad eyes. 'You have come to love Germany, Pink,' he said. 'I know, because I have felt it. But there will come a time when you will find it very difficult not to hate Germany. And then, always, always you must remember these months you have spent in Freiburg. Remember the happy things, the good things; in those you have seen the heart of our people. The cruelties and foolishness, the stamping boots and the coarse voices of command, the pitilessness of our people toward those of different beliefs and race – when you recall those things remember that they are the symptoms of a disease. When a person has a terrible disease you may easily be revolted; but if that person is someone you love, then you know in your heart that under the disfiguring symptoms the true person is still there, possibly in great pain. You forget the symptoms, except in so far as you help that person you love and admire to be rid of their sickness and to recover.'

Ten years, Spemann had said on that night. His estimate was not very wide of the mark, for just under eleven years later the old merchants' houses in the Münsterplatz lay in smouldering ruins around the scarred fabric of the superb cathedral of red sandstone as the last of the bombers faded away into the distance. His own laboratory was no more than a heap of charred stones and twisted pipes, indistinguishable from a thousand others. Only the torn wings of huge exotic butterflies blowing in the dust might have indicated to some that the place had once been a zoological laboratory.

The snow now lay crisp in the streets as we arrived in Freiburg, fresh from docking in Strasbourg. The familiar post bus was waiting warm and hospitable beside the station and soon we were passing through the edge of the town toward the snow-blanketed forest mountains. The bus took us close by the Schwabentor, one of the two gateway towers of Freiburg which had stood for centuries, and I was delighted to see that its face still carried the immense picture of a wagoner with two casks on his cart and a cat running beside.

Ever since I first wandered out of the city towards the hills I had been intrigued by this mural on the Schwabentor, the gate which straddles the road entering from the east. Schwabentor means Swabian gate, and certainly Swabia might be reckoned to lie somewhat in that direction; but perhaps it also takes its name from the Swabian carter who is the subject of the picture. Of course there are different interpretations of what the man is doing with his barrels of gravel loaded on the cart, and one of them relates that the carter was commissioned to bring to Freiburg two tons of gold pieces to help pay for the construction of the cathedral, but when he arrived the casks were found to contain only stones. Suspicion naturally fell upon the man himself, although all Swabians are traditionally so stupid that one can hardly suppose he would have thought of performing a substitution. However, the good fellow had his own suspicions and soon made his wife (the cat in the mural) confess that she was a witch and had personally magicked the transmutation. He also learned – presumably not from his wife – that any spell would be broken if he were to chop in pieces the creature which had cast it, so he promptly took an axe and reduced his wife to small fragments, whereupon the stones were found to have become gold once again.

More pleasant is the tale that a rich Swabian farmer had heard of the beauty of Freiburg and so he decided in his impetuous Swabian foolishness that he would buy it for himself. Stowing all his money into two casks he set off for Freiburg, where he asked the people how much they wanted for their city. He was mortified to find that the value was a thousand times that of his savings, but to show that he was not such a man of straw as the Freiburgers might suspect he opened the barrels to show them his gold. Unfortunately it proved to be gravel. This delighted the onlookers, but it also convinced them that however thick the Swabian men might be their women were not necessarily so stupid – for it was the wife who sensibly had substituted the stones for the gold before her husband set out on his ill-conceived journey.

The road to St Märgen winds up from the plain and after an hour our bus reached St Peter, its immense abbey church of red sandstone confidently standing as one of the greatest glories of baroque in the Black Forest. Once again we were on the trail of Ursula's water-borne maidens, for it is said that an Abbot of St Peter and the Archbishop of Cologne had been close friends during their student days, and amid their theological studies they made an agreement that the one who should climb highest up the branches of the ecclesiastical tree would give the other a valuable present. The result some decades later was that the one who became archbishop presented the other with the bones of seven of the eleven thousand virgins from England who accompanied Ursula on her voyage upon the Rhine.

I had been to St Peter before – by bus, on foot, or ski-ing in a rather ungainly and grandfatherly way from the top of the Kandel or from St Märgen. One day when I was sitting in the inn the St Märgen barber came over to me and showed me some pages written in 1925 at the age of 89 by a member of his family, Benedikt Schwär, so that others might know of the panic which gripped St Peter in the 1840s.

'At this time my father was already in London: he had established a good business there', wrote Benedikt Schwär. (The business would of course have been a clockmaker's, as Black Forest clocks

were in great demand in England. The barber told me it was
'Schwär's, in East Street', but probably it has long since vanished.)
'Then came the fateful year 1848. He left England at the beginning
of that year. One morning at the end of March we three were
having lunch when Abraham the Merchant came tearing into the
yard with neither hat nor coat, threw some money on the table and
said: "That's yours, you lent it me. The French are coming, they
are already down there in Eschbach!" (Eschbach was only three
miles down the valley.) My father had given him the ten crowns a
little while before to buy him some things. Well, that was the end
of the meal. Father ran up the slope to the court of the monastery
with me behind him. The whole place was full of people, all talking
at once. "We must flee, and hide our money," they were saying.
Mayor Weber, who was a builder, said "I know a good place. There
is an empty space in the monastery kitchen, under the big range
which I put in." No sooner said than done. The floor was broken
up with pick-axe and crowbar, and Bühl-Lenz the police constable
was given the task of going up to St Ursula's Chapel, where there
is a good view of the valley in the direction of Eschbach, to watch.
"And when you see the French, run back to the courtyard and tell
us at once!"

'During this time the men arrived with their money. Headmaster
Braun had filled a fairly heavy leather bag with thalers, Kessing
the Priest brought money in a purse, and my father produced a
leather belt which he had brought home from England, in which
he kept his silver money and also some pieces of gold he had brought
back from London. Then Kreutz the Miller and Waldvogel the
Tanner arrived, each with his money in a cut-down fruit sack
bound with a string. Last of all came Abraham the merchant. He
had packed his thalers in an old sow's bladder and sealed it with
wire. The young men (theological students, as the monastery had
been converted to a diocesan seminary, which it still is), about 50
of them, together with Professor Länder and Professor Knittel
and Vicar Held set off up the Schmittenbach brook to the safety of
the high forest.

'We hid things too. My father hid his English barometer, which
was carried up into the eaves along with other things. Old Frau
Kleiser who lived in our second floor brought her bedding and

linen down the ladder into the cellar, where there was a big empty
tun. My father unscrewed the little door (by which even now boys
are squeezed in to wash out such barrels), stuffed the things in,
pushed them right to the back with a crutch, then screwed up the
door again. Then everybody got ready to flee, the money-hiders
too, with their tools. In came a woman, right into the monastery
kitchen, and saw what was going on. Then she went away to beg
something. This woman was known to everyone as "the big chatter-
box". She hadn't the most prudent of tongues and was well known
in the monastery, as she often worked there. "Our whole work is
now a waste of time", said Headmaster Braun. "Once the French are
here, that woman will tell them everything, and all our money
will be gone."

'Meanwhile it was already midday, as Sexton Schwab had tolled
the bell. People had calmed down a little, as no French had come.
The hole under the range was filled in, and people gradually went
home. But good police-officer Bühl-Lenz was still standing at his
post watching down the valley for the French, who never came.
And if he were not dead I think he would still be standing there,
for neither the mayor nor anyone else ever remembered to tell him
he could go home.'

St Märgen sparkled a welcome to us, its few hundred feet of
elevation above St Peter making the difference between a little
snow and a heavy blanket of white on the houses and trees, the
fence posts, and the roof of its own twin-towered church, less
magnificent than that of St Peter but tall and stately. It is these
towers which one sees from far away among the hills – and even
(with exceptionally good eye-sight) from the summit of the Feldberg, the highest hill in all the Black Forest. Now in its Christmas
card dress the village looked very different from when I came to it
across the sunlit meadows when walking the Western Trail. Then,
the large-eyed cows paused in their bell-ringing to watch me go by.
Now they were all in their winter quarters, the steamy warmth
from their bodies helping the farm families with their heating
problems.

Walking in those summer days some years back, from above the
Golden Raven I dropped down, down, and still further down towards the depths of the Wildgutach, one of the wildest valleys of

all the forest, and on my way I came quite unexpectedly upon the Balzerherrgott, which being interpreted means Balthasar's Lord God.

Who Balthasar was I cannot say, except that he had a little small-holding tucked away in the woods, a property of which all trace has long since vanished. All trace, that is, except the Lord God, the Christ. Somewhere Balthasar must have found the stone figure and brought it to his home in the Black Forest. The Christ was set on a cross of iron and placed under a solitary beech tree which served to give some shade to such poor cattle as Balthasar could muster.

What fate overtook Balthasar I do not know either. Maybe he was murdered by forest robbers, or died of sickness. The family left their home on the hillside and soon it decayed and collapsed. Nothing remained except the Christ, still hanging upon his cross like so many others in that Catholic countryside. As time went by, the Christ became the target for the stones of shepherd lads – or so I have read, though I think it unlikely that any forest lad would stone a Christ for fun, for only in our own day would he be sure that no terrible retribution would overtake him. More certain is that a frustrated hunter once turned upon the crucified figure in a fit of destructive rage and shot off his arms and feet. At last the cross fell, the mutilated Christ lay on the ground. It was a shepherd lad who raised the figure again and leaned him against the beech tree.

A beech is one of those trees which produces a thick growth around a wound or obstruction. Soon the new wood began to creep round the sides of the crucifix until the cross itself was almost entirely engulfed. The two ends of the crossbar projected from the bark on either side, and eventually the forestry overseer had them cut off with a hacksaw – though I cannot imagine why. So there the Christ of stone was held, gripped by the beech which raised him ever higher from the ground and closed its protecting flesh more and more over his naked and mutilated body. Only the head and some of the ribs were visible, and as though to remain true to the legend of how he came by his red breast, a robin built a nest in the safety of the crown of thorns. That I learned from my friends at St Märgen, for when I passed that way the robins had long since gone, the spear-thrust had been covered by the advancing fold of beechwood, and only the head looked down upon me from the broad stem of the tree, a fine head, gothic and greyed, bowed with the sorrows of humanity and immeasurably sad. A few more years, and the Christ would be gone, folded away inside the tree-trunk to astonish a saw-mill operative a century or two later.

From St Märgen I headed south-eastward to pick up the red-lozenged trail only an hour's walk distant, and made for the Höllental (or Hell's Valley) below. To starboard I could see the cluster of houses of Breitnau, and behind them the hill over which I had once fought my way through knee-deep snow to the house of Oma Waldvogel. It was partly her name that led me there through such exertion, for it is not every day that one comes upon a person called Granny Woodbird; but there was another reason also. I wanted Granny Woodbird to make me a pair of slippers.

The old lady seemed enormously aged even if she may only have been eighty-six, and she was sitting in the warm, wood-scented parlour of a peasant house with some of her many grandchildren around her. Two little girls were pushing small bundles of straw under the surface of the water in a tin bath while granny pulled out a wisp and plaited it like a pigtail, continually adding more of the wet straw as the rope grew ever longer. Already some twenty or more feet of straw plait lay coiled on the floor between her feet.

I introduced myself as a customer. I would like a pair of shoes, I said. With flowers on the toes? Yes. And for indoor or outdoor? Oma Waldvogel explained that if one was going out to milk the cows and had to cross a snow-filled yard her special rubber soled variety was the better. The soles were thick and non-slip. They had a tread like a motorcycle tyre, which was not so very surprising as they happened to be cut out of motorcycle tyres.

I chose the outdoor model, and the old lady measured my feet and called to another child, who opened a wooden chest in the corner of the room to bring out a number of carved wooden lasts with which to compare my feet. Eventually we found one of the correct size, and after leaving a tracing of my feet on a piece of brown paper I paid for the shoes. Granny Woodbird told me that one of the children would ski across to the road and put them on the evening bus to St Märgen two days later. If I met the bus the shoes would be there. And so they were, as fine a pair as ever I have

had. Tyre-soled, half an inch thick, with their body of straw-plait
rope padded and lined with part of an old woollen pullover, the
rim edged and bound in scarlet and the toes adorned with a bunch
of pink and blue flowers in wool; for years they brought back to
me the memory of the forest and its people, and on cold evenings
aboard the *Thames Commodore* they kept my feet wonderfully
warm. In their cosy insulation I steered the two days of hard slog
upstream from Karlsruhe to Strasbourg.

The Höllental is rightly named. The road that passes through
it is a main route from Paris to Vienna, and so much traffic roars
along the tarmac that to live anywhere in the valley must certainly
be hell. Had the Black Forest Association not provided a footbridge
I doubt if I would have managed to cross the roadway at all, so
furiously did the Mercedes and Volkswagens sweep by, defying
any pedestrian to dare risk his life in their territory.

Another hour and I was walking alone among the rosebay and
raspberries toward the dark wood at the edge of the bald-headed
Feldberg, the highest mountain in all the forest. At the foot of its
sheer bluff I came to the mysterious deep blue water of the Feldsee.
Part of the strangeness of this exquisite patch of water may derive
from the many evil spirits contained within it, for in times gone
by the lake was a receptacle for just such creatures. It was the
custom to ban a wicked sprite into a flask, and this could be done
in a variety of ways. One method was to call a priest, who put a sort
of spell upon the unwanted imp or whatever it might be, and
having thus immobilised him crammed him into the bottle.
Another was the ingenious ruse used by Paracelsus, the doctor and
chemist of Basle, who taunted a spirit and betted him that however
clever he might be he could not squeeze himself into a medicine
bottle. Which being accomplished, the doctor quickly put in the
stopper.

Embottled spirits were traditionally carried to the top of the
Feldberg cliff and then flung far out to splash into the deep water
of the Feldsee, and when I reached the shore and sat there a while
to marvel at the deep green images of the sombre pines standing
inverted in the lake I noticed that there were fragments of green
glass on the beach. But of escaped spirits I saw no trace. Only far
above me there stood a row of tiny figures at the edge of the

precipice, visitors who had been swept up there by the chairlift
to enjoy what must be one of the wildest and most magnificent
views in all Baden.

The Feldberg area is more visited than any other part of the
Black Forest, and in summer it streams with cars and coaches and
inclusive tours. Then quite suddenly one is in the wilds again,
with here and there a clearing and an upland farmhouse, or a patch
of open meadow cropped short by the tireless cows. Six hours from
the Feldberg's group of hotels I came next day to the Schwarzwaldverein's excellent *Wanderheim* on the Hochkopf, as pleasant
a place to spend the night as ever I could have found; but one can
hardly go to bed at lunchtime, and as I still had 50 kilometres to
Basle and only two more days until my plane home to London I
thought it prudent to walk ahead and drop down from the main
path to Todtmoos. This little town is famous as a health resort for
lung diseases and is well supplied with sanatoria, specialists, nurses
and the like, but it happens also to be a resort in the more ordinary
meaning of the term, and as I arrived there on a Saturday in the
height of the festival season it was not surprising that no bed was
to be found.

I went from pension to hotel, from hotel to guesthouse and
clinic and back to pensions again, but in vain; and by some
master stroke of local genius the municipal accommodation bureau
was closed at week-ends — the only time when it was likely to be
needed. Yet it was interesting to discover the way in which a sole
walker was received during the season of big tourist business. A
few of the landlords were genuinely sorry they had no accommodation, but more were just plain rude.

'Get along out of here', the owner of a pension shouted down
to me from a window. 'We've no time for walkers. That sort of
thing is long out-of-date.' Like others, he had no use for such
idiocy. Besides I would not be paying for a garage as well.

A few were openly hostile, and when at last I realised that I was
wasting my time trying for a bed in Todtmoos I marched out of
the town and walked on to Schwarzenberg. One of the first houses
I came to had a notice in the window that there were rooms
available.

'But not just for one night', said the woman, 'I mean, just think of it. The laundry and so forth – why, it wouldn't be worth my while. And certainly not for a walker. The very idea!' She looked me up and down as though I had foot and mouth disease. Her little dachshund turned up his nose, sniffed, and averted his eyes.

'Of course if you only want to stay for one night I suppose it could be arranged,' she added grudgingly, glancing at her watch. Evidently the chance of trapping another visitor was running out. 'I'll let you have bed and breakfast, only you must pay one full week's board, naturally.'

'Naturally,' I said. 'But I would prefer to sleep in the wood and have the more congenial company of the insects.'

I asked at the sawmill, at a farm, everywhere. The real villagers were all as pleasant as could be and they hopefully referred me from one house to the next until eventually I reached the further end of Schwarzenberg. The last house but one was a pretty little farmhouse with a roof that seemed to fall over its ears and almost hit the ground. Every window was gay with geraniums, and in a small bed in front the begonias and dahlias were blooming as exuberantly as in my own garden at home. Among the plants two little gnomes in red caps were leaning on their spades just as though they were the energetic gardeners responsible. It all looked so delightfully gay and inviting that I decided I would be content if they would just let me sleep in the barn.

I knocked. A woman in her thirties opened the door and looked at me uncertainly. 'I don't really know what to say,' she explained. 'I'm not sure what my husband would think of it.'

So I sought out the husband, the father of the three lovely children who were with him in the cowstall.

'I don't know really,' he said as he looked up from the pail. 'I'm not sure what my wife would think of it.'

A sound married couple, I thought. Neither would do anything the other might not wish. I would be happy in such a house where things were just the way they should be. Yes, even on the floor I would be content.

'Of course we really aren't equipped for taking guests,' said the woman.

'No,' the farmer agreed. 'The famous economic miracle the government is always talking about has not exactly reached the smallholder, you know. The best thing they could do with homes like ours would be to put a match to them and start again.'

'We live very simply,' the woman added. 'There's no running water in the rooms. Just one tap in the yard.'

I hastened to reassure her that I did not expect them to keep Italian waiters in tails. When I casually mentioned that I had a brother-in-law who was a hill farmer with sheep the last hesitations vanished and I was invited in.

In many respects it was the pleasantest of my nine nights on the trail. We rose with the cows at half past five and sat long over a wonderful breakfast of grape tart and coffee, talking of agriculture, sheep, pigs, pesticides, forestry, timber, and what things were like on a Northumbrian farm. All the while the smallest boy with his fiery hair helped himself to the grapes on the pastry of others, until at last he was threatened that the Man would bundle him into a sack and carry him off.

The Man was myself. With his large round eyes the boy looked at me, not in fear but hoping that such an exciting adventure might really overtake him and he would indeed be bundled away in a bag to the strange story-book country of England. The mere possibility made him lean across and take all the remaining grapes off his father's plate.

VIII

Encounter on the bridge – Strasbourg on the Ill – the
porridge-pot from Zürich – end of the Schwanau raiders –
lost wine of King Henry – the cathedral clock – two inns of
Strasbourg – two routes upstream – fate of Turenne – the
English potato-man

I FIRST discovered Strasbourg ten years earlier, when the
Commodore carried us thither by way of the Meuse and the
Rhine-Marne Canal, a waterway which must rank among the most
beautiful in France where it drops down through the forest valley
of the swift and trout-laden River Zorn from the Vosges summit
towards Saverne and the Rhine plain. On her first visit of many
the *Thames Commodore* followed the same route. She had deposited
some friends at Nancy, and my wife and I had a week in which to
cross the divide and reach the centre of Strasbourg to await three
others who were flying over from the United States to join her for
part of her long maiden voyage, which had begun at the London
Zoo and was to end at Besançon.

After seventeen years of inland voyaging I thought I knew all
the possible situations one might encounter, but I was mistaken.
On our way down from Saverne we drew in for the evening at a
little quayside beside a bridge, far out in the country, and after
basking on deck in the rosy light of the summer sunset we went
below and eventually turned to making the supper. Miriam was
cooking something in the galley when there came a noise which
sounded midway between a clap of thunder and somebody dropping
a crate of tin trays. One single violent, juddering crash was
followed by a metallic avalanche, then silence. The ship gave a
slight tremble, and then was still again.

'What on earth was that?' Miriam asked.

I had no idea. 'Sounded like a car dropping from the skies,' I
said, not very seriously. 'It wasn't anything on board.'

142

'No, but the whole place shook. I felt the boat rock.'

'Perhaps it was the devil flinging a dolmen,' I suggested. 'He was always throwing things at Strasbourg Cathedral, long ago.'

And there we left it. Neither of us so much as glanced out of the window.

After supper we decided to go ashore to the inn beyond the quay, and as I jumped down in the darkness I tripped over a wire, then another. The quayside had been clear upon our arrival, but now it seemed to be covered with a spider's web of cables. The cause was not hard to discover, for the wires led to a broken telegraph pole beside our stern, and lying across our after mooring line was a blackish boxy shape which turned out to be a delivery van. It was upside down, its wheels ridiculously reaching for the stars, and the rear doors were open. Scattered about the canal bank was a mass of fruit trays and a hundredweight or more of squashed peaches. How thoughtless people were, I considered, to drop their confounded internal combustion engines on our mooring, to say nothing of entangling us in telephone wires.

I went back for a flashlamp to help Miriam over the debris and with it we looked inside the inverted van. There was no corpse, nothing but the sort of confusion one might expect to find in any rolled-over vehicle. As we examined it we became aware of mutterings and creaking sounds from the bridge immediately above, and walking up the ramp we found a police lieutenant, a sergeant and two garagistes trying to bend the front end of a Renault saloon straight enough for the wheels to be freed. At the moment its toes were turned out like those of a circus clown and the tyres were jammed against other parts of its body. The flattening of its face on one side gave the car a sadly psychopathic appearance in the beam of our lamp.

The police were grateful for the light, and they took me for some ever-watchful official of the canal – at least, I heard myself referred to as the Monsieur from the Department of Bridges and Highways. Miriam asked them what they were doing. (Ladies always make these helpful enquiries. One has only to have a puncture and be labouring away with a rusted jack and a wheel-brace that doesn't fit, to find that some amiable woman passing by will just pause long enough to ask if you had noticed the tyre was flat, and were you going to change the wheel.)

The lieutenant straightened his back, saluted politely, and said they were trying to disencumber the bridge. More than an hour before, the lady – and here he bowed towards a mute figure sitting disconsolate on the parapet – the lady had suffered an encounter with her car. It had remained immobile ever since, and the bridge was blocked. However, a crane would soon arrive. The genius would provide one. (By this he meant the military engineers, who are known in France by this pleasantly flattering title.) The second vehicle was not encumbering the bridge. It had removed the telephone system – hence the delay in establishing contact with the genius – and had come to rest on the quay.

I asked him if he had any idea what could cause two automobiles to drive along a straight road towards a bridge which was obviously wide enough for both, and strike each other face to face with such unerring aim. Could it be that some degree of *ivresse* was involved?

The lieutenant said that to judge that was outside his province. Both drivers had been asked to yield of their blood, and the merchant of fruit had been taken to hospital because he felt bad in the head. No, he was not seriously hurt, but his van had made several inversions before it came to repose by the canal. As for the cause, of that he had no doubt at all. If I were to look over the bridge I would see a boat, a *très beau bateau* indeed. It was not often that such a sight was to be seen on the canal. Both drivers had seen it at once. '*Ah, quel beau bateau, quel joli bateau*' they had said to themselves – was that not so, madame?

The woman on the parapet nodded. She did not seem to want to discuss boats just at the moment.

'*Oui, oui!* That was it. They had both turned to look at the pretty boat, and *Boum!*'

Strasbourg has one of the largest inland ports in the world, and in France there are only three sea-ports which exceed it in size. Yet the city itself is not on the Rhine but lies astride the clear, swift and rippling River Ill, which flows past a succession of waterfronts each of which is a painter's delight. The corner of the Petite France, where a fairy-tale lock-house looks across to the black and white tannery house is one of the most picturesque sights

Strasbourg, the River Ill

in the whole country, but this is only one of many. The vast
building of the old customs house, now a restaurant, is a magnificent
piece of medieval architecture, and below that the great sandstone
palace of Cardinal Rohan stands majestically beside the stream.
There is a riverside walk where ladies exercise their dogs, and
whenever we have docked in the city we have saved our cutlet
bones for these twice-daily visitors to our berth.

This berth is pleasant indeed, being just where the Canal des
Faux Remparts joins the Ill at the Quai des Pêcheurs. The wall is
that of a lock now vanished, the pen being replaced by a pleasant
little lawn with flower-beds, just as though it has all been laid out
specially for our own reception. No traffic uses the canal, and even
the river carries only a daily trip-boat in the summer, but one can
row half a mile along the ring canal to the market and buy eggs
and country cheese, vegetables and peaches – or, in the winter,

Christmas trees. Just by the bridge at the junction of the streams a simple and ancient church, the Wilhelmskirche (St Guillaume) stands rather squashed out of shape by the awkward angle at which the streets meet, and it has a pleasant unpretentious spire.

On the Sunday before Christmas I walked across the bridge to the morning service, which was in German. Strasbourgers, like most Alsatians and many Lorrainers, speak German, and all official attempts to dissuade them by putting up official notices in French and recruiting the police from other parts of the country have been a singular failure. There is indeed a Protestant Church which functions in French, but German is the more usual – and rightly so for was it not the language of the Reformation, which began in Strasbourg itself before stirring Luther to activity?

During the service my attention and my eyes were wandering as they sometimes will, and suddenly I saw the name *Zürich* on a commemorative tablet on the wall. The inscription recorded the gratitude of the parishioners to the Guilds of Zürich, who had sent them the sum of one thousand pounds in the great distress which followed the bombardment of 1870 in the Franco Prussian war – a callous attack which incidentally destroyed almost the whole of the incomparable collection of medieval illuminated books in the library of the cathedral. The Guilds of Zürich, I pondered; then suddenly I remembered. The porringer! Yes, the vow of the great porridge pot had been fulfilled after all.

It happened this way. In 1576 there was considerable unrest in the city, and to prevent disturbances the magistrate boldly decided to distract the people with a great contest of shooting with the arquebus. It might seem highly dangerous to invite shooting societies into a city seething with discontent, but he had judged rightly and the scheme was a great success. Strasbourg went *en fête* and from far and near the teams of marksmen responded to the challenge. Among them were fifty-four from the Guilds of Zürich, trade guilds of which many exist in that city to this day and are very similar to the Livery Companies of the City of London.

In those days the journey from Zürich on the River Limmat to Strasbourg on the River Ill was most easily accomplished by water, but the distance was considerable. Although the voyage was entirely downstream one had to reckon four days, but the Zürichers decided to make the run in a single day of strenuous non-stop rowing. As a demonstration that it could really be done, they placed in the centre of their boat a large iron porringer, which was filled with hot gruel at Zürich. The 'original' pot is still to be seen in the museum by the Ill in Strasbourg, though I have never thought that it was very probable that the worthy Zürichers would have left it behind – and, if they did, that it should have been so carefully preserved for nearly four centuries, even if it suffered a chipping in the bombardment of 1870.

The oarsmen of Zürich performed their extraordinary feat, which even today must be a challenge to any boat club, and they were received in Strasbourg with wild enthusiasm. Their leader then made a speech of thanks in which he declared that if ever Strasbourg were in need the Guildsmen of Zürich would come to their assistance in less time than it took for a pot of porridge to cool – for the cauldron in their boat was still hot enough for the contents to be served to the astonished Strasbourgers.

All these details are known from verses written by one Johann Fischart, who witnessed the victorious arrival of the Zürichers in the centre of Strasbourg nearly four centuries before the *Thames Commodore* lay at the same quay with her Christmas tree aloft. His poem was printed the following year, and a copy is to be seen in the Rhine Shipping Museum in the harbour at Basle. The title page has a line-block of the boat and oarsmen, whilst hot and steaming in the centre of their vessel stands the great cauldron of porridge.

In this dramatic way the men of the Guilds promised their friendship:

> *Zu zeigen dass sie allezeit*
> *Den Freunden so zu Dienst bereit,*
> *Wie aus der Ferne sie herbei*
> *Noch bringen konnten heiss den Brei*

> *To pledge that if their aid were sought*
> *They staunchly by their friends would stand,*
> *As swiftly as they now had brought*
> *Hot porridge from their distant land.*

F

Of course the Zürichers were not the only ones to travel down the Rhine to the great shooting match at Strasbourg. Thirty men of Basle rowed there also with fife and drum and banner at the masthead, the oarsmen in white trousers with smocks of black satin, and on their heads black berets with white feathers to complete the uniform. They brought no hot porridge, but their gifts for the Strasbourg city council comprised a live deer and four live salmon delivered in long containers. Nor were these ships of the marksmen in any way exceptional, for in the Middle Ages the great waterway of the Rhine was the best and safest transport route available – just as it had been in Roman times. Already in 1209 Rhine-ships from Basle are mentioned in the customs regulations at Koblenz, and there was sufficient traffic in the fourteenth century for Walter von Geroldseck to establish the fort of Schwanau (Swan Island) with a force of tough raiders to prey upon the ships plying between Basle and Strasbourg.

Geroldseck had designed his lair ingeniously. An outer defence of swamps surrounded a system of deep moats filled from the river itself, and within these a ring of massive walls made the keep as good as impregnable. When a ship was sighted from the tower the soldiers would go down to the shore and fire with crossbows and heavy catapults until the vessel had been forced to land, so that the passengers could be seized and ransomed for a goodly sum – or, if they had no money or wealthy friends, just robbed and murdered. So things proceeded until 1333, when the two cities organised an attack upon the place.

The first step was to bring up a bridge of boats over which battering-rams and catapults could be brought up for a siege at close quarters. Luckily a spell of exceptionally dry weather parched the marshes and drained the moats, and then the attackers began their bombardment. It was not only stones that they hurled upon the Schwanau but cartload upon cartload of garbage, manure and human excrement until the living accommodation and the wells of drinking water stank so fearfully that the garrison could hardly continue to hold out. Next followed a deluge of flaming missiles until at last the castle was ablaze. When eventually the garrison of sixty men capitulated the merchants and shipmen of Basle and Strasbourg made short work of them. One very old man and a

young lad were spared, but the rest were promptly beheaded –
except for three tradesmen. These were bound, placed upon the
largest catapult and hurled to splash against the stout walls. And
that was the end of the Schwanau.

In spite of the rocks and shoals, once the Schwanau had gone
the Rhine was a much safer route than a forest road beset with
robbers. Every conceivable cargo passed down it. In 1417, a
consignment of 250 tuns of wine was loaded at Basle for convey-
ance to London as a present from the Emperor Sigismund to King
Henry V of England. Unfortunately this wonderful gift never even
reached the North Sea, for the Duke of Brabant had heard that it
was on the way and he ambushed the convoy in the Dutch reaches,
and seized the entire lading. The result was of course that the
Baslers were determined to get their money back, and for decades
they seized every Dutch ship, cargo, man or mouse which they
could lay their hands upon.

Then in 1431 came the famous Council of Basle, one of the great
and long drawn out gatherings of the Roman Church, purposely
held in that city because of the transport facilities which the Rhine
provided. Cusanus the theologian and scientist travelled to it by
boat from Bernkastel on the Moselle, and bishops and cardinals
came by water from all over Europe. Nor was this in any way
unusual, for travellers of every description used the river. Clerics
and peddlers, Jewish traders and imperial emissaries, scholars such
as Adam of Usk from Oxford and Erasmus from Rotterdam, the
raftsmen with their long sweeps, pilgrims heading for Rome,
negotiators bound for the peace talks in Münster, all these
travelled the Rhine. Perhaps the upstream journey was slow, but
where was the need for hurry?

Few people know Strasbourg intimately, though every day in
the holiday season parties of visitors arrive in the cathedral square
to watch one of the performances of the famous clock with its
collection of jacks and moving figures. The ingenious astronomical
section shows the night sky, the state of the moon, and the date.
Once an hour the cock of St Peter crows, and at every quarter
Death shows himself but rapidly retreats when he sees the figure
of Christ. Only at the full hours is he permitted to appear briefly,
unvanquished. Yet all this is only a small part of the programme

displayed by the ingenious mechanisms built in the 14th century by a clockwright named Habrecht, whose desire was to provide Strasbourg with the finest clock in all the world. This he certainly did, and his work has drawn visitors for centuries.

'The famous cathedral clock is the Phoenix among the totality of clocks in Christendom', wrote Thomas Coryat in 1611. 'It excels by far all those I have seen, even that of St Marks in Venice and that of Middelburg in Zeeland – indeed it surpasses all others as a fair young lady of eighteen years, who is continually at pains to show off her beauty to the very best advantage surpasses an uneducated and coarse frump from the country, or a rich pearl of the orient compares with a mere common lump of amber.'

It is difficult to reconcile this praise with the legend that for nearly five hundred years the clock never worked, but it is still alleged that the realistic authorities of the city made quite sure that no other would have a clock to rival theirs by the simple expedient of forbidding its maker to leave Strasbourg. It then occurred to them that he might perhaps nevertheless at least design and build the mechanism for some greater masterpiece, and they took care of this by putting out the clockmaker's eyes.

Yet the council showed itself to be not entirely ungenerous, for when the blind and impoverished Habrecht sickened and was clearly dying they granted the one last wish that he might be taken to the mechanism of his clock in order to carry out a slight improvement. Taken to the rear of the clock he felt the wheels and spindles with his hands, then deftly manipulated the works. The clock stopped and no threats could persuade the sick man to start it again. After his death several attempts were made to restore the works to order but in vain. It was not until centuries later, in the 1830s, that a master clockmaker at last brought the mechanism into working order again.

As for the truth of this tale, the first cathedral clock was made in the fourteenth century, and then as now a cock crowed and flapped its wings at every hour. At the same time the three sages from the east bowed before the virgin. Eventually this piece of machinery failed and in 1547 a new clock was ordered to be designed by three leading mathematicians of Alsace. Twenty years later their design was still incomplete and another professor of mathematics was called in to finish the calculations. Two mechanics (one of whom was indeed named Habrecht) then built the machinery, which ran for two centuries and very rightly stopped in 1789, no doubt disapproving of the foolish conversion of the cathedral into a 'temple of reason'. Fifty years later a skilled mechanic was called in, and after four years he had modified and rebuilt the entire works and added motion to all the figures which were formerly fixed, so that now a regular cavalcade of seasons, ages, genii and Biblical figures leaps to life as the hour strikes.

Yet the story of the blinded mechanic may well reflect something of the harsh and pragmatic way in which the city fathers were in the habit of dealing with problems. Certainly they wasted little time upon malefactors, who for minor offences were ducked in the Ill but if guilty of more serious crimes were merely bound hand and foot and had a suitable weight tied round their necks before they were dropped from the parapet of the Pont des Supplices (now the Pont du Corbeau, a short way upstream of the *Thames Commodore*'s berth). But once again the burghers were generous to the criminals during the days before their involuntary demise, for the city kept a 'house of the condemned'. This building formerly belonged to a wealthy and respectable couple whose only child was a son who – like so many a young man today – kicked over the family traces and took to drugs. His particular leaning was towards alcohol, and in one of his drunken bouts he killed somebody. All entreaties that he was unaware of what he was doing were brushed aside. Murder was murder, the magistrates said. There was no reason for the young fellow to take leave of his senses through drink if he did not want to. He would be executed (by drowning, I presume, as this was long before the days of Doctor Joseph Guillotin and his ingenious pain-reducing machine) and the only concession would be that he could spend his last days at home.

The shock, or perhaps the sheer strain of having their condemned son living on the premises, was too much for the parents, both of whom died not long after the execution. Their house was left to the city, and in their memory the curious custom was introduced by which condemned criminals were entertained there for several days at the public expense and allowed to eat and drink as much as they wished. It seems, however, that many of the condemned suffered from a certain loss of appetite and took little advantage of this act of generosity.

My wife and I always looked forward to our arrival in Strasbourg for a particular reason – or rather, for two. One of these was the onion tart in the 'Zuem Hailiche Graab'. It is not every day that one can find an inn named the Holy Sepulchre – maybe there once was a religious institution of that name nearby – but it was the tart more than the name which drew us time after time. Somewhat like an old London coffee-house, the Holy Sepulchre had its long tables with high pew-backs, and along either side were seated dozens of broad-faced, heavy Alsatians, munching the landlord's special onion tart as an accompaniment to the excellent wines of the foothills of the Vosges – the Pinot and Tokay, and especially the aromatic Gewürztraminer.

The other reason was the 'Lohkäs', an unpretentious little inn close by the lock of the Petite France, which we could reach by the bankside walk of the old towpath. Here it was a case of *choucroûte garni*, but even more of the great automatic organ, an aristocratic fore-runner of the juke-box and every inch of ten feet in height. It was always worth the half franc in the slot to set the thing in motion, even if the music left something to be desired. The sounds were produced partly by wooden bars of the xylophone type and partly by organ pipes, but as some of each variety were missing and shrinkage or damp had so changed the pitches of the two systems that they bore no relation to each other, several verses of a tune could be played before anyone present could identify it as an extremely familiar air. Yet the music was largely irrelevant, for it was the accompaniments that mattered. The machine was built so that its upper storey represented an Alsatian house, and as the instrument ground and wheezed its way through the tune the doors of the various floors would open and close, a maestro in tails would peer through his spectacles as he beat a tempo which knew no correlation with the music, an Alsatian boy danced endlessly round the parlour with his pretty girl, and the cymbals were clashed by a monkey. Below, an early locomotive in shadow would reappear two or three times a minute, puffing its way to haul a train of boxy coaches across a high trestle bridge which spanned a violent torrent, the water seething blue and silver in its ingenious flickering. But the *clou de la collection*, the nail of the whole affair, was the devil. From time to time his pointed ears would appear over the edge of the chimney of the happy Alsatian house, then slowly he would rise until his whole evil and smirking face could be seen projecting from the flue. Whether it was the world in general which displeased him or only those who were eating their sauerkraut in the Lohkäs I do not know; but after turning his head to look at us he would flush scarlet with rage, or maybe from the sheer heat of hell, and after flashing fire from his eyes he would retreat into the chimney again to think things over.

On her maiden voyage the *Thames Commodore* headed on towards Basle by taking the Rhine-Rhône Canal, which leaves Strasbourg at the Hospital Lock and turns a sharp corner to aim straight for Mulhouse eighty miles distant. At least, that is what it used to do, but with the development of the Grand Canal d'Alsace most of the course had by then been allowed to decay and only the first few locks were still kept open, enough to provide a route for the slower and more underpowered barges to the still water at the foot of the giant lock of Rhinau on the G.C.A.

An hour out of the edge of the city we drew into the bank and settled down for the evening in a scene of incredible beauty or astonishing dullness – according to which way one regarded it. Ahead the canal ran like the convergent perspective lines of a student artist to finish in the tiny dark rectangle of the gates of the next lock up the line. The water lay brown as cocoa, unruffled by the slightest breath of wind or even the plop of some hopeful young fish. Beside it the towpath on one side and the rusting traction rails of the electric mules long since sent to the knackers yard drew their own unswerving lines through the grass and willowherb, each of them flanked by an expressionless file of slim poplars, not one of them an inch out of place except where, immediately opposite us, a brief gap had been wrenched by lightning or gale. Somewhere beyond the trees a plume of smoke rose straight upward from the stack of the Erstein sugar factory, and far in the distance to our right the high ridge of the Vosges lay concealed by the haze, revealing its presence only as an invisible something behind which the sun was soon to sink to rest until the following day. As a boatman I found the scene wonderfully peaceful, but its sheer loveliness was only brought to my notice through one of our new guests, Florence Wheelock, who was so enraptured by it that she would contentedly have spent all night on the deck watching the orange change to amber and red, then to violet and an ever deepening blue until the night stars stared clear and unwinking upon us from above, and the first droplets of dew began imperceptibly to distill on the decking.

In contrast to this soft and idle route, our next departure southward from Strasbourg was by the Rhine itself. One more lock of the G.C.A. had by then been completed, and I reckoned that two hours hard labour up the swift March flow would be easier and quicker than to take the old canal again up to Rhinau.

It was a cold morning and a wet one when I started up the engines and sidled the ship out from the quayside where she had lain alone for three months under the eye of a nearby concierge, a professional hunter whose window looked out over her super-structure. I had of course taken all her cooling system to pieces for the icy months when Strasbourg lay gripped in its customary winter freeze, but as soon as I had reconstituted her arteries and veins she cleared her throat and started without hesitation, as anxious as myself to head south into warmer climes. The River Ill was so swollen with the thawing snows of the Vosges that the towpath was under water, but she shot the bridges in great style, flashed her papers at the customs post at the entrance to the harbour basins and set off through the port.

Even on a Sunday morning the Autonomous Port of Strasbourg was a fine sight. Not a ship was on the move, but along the miles of quays the motor vessels of the Rhine trade lay waiting for Monday and the return of the dockers. A few surviving giant lighters with high-perched steering wheels, groups of powerful modern pushers resplendent in the bright paint of their several liveries, tugs and cranes, fuel boats and tankers, dredgers and work-boats, harbour launches and customs craft, the hundreds of ships lay still, hardly deigning to let their heavy bulk acknowledge our passing by even the slightest of tremors. Basin after basin we threaded until the Écluse Sud came in sight. Three loud blasts stirred the keeper from his seat by the fire, and soon we were dropping between the wet walls of the lock to the lower level of the Rhine beyond.

It is always an exhilarating experience to steer out into that great river. Ever so slowly one bobs down the gulley from the lock, watching for the mast tips of ships sweeping down beyond the dike. At the end of the mole there is a confused patch where the water swings back to circle over the silty shoal before resuming its journey downstream, then suddenly the current strikes the bow so forcefully that one wonders whether even the full power of two hundred and sixty unleashed Perkins horses is going to drive the stern round and head her up into the surging river. A swashing of waves and then she straightens out, her nose pointing upstream, the water foaming swiftly past her flank although the bank glides by so very, very slowly.

The Rhine is curiously remote, for the towns lie way back from the river, nearer to the rising ground which to starboard reveals itself in clear weather as the Black Forest. It was from one of the lesser heights where the forest drops to the Rhine plain that the Margrave of Baden looked towards the river, which the troops of Louis XIV had just crossed, and through his glass made out a figure riding upon a white horse at the head of the invading forces. Quickly he summoned one of his best gunners and pointed out the distant figure, asking whether there was any chance of hitting him at such an exceptionally long range. The gunner said that he could at least try, and he primed a cannon. At that moment the French halted, their commander sitting astride his horse beneath a walnut tree.

The bombardier lined up his gun, raised the muzzle to give the longest possible flight, lit the fuse and stood back. The ball flew high over the fields and eventually by a lucky chance struck the trunk of the walnut tree with such violence that one of the main limbs fell off and came down upon the horseman, flinging him from his steed. He hit the ground so hard that he died.

Such was the extraordinary end to the brilliant military career of Marshal Turenne, and to remind the French of what might happen to their generals the plot of land upon which the tree stood was presented by Baden to the French nation.

Somewhere in the plain Offenburg lies hidden, a place that is little more than the railway junction for the line to Kehl and Strasbourg. Though it is invisible from the river I changed trains there many times in the 1930s but never did I stray beyond the station. Had I done so I might have seen in front of the town hall a statue of Sir Francis Drake, very fine in an admiral's uniform and standing upon a wreath of potatoes. His presence is hard to explain, for he never sailed the Rhine. His statue was chiseled by a sculptor of Strasbourg who later presented the work to Offenburg, possibly because he thought the space before the town hall needed embellishment. The same sculptor seems also to have been under the impression that it was Drake who first imported potatoes from the New World. Offenburgers could hardly be expected to know much about this English corsair, and so to the townspeople the statue became known quite simply as the *Kartoffelmännle* – the little potato man.

The run to the foot of Gerstheim lock is unspectacular. To starboard the Rhine is flanked by mile after mile of French copse, the poplars scattered at random and tangled with brushwood. To port the copse at first sight appears similar, but it is German and therefore orderly. The ground is clear, the trees in sentry rows of such precision that as each line of them passes abeam one is aware for an instant of only a single poplar, so exactly does each tree stem hide the one beyond it. There is little traffic on a Sunday morning, but before Gerstheim's broad cut comes into view we have overhauled two ships, one heavy laden with trunks of mahogany from African forests, the other with containers trans-shipped in Rotterdam. The water is smooth in the lock-cut and it will be so for most of the long haul ahead to Basle. A rise of forty-five feet in the giant pen, another great step at Rhinau, and to starboard the clouds part to reveal the massive ramparts and turrets of the distant Haut-Koenigsbourg standing like a sentry on its shoulder of hill, and behind it the blue mass of the dark forested Vosges. The great castle had long been ruined and dismantled when the nearby town of Sélestat bought it as a wreck. After the Germans took Alsace the town council, lacking any funds to undertake such a vast piece of restoration, hit on the idea of presenting the ruin to the Kaiser, who poured money into rebuilding the whole complex of buildings according to the best and most expensive antiquarian advice. With

On the Grand Canal d'Alsace

the Treaty of Versailles, Séléstat became French again and inherited its once shabby gift in excellent condition.

The Vosges appear in the distance very much like the hills of the Black Forest on the further side of the Rhine plain. And similar they are, yet at the same time strangely different. In both cases the tops of the mountains are smooth and round, but whereas the Black Forest has its flourishing upland farms the Vosges summits are bare and open, with herds of cattle grazing on poor and rough grass. The Black Forest has butter, the Vosges cheese, and all because of the shape of the country. To the west the country falls away very gently, and the prevailing westerlies are lifted gently to drop damp mist and fine rain for much of the year. I have yet to take the southern branch of the Canal de l'Est through Épinal without standing out for hours on end to work the locks in a drizzle.

The fine rain of the Vosges is excellent for making a vast area of boggy pasture, but once the air passes the summits it falls down the steep slope to the plain and as it does so the compression heats it and so makes Alsace the hottest part of Europe north of Italy. The warm air then blows over the plain and hits the steep side of the Black Forest to be thrown up high. It is made cold quickly, and that makes what rain is left fall out. It is violent rain if it is rain at all, and in millions of years it has rained enough to break up the German hill tops into good soil for agriculture. The Black

Forest has farms and mountain villages but the Vosges have none. The villages are down in the valleys and so in winter are the cows. Not until St Urbanus' day (25th May) do they trail up to the highlands again, the cheesemen and their dogs following them.

To make butter involves a churn and a separator, a sterilizer, clean cow-sheds and everything a Black Forest farmer would have to hand, but in the Vosges the herdsmen sleep in huts or rough shelters, setting the milk in pans to convert it slowly to cheese. Excellent cheese too; the Münster of Alsace is always a favourite aboard the *Thames Commodore*.

Above Rhinau lock a third group of hills appears, humbler but much closer, a group of little volcanic cones which are set so close to the Rhine that one chugs close alongside their wooded slopes. These miniature mountains are the Kaiserstuhl, the Imperial Throne, one of the warmest and strangest areas along all the Rhine.

IX

IT WAS on our earliest voyage up the Rhine valley that I consulted
a village policeman and asked him where we might see a wine-
making establishment. He considered, then 'phoned to the little
Kaiserstuhl village of Kiechlingsbergen, where every inhabitant
from the priest and doctor to the farmer and innkeeper had his
own little patch of the hillside and produced cooperatively such
excellent wines that I believe they are only obtainable in Britain
in the private cellars of the German Embassy. Maybe they cannot
even be found there. Certainly they are exceptionally good. As the
manager of the vineyards explained to us,

> *Ehrlich, schaffig, hoffnungsfroh*
> *sind 'Kiechlingsberger Lüt'*
> *Dü merksch an ihrem Wi des scho,*
> *probier' ne wenn de wit.*

> *Honest, gay, industrious*
> *are Kiechlingsberger men.*
> *A goblet of their golden wine*
> *– you'll find it proven then.*

And with that curious tendency that German vintners have to
explain the basis of their trade in rhyme he pointed out with a
more familiar verse that many of the wines had ecclesiastical
names – Churchpath, Calvary hill, Deans field, and so forth – for
very good reason. It was because:

> *Die Mönche wussten fruher schon*
> *wo wächst ein guter Wein.*
> *D'rum merk Dir, edler Musensohn,*
> *dort schmeckt er heut' noch fein.*

The slopes to yield a noble wine
the monks knew long ago,
So mark you well that there it is
that still the best will grow.

We had arrived at the time of year when there was nothing to see. Nothing, that is, but a long, cool, vaulted cellar with rows of tanks in fibre-glass, and the long pink snakes of pipe which led to the pumps. But though the wine might be stored at some stage in synthetic material it still had to mature for the vital part of its life in wooden tuns. This, he explained, was partly to allow a certain 'breathing', a concentration of the wine by evaporation through the wood. A definite percentage of the fluid would disappear in this way, and a full barrel would later be found to have a sizeable empty space above the liquid. This minus quantity he termed the *Mäusefrass* – that which the mice have eaten. Of course the mice could only be allowed to make off with just the right amount. If they were to nibble too voraciously at the contents of a tun, then the wine would not be of the right consistency and there would be less of it. Too much *Mäusefrass* was lost money for the honest, gay, industrious priest and innkeeper, farmer and doctor and baker. It was the manager's responsibility to see that the mice did not get away with too much, so he kept a cat to control the matter. And there it crouched, a sleek well-fed, beautiful white cat in porcelain, artfully perched on top of one of the tuns, from where it had a clear view down the aisle of casks.

I had once before been in a Kaiserstuhl cellar, but that was back in the 1930s. The landscape now seemed changed in some way, and soon I realised that this was because the *Hohlwege* had disappeared. When first I saw the Kaiserstuhl hills they were crossed by a number of tracks which had been cut down ten feet or more into the yellowish soil. Whether this was originally due to land erosion, to wind and rain beating upon pathways, I am not certain, but now those warm and pleasant gulleys had nearly all been filled in level with the land beside them so that farm machinery could move about more easily.

The *Hohlwege* had soft and sandy sides, and were inhabited by ant-lions, which otherwise I have only seen in the pine-woods behind the shore immediately west of Cannes, where they live and thrive by the million. An ant-lion (*Myrmeleon*, as zoologists call it) is not dangerous to humans, but to ants it is a regular lion. It was to watch the creatures devour their prey that Professor Bruno Geinitz once took the zoology students cycling out from Freiburg. At least, that was the official reason, but we later discovered another.

At first glance an ant-lion is easily overlooked, but the professor's sharp eyes quickly located the insects in the sandy slopes of the lanes. More correctly, he spotted the tiny craters about one inch in diameter which appeared empty until we examined them very closely and could see in the bottom of each a tiny pair of curved pincers protruding between the grains of sand.

The professor caught an ant and slid it deftly down a piece of grass so that it fell into the crater near the top. The moment the ant touched the side there was tremendous activity at the bottom and we saw that beneath the pincers was a small flat-topped head which jerked violently upward and catapulted the sand grains that were lying on it at the unfortunate ant as it scrabbled desperately on the insecure slope, dislodging the sand under its feet, but making very little progress towards the top. The ant-lion ducked its head to load more sand then fired again, and again, and again, a continual barrage of sand particles. Sometimes the creature missed its aim but most of the shots hit the ant and hampered it. At the same time the head was loading from directly beneath the ant and causing minor landslides to bring the quarry nearer.

After perhaps a dozen salvoes of sand the ant-lion scored such a well-aimed hit that the ant fell straight between the sharp curved pincers and was drawn quickly beneath the surface of the sand. The meal did not take long, and soon the flat-topped head was back again, firing some of the dislodged sand clear of the crater to prepared the trap for the next ant, and also ejecting the remains of the first victim.

Scooping with his fingers the professor quickly unearthed the entire ant-lion. Less than an inch long it had a fat body topped by the curious little catapult head which seemed as though fitted with a spring and trigger.

'Now watch,' he said, and he dropped the creature on the sand. Wiggling the hind end of its fat body, the animal quickly burrowed

162 SMALL BOAT ON THE UPPER RHINE

downwards, hind-end first, and within a few seconds it was gone. Only the regular spray of sand showed where it was busily excavating a fresh crater.

From the point of view of invertebrate zoology we had now seen what we had set out to find, but Professor Geinitz casually remarked that it might be rewarding from a strictly scientific point of view to visit one of the cellarage establishments where the grapes were crushed to make the fine wines of the Kaiserstuhl, so we cycled away to the buildings of the Vintners' Cooperative at Ihringen.

Most of the establishment was underground, in a cool and dark cavern cut deep into the hillside. The cellarmen below ground were very pleased to have a visit from a party full of youthful zeal for learning how everything was done, and with candles in their hands they led us between the rows of wooden tuns propped on trestles. At one of the casks they stopped to draw off a quart or two and to fill a glass for each of us.

Was it good? We said Yes, it was good.

We all moved on a few feet. This one, the cellar-master said, was better. We must drink up and try it.

How was it? Better than the last? That was because it was a year older.

Now back another year. How about that? Ah, yes, but just wait for the next one.

And the next. . . .

And the next. . . .

And the next. . . .

All through the tasting the professor kept up a flow of earnest conversation about sugar content and micro-organisms, and varieties of vine that were immune to leaf spots and rusts. He drank glass after glass as though it were water, but I found after a while that my earnest attention was beginning to wander. I was aware of a curious champing sound like a printing-press somewhere in the back of my head, and when I moved forward I never felt my feet touch the ground. I thought I heard a thud somewhere behind me and a strangely inane laugh. Turning round I saw in the dim light one of my fellow zoologists sitting helpless on the floor and making repeated but quite unsuccessful efforts to rise.

Suddenly my own legs crumpled beneath me and I found that I too was quite unable to move them.

'Yes,' I heard the chief vintner say, 'The juice of this particular grape has the property of paralysing the legs.'

'Very interesting,' commented the professor. 'Perhaps its action is at the synapses of the motor neurones.'

'Perhaps,' said the vintner handing him another glass. But I was relieved to hear him add, however indistinctly, that the paralysis was only temporary. It would wear off in an hour or two, he said.

'Very interesting,' said Geinitz again. 'Very interesting indeed. Certainly a subject for proper research.'

I never discovered how the professor managed it, but in his trial of strength with the vintner he emerged completely victorious. Most of his invertebrate zoologists were lying between the vats in a state of paralysis, but Geinitz made the tour of the entire cavern, stepping over their bodies, sampling another vintage, savouring it, and talking biochemistry. I suspect that his knowledge of the subject had enabled him to take certain mysterious counter-measures in advance, but if so he kept his secret well.

The vintner was right – the paralysis was not permanent. It passed off slowly, and in ones and twos the class of zoologists eventually began to stagger out of the cave like the prisoners released from a dungeon. Outside in the sunshine Professor Geinitz stood smoking a cigar and waiting patiently to welcome them with an indulgent smile.

'Very interesting, don't you think?'

We agreed heartily. The fifteen miles back by bicycle proved interesting too.

I also visited the Kaiserstuhl on another instructive tour, when we went to find the swallowtail butterflies and the rare orchids. This was not a laboratory trip but a voluntary extra. Once a week there was a lecture outing on 'Indigenous Flora and Fauna', and early in the morning we would assemble at the Schlageter Memorial to await another and very different professor, a man who had a larger beard than Darwin and a high domed head which hinted at immense wisdom. He was as polished as Linnaeus, gentle as Gilbert White and reverent like John Ray, and he wore a deep black cape and a broad-brimmed hat that would have suited the

Quangle-Wangle Quee. He was almost a caricature of the old style naturalist, yet even to smile at his appearance would have been impossible. His presence commanded instant and genuine respect.

Professor Aschenheimer would arrive just as the clock struck eight, and sweep off his broad hat in greeting. To the girls he bowed with such genteel courtesy that they were impelled to curtsey rather clumsily in reply. He would draw out an antique gold watch, study it curiously, listen to make sure that it was still going (it had never stopped during the half century it had been in his pocket) and replace it. Then with a soft 'So!' he would turn and head off briskly towards the edge of the town with us at his heels.

From the moment we left, the professor never stopped talking for more than a few seconds. His voice flowed gently in the most perfect High German that was a sheer joy to hear, and never for an instant was he boring. At nearly eighty his sharp ears picked up the slightest sound – a distant willow-warbler, a squirrel biting at the base of a fir cone, the faintest click of a beetle. Nothing escaped his notice. The smallest insect, an aberration in the veins of a leaf on a wayside bush, all these he saw and discoursed upon as he forged ahead in the hot sunshine with ourselves struggling to keep up with him.

Sometimes we covered only a few miles but on other occasions our circuit would be twelve or fifteen. Always, at exactly the right moment he would stop with another, 'So!' and draw out from under his cloak the spotless white serviette which contained his lunch. We flopped down on the ground to rest, but he invariably continued to stand, interrupting his meal to explain the chemistry of the pigment of an orchid or the mating behaviour of a curious worm he had seen under a bush.

Aschenheimer was a figure from the past. Within his immense head he had a library of the most astonishing details of every living thing that walked, crept, flew, or rooted in the ground. He was never stumped, not once. He knew the group, class, order, genus and species of everything, its behaviour and life cycle, its haunts and habitats, and every word he spoke was of the most absorbing interest. Yet he was perhaps the last of a dying race, for the naturalist is today extinct. The modern scientist is an expert in his own narrow line and only too often quite ignorant outside it, nor can he usually hold the attention of his hearers for more than a couple of minutes, so strange is his specialised language. When out with Professor Aschenheimer I always had a curious sense of the changing pattern of knowledge and a strange fear that he would die before the next week, his immense store of knowledge perishing with him. Yet every week he was there, with his watch and his white serviette and a vigour that shamed the newer generation that accompanied him on his walks, and whom he filled with a reverent curiosity about their fellow-creatures which would remain with some of them throughout their lives.

At the southern end of the Kaiserstuhl the land flattens off and then bursts up in a sudden lump of rock, the Mons Brisiacus of the Romans, now the site of the little town of Alt Breisach. Beside it the Rhine water jumps the high step of the barrage of Vogelgrün, whilst across the river an idyllic little canal winds over the country to the almost forgotten inland port of Colmar in Alsace. Alt Breisach has a harbour, the only one between Strasbourg and Basle, and so it is a place where the *Thames Commodore* has often drawn in for a night's rest. And Breisach being what it is, she has not always been in a hurry to proceed.

It is a wise precaution when approaching Breisach not only to be on the watch for shoals where the old Rhine bed rejoins the outfall from the lock, but also for the water-spirits. Three of them are attached to the reach immediately beneath the town, and they are said to sing in the river with a lure quite equal to that of the Lorelei of the Rhine gorge, but whereas Lore would deliberately try to lure barges to their doom on the rocks at the foot of her *Ley* or cliff, the three singing *Nixen* of the Breisach reach are fore-tellers of doom. Somebody is going to be drowned, just as they themselves once met their deaths as gay young girls who swam out from the shore and were sucked down by a whirlpool.

At the edge of the town and downstream of the tanker jetty a vast gateway stands at the edge of the Rhine, leading nowhere at all. It was designed by Vauban and is a most imposing structure from the great days of the Roi Soleil, and of course its somewhat ridiculous position has been forced upon it by the drop in the level of the Rhine below the Vogelgrün barrage. It was built as

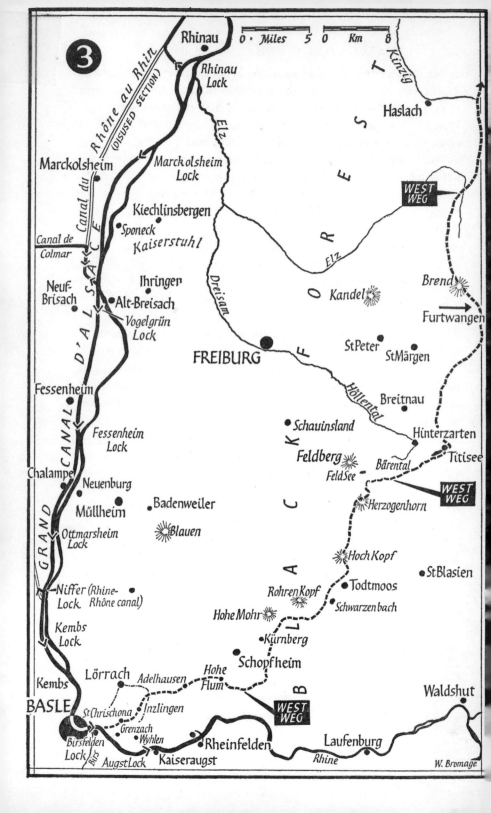

part defence, part triumphal arch for the French armies crossing
the Rhine on their route to conquests farther east. Magnificent it
certainly must once have been, even if now the drawbridge is
rusted and only the mating ducks and the *Thames Commodore*
move slowly past it in wonderment.

So boldly does the magnificent romanesque cathedral of
Breisach stand on its rock overlooking the Rhine that it is hard to
realise that this tight-clustered town was more totally destroyed
during the Second World War than was Hamburg or Cologne, or
indeed any place other than the shippers' town of Emmerich where
the Rhine crosses into Holland. Breisach stood immediately in
front of the muzzles of the big French guns across the water, and
its elevation also made it an excellent spotting platform. Not all its
Martin Schongauers or the fame of its glorious carved altarpiece
could save it.

This astonishing piece of work is renowned for three reasons –
its vast size, its brilliant carving, and the curious fact that its
creator is unknown beyond the fact that he created the work in
1526 and his intials were H.L. In German art books he has the
simple and straightforward title of 'Meister H.L.', but tradition
in Breisach identifies him as a certain Hans Liefrink, a young man
who fell in love with the beautiful daughter of a wealthy town
councillor. Naturally this important person was not inclined to
part with his daughter to a mere travelling apprentice, and a wood-
worker at that. Sadly Liefrink took himself off to Nürnberg, but
not before he had sworn eternal devotion to his girl and planted
in the corner of her garden a rose-tree so that the flowers might
remind her of their love.

Time passed, and the day came when the prosperous Breisachers
wished to adorn their cathedral with a work of art which should
have no equal in all the world. The advice of Albrecht Dürer was
sought, and as he recommended a young woodcarver of Nürnberg
named Liefrink the worthy Hans was invited to his own town of
Breisach and commissioned to carve an altar finer than any in
existence. He called once more at the house of his true love's
father who was now somewhat better disposed towards him; but
unable entirely to swallow his pride the councillor jestingly brushed
the young artist off with a remark to the effect that he might

certainly have the daughter if he could carve an altarpiece higher than the ceiling of the cathedral nave. This, if taken seriously, meant that to win the girl Liefrink would have to carve a work more than forty-five feet in height, a formidable task indeed. Besides it was not easy to imagine the cathedral containing something higher than its own roof.

But that same evening Hans met his beloved in her garden and together they went to look at the rose-tree he had planted. It had grown strong and healthy and the weight of bloom caused its tip to bend right over and point downwards. In a flash Hans saw the answer to the mechanical part of his problem.

And that, they say, is how Breisach's amazing triptych, brilliantly carved in lime-wood, came to be made higher than the ceiling, so that only when the craftsman had steamed its central pinnacle and bent it over permanently could it be brought into the cathedral at all. It was a pleasant way to win a beautiful bride, and I have always thought that the Meister H.L. must have made an excellent husband.

If the year 1945 saw Breisach second only to Emmerich in the extent of its destruction, that town of the Lower Rhine had a certain inherent internationalism on account of its trade, and so the lot of being chosen for a referendum fell upon Breisach. In 1950 the natives voted in secret ballot on the question 'Do you wish political and economic national boundaries within Europe to be removed, and all its peoples to be merged into a single European Union?'

That nineteen out of every twenty Breisachers answered 'Yes' astonished everyone; traditional animosities were evidently not so strongly inbuilt as might have been expected. And to commemorate Breisach's determination to head towards a united Europe the 'Europa Flame' was lit in the cathedral and solemnly carried to the top of the Eckartsberg, a vine-clad hill at the edge of the town where a ruined tower looks out beside a group of pines to watch over the Rhine. I first saw its curious green glow eight years earlier, when chugging up the old Rhine-Rhône waterway in the *Commodore*, and I remember being greatly moved by the sight. Here at last was a sign that something better than national pride was stirring in the hearts of men. I imagined the lads and lasses of the little town walking arm in arm up the steep path through the vines and looking into each other's eyes in radiant confidence that the future was not all darkness.

That being so, it came as something of a surprise to me to find that when I now urged our friends up to the top of the hill to see it, the flame had vanished. The bowl was there on its pedestal and it contained some white excrement from the sparrows that now used it as a convenient perch. But the pipe was disconnected and obviously the flame had long been extinct. In a mixture of disappointment and surprise I ran down the path and presented myself at the police station. What, I demanded, had happened to the *Europaflamme*?

The officer smiled. 'It has been discontinued,' he said briefly.

'You mean the people of Breisach have changed their minds?'

'No, Herr Doktor. But the flame was an inconvenience.'

'An inconvenience! It was said to be the outward and visible sign of an inward and idealistic hope,' I retorted angrily. 'Who found it inconvenient?'

'It was the Nato base in Alsace, Herr Doktor. The green light confused the pilots of the jet fighter planes. The American command demanded that it should be extinguished.'

'What! I suppose they wanted the ideal forbidden too. Anyway, I think it's a damned disgrace. What on earth will the younger generation think if you meekly extinguish the peace flame to please some damn fool commanding officer?'

The police officer nodded in sympathy. 'I agree, Herr Doktor. It is a scandal – but there it is. Perhaps you could write to the mayor. Maybe it would help.'

I wrote to the mayor, but I never had a reply. Four years later we again drew in for the night at Breisach. No hopeful glow of green lit up the darkness of the Eckartsberg. The jet mentality had evidently won.

Only on the night of 11th November does a flickering glow light up the Eckartsberg. This has nothing to do with armistice, or remembering the slaughter of two world wars, but comes from torches carried by the members of the Guild of Fools, who march thither to the sound of drum and fife to inaugurate the annual carnival. The Master Fool makes a speech, the town band strikes up the March of the Fools, and over the Rhine in Alsace the people know that even if the Europa Flame has gone, the Fools are on the march once again.

In fact Breisach is a great place for fools and it is the home port, as it were, of one of three five-hundred-year old guilds of the upper Rhine which enjoyed special privileges granted to them by the emperors. The Guild of *Gaukler*, which included tumblers and acrobats as well as strolling players and conjurors, came to be particularly attached to Breisach, probably on account of its favourable position on medieval routes by road and water, and also through local patronage. Every year about the time of Lent Breisach has its Gauklertag, a day when comics and clowns and professional fools pour into the town to celebrate and generally play the genuine fool.

Towards the end of the fifteenth century, Breisach was under the rule of a Burgundian bailiff, Peter von Hagenbach. He knew well that it paid to cultivate the fools, and sometimes he led the way in riotous hilarities. One year he decided that the carnival should be more boisterous than ever, to celebrate his own marriage. He accordingly levied a tax to pay for the fun and after dinner he led ten dances (probably something like a conga) 'over the tables and chairs', the whole company being obliged to follow him – with the result that many a pretty maid was exhausted by the effort and 'two pious ladies did not survive the year'.

Hagenbach was cruel and a heavy drinker, and the people of Breisach never knew what he would do next. One Easter Monday he ordered all the men and women of the town to appear on the rampart at the edge of the Rhine. There – or so it was believed by those who had already experienced his methods – he intended to slaughter all the men and to put the women aboard leaking barges to drown in the Rhine. The burghers declined the invitation, and the bailiff imposed a fresh tax. Four who refused to pay were seized and executed. This was too much for the people, who rose united, seized the bailiff and imprisoned him. A court of Swiss and Rhinelanders was hastily summoned and Hagenbach arraigned, tried, condemned and executed all within a single day, amid scenes of public rejoicing.

It is sad that the Second World War should have brought about the destruction of the tower in front of the castle (already destroyed by the French in 1745), for that tower was a memorial to Gottfried Tulla, the man who first harnessed or at least bridled the Rhine. Today almost the whole of the river above Strasbourg has been reconstructed as the Grand Canal d'Alsace, but this mighty transformation of the river into a succession of broad pounds separated by barrages and locks has given the Rhine not a second form but a third, for a century earlier the river bed was already radically altered from its natural state.

Originally the Rhine flowed down from Switzerland as a diffuse mass of loops and channels, backwaters and rapids, dotted with hundreds of islands and obstructed by shifting shoals of gravel. The course was in places more than a mile wide, and this explains how medieval craft could make their way up the river hauled by mules or horses. They invariably took the comparatively slack water of minor loops and followed channels away from the main flow, whereas the rafts and ships outward bound would choose instead those parts of the watery maze in which the current was fleetest. But the river was so capricious that with every flood new channels could be formed, and it is even alleged that the citizens of Breisach went to bed in a town on the left bank and awoke next morning to find themselves on the right, the entire course having changed overnight. That was in 1296, and even if the term 'overnight' was probably added later by some imaginative historian who had made no time-and-motion study of erosion there is no doubt that Breisach began the summer flood season as a town in Alsace and ended up in Baden.

Nothing was done to improve the behaviour of the Rhine until toward the end of the eighteenth century, but in 1778 Baden and France concluded an agreement for the correction of the Rhine bed. Yet in spite of all the efforts of the Baden government to have the joint plan put into execution the French would not stir. Then as now they proved difficult partners in a joint enterprise and the only works they were prepared to carry out were such as would divert the channel to their side and leave Baden in possession of the shoals. It was at this stage that Tulla was put in charge of Baden's share of the work.

Gottfried Tulla came from a family of Dutch Protestant

refugees which had emigrated to Germany at the time of the Thirty Years War. As the eldest son of his parents he should by rights have taken holy orders, but as a boy he showed such competence in mathematics that the family tradition was broken and he was diverted towards hydraulics and mining engineering.

Tulla's scheme was to reduce the Rhine to one single channel, banked with masonry, blocking off the side-arms which rambled about the plain. He also cut off the loops and cat-elbows, thereby shortening the course between Baden and the frontier of Hessen by as much as fifty miles. But he realised that nothing could be done in the upper reaches without the cooperation of the French and that a common mind was a prerequisite of any action. In his efforts to achieve this he was of course hampered by the Napoleonic wars, and he also had critics in Baden itself who maintained that his scheme was either impossible or would cost enough to bankrupt Baden, or both. Nothing was achieved until after the defeat of Napoleon, when the Palatinate was ceded to Bavaria, a land which immediately accepted Tulla's ideas. A start was made in the Karlsruhe area, where six short-cuts were excavated. The water level fell by nearly five feet, but when in 1824 an exceptionally violent flood laid waste the country further upstream, Karlsruhe was not inundated.

As a result, Bavaria and Baden were encouraged to make a further agreement for works in the Speyer area, but these were still incomplete when they had to be suspended as a result of representations by the riparian states further downstream, which feared that their own flooding would be made worse if Tulla sped the floodwater so effectively on its way. It was not until after Tulla's death that the next generation of engineers succeeded in convincing others that these fears were groundless, and the works were again taken up. Not until 1840 did the French cooperate along the Alsatian reaches, and the correction of the Rhine according to Tulla's plans was not completed until 1879, just over a century from the time when the negotiations with France were begun.

Tulla's object was not to improve the river for navigation, but to rid the Rhine plain of its disastrous floods and also to remove the swamps which had for so long been a source of disease. In fact the works made the river flow much faster, and the water above

Mannheim fell away to such an extent that all navigation above that city ceased. A quarter of a century was to elapse before Alsace-Lorraine (then Prussian), Baden and Bavaria banded together to carry out groyning in order to make navigation possible once more as far up as Strasbourg. Basically the scheme was to place alternate sets of groynes along either side of the river to throw the water first one way and then the other so that it would get tired of trying to run straight. The notion proved successful and the system survives to this day as the reason why, once every kilometre and a half, the *Thames Commodore* has to cross the opposing traffic and change sides, hauling out or in the blue flag on a staff to starboard to show that she knows what she is about.

In so far as Freiburg has a port at all, its harbour would be Breisach, for the university city lies far back from the Rhine and astride its own little river, the Dreisam, which bubbles and churns its way down from the Black Forest toward the plain. I had hoped to be able to take our American friends into Freiburg, if only because one of its former natives, Martin Waldseemüller was to a very real extent responsible for America itself. Waldseemüller was a cartographer, and in the year 1507 he drew a map with the title *Universalis Cosmographia*, as a companion to his booklet *Cosmographiae Introductio*, an Introduction to Cosmography. That map carried for the first time in history the printed name 'America', and in the *Introductio* he specifically proposed that the fourth continent which had been 'discovered' by Americus Vesputius (i.e. Amerigo Vespucci) 'should be given the name Amerigae, or maybe Terra Americi, the Land of Americus; or better still *America*, because Europa and Asia already have feminine names'.

Besançon, however, was calling us urgently, for our companions were anxious to be in time for the opening concert of the music festival, and before we turned from the Rhine to cross the divide by the Belfort Gap I was determined to forge upstream to the limits of navigation in Switzerland. So Freiburg had to remain unvisited on this occasion and I would have to be content with the memories of the uneasy days thirty years back in history.

From Freiburg to Basle is an easy run up four great stairs of the Grand Canal d'Alsace, each leading to a broad and deep section of artificial waterway twice the size of the Suez Canal. Its construction was authorised by the Treaty of Versailles, which empowered the French to construct a number of hydro-electric barrages on their own territory and divert the Rhine into a vast new concreted canal on the Alsatian side. Maybe the Germans were then in no position to argue, but by this ingenious means the French not only appropriated the whole of the Rhine energy to themselves, but by drying the original bed of the Rhine and transferring the whole waterway to their own territory they neatly deprived Germany of the possibility of importing and exporting by water, and any factories in Baden had to use rail and road instead. But another consequence which even the French engineers had not foreseen was that the works converted their own Alsatian plain, a hot and rich and once extremely fertile area, into a desert. The land needed a constant supply of water to make up for loss by evaporation, and this water came from the Rhine. Once the flow had been diverted into a new neat bed of concrete the water could no longer soak out into the soil. The land was parched, to either side of the Rhine the crops died and the trees withered. In places the water level in the soil dropped by more than thirty feet, and the villages were faced with ruin.

The solution was, of course, to make breaches in the huge concrete gutter and allow water to leak out again, and also to change the system in such a way that the original Rhine bed would still be filled with water, at least over reasonable lengths. This meant that between the locks the channel would once again have one bank in Germany, the other in France, and both countries would be able to develop their own ports. This new 'loop' system is in use along all the river from Vogelgrün to Strasbourg, but above that the Rhine itself is no more than a sad-looking ditch, broad and stony, often dry or only ankle-deep, and with the groynes projecting from its sides like the ribs of a fossil reptile.

Opinions about the G.C.A. differ. A bargeman will think it excellent, for its deep water with little flow makes navigation easy for him. Nature-lovers are more likely to see it as a menace on account of its disturbance of the water levels, and also as a horrid gash across the landscape. How many million cubic yards of gravel had to be excavated I do not know, but it was all piled along the sides to make a double line of sterile shingle mountain range which in places was sixty or seventy feet high. It was many years before anything could be induced to take root and grow on such an inhospitable foundation, but after nearly twenty years of effort some parts had been clothed with bushes and even fir trees. There was vegetation enough for one stretch of bank to be fenced off as a bird sanctuary.

The G.C.A. had only just acquired this new and better dress when work began on the Europort, far away in the North Sea, below the Hook of Holland. Millions of tons of concrete were needed, and quite suddenly the G.C.A. found itself in possession of an almost inexhaustible gravel mine. Nearly all Swiss imports of raw materials come up the river by ship, but as the exports tend to be watches, magnetos, medical drugs and satisfied tourists the ships return down the river empty. Or rather, they used to do so, but we now found them pulling into jetties in the G.C.A. where a conveyor-belt would fill them with gravel for the Europort works. The pleasant, hardly established copses were being grubbed out, the warblers sent into exile and the mountains of shingle-wealth shovelled away to leave once again a pair of hideous arid scars up the valley.

Above Breisach no town short of Basle is actually on the river, but Neuenburg on the one shore and Chalampé on the other come as close as they dare, and a bridge joins the two. Neither is much of a place, for both were in the field of wartime fire, and had to face the consequences. As for Neuenburg, the *neu* or new in its name relates to the year 1496, when the ever-shifting gravel banks in the river so deflected the current that the original village was undermined and the inhabitants had to remove themselves to a new position, leaving their houses to be washed away.

If Neuenberg was annihilated during the Second World War, it had a narrow escape three centuries earlier, when the Thirty Years War brought the frightful Swedes villaining up the valley to leave a trail of stories in which the wicked men or those in league with the devil are invariably Swedish. Yet I think the officer in this particular incident cannot have been altogether bad. He had a dislike of massacres – an unusual quality in those troubled times – and he would never break his word.

It happened one day that the villagers set upon a Swedish

patrol and killed every man in it. 'When we come to Sweden you can do the same to us', they cried exulting.

When the news reached the Swedish commander he swore a solemn and fearful oath that he would revenge himself upon Neuenburg until not a dog remained alive within its walls. With this resolve he went to bed, but in the pleasant dawn of the following day he regretted that he had sworn such slaughter, and calling his chaplain he asked to be absolved from his vow. The dutiful priest said that he could not remove the vow, but if the alternative was to be a blood bath the general would commit a lesser evil by merely breaking his oath. The officer thought this a specious argument. If the vow had to stand he would in all honour carry it out. He dismissed the chaplain and thought deeply to find a solution of his own.

Meanwhile the frightened Neuenburgers had closed the gates and shut themselves within the walls. Eventually the Swedes appeared before the town and set about the gates with axes. Then the officer himself rode in at the head of a force of cavalry. No man, woman or child was to be hurt or molested, he ordered, but – just as he had sworn – not a dog was to be left alive.

The death roll on that day was made up entirely of canines. Nineteen great butcher-dogs are said to have been slain, and I can only suppose that these were the skulking kind of mongrel one may often encounter nowadays haunting a butchery for bones and offal. There also perished three sheepdogs, eight retrievers, twelve little dachshunds and sixty-four poodles – a list which gives an interesting insight into the variety of pets kept three centuries ago in a modest village beside the Rhine.

X

The southern Black Forest – Chrischona and her sisters – the
forest gnome – tragedy at Istein – Vogel Gryff – drummers
of Basle – steam on the river – Basle of the chemists – birth
of DDT – Susanna and Lucia

FROM the top of the shingle banks by the Neuenburg bridge I
could see over the foothills where the excellent Markgräfler
wines were maturing in the cellars, across to the hazy blue domes
of the higher mountains of the southern Black Forest. Somewhere
behind them lay Todtmoos where I had been rejected, and
Schwarzenberg where I had been received so hospitably. When I
set out from that happy farmstead I still had a final day of woodland ahead of me before I should reach the open farmland of the
foothills in the angle where the Rhine makes its right-angled turn
through the city of Basle, a day of lonely walking among the silent
pines. It has always surprised me how devoid of bird song the
forest is, and on that morning I walked for hour after hour without
being aware of anything more than the clicking squeak of a tit,

far up in the branches overhead, or the ticking of fir cones creaking open in the sunlight. I met no other walkers either, but now and again I could hear from deep in the forest the metallic sounds which told of the tireless activity of the lumbermen.

Sometimes it was the distant ring of an axe crisply trimming the branches from a felled tree, or perhaps my ear would catch the neurotic whine of a mechanical saw, or the pleasant jingle of chains on a lumber wagon, sounds that came from either the gangs of woodsmen or perhaps from the Lehlifotzel (or Pfaffestegjockeli as some might call him), an individual who might often be heard but only rarely seen as he made his way through the forest towards Basle, his ghostly cart laden with equally ghostly wood. In his lifetime the Lehlifotzel was a crafty dealer in firewood who would so steer his wagon that the hub of a wheel would strike against the corner of a stack of logs and bring the timber tumbling to the ground. Quickly he would jump down and add a few logs to his own load, and by such ingenious means he eventually became a prosperous fuel merchant. But he had overlooked the fact that the world is governed by a just moral law which eventually catches up with even the most crafty of crooks. When he died in affluence his spirit was condemned for ever to drive the loads of wood along those same forest tracks.

I am not sure how this particular individual met his death, but the original of another wood-thieving ghost of the Black Forest came to a dramatic and violent end. This man was a good-for-nothing smallholder in the Schapbach valley, an atheistical sort of fellow who was also a bad farmer. As his farmstead became continually more run down he took to the bottle and persuaded others to join him in boozing sessions and gambling. As one might expect, the family of this inadequate fellow was soon upon the brink of destitution and it was then that he had an idea. The river that flowed past his holding was used for rafting and floating down lumber. Nothing could be simpler than to help himself to the timber of others, he thought.

So the fellow began to fish out the logs under cover of darkness, carefully stacking them beneath other timber which he cut from his own small portion of the woodland. Little by little he built up a thriving business, and when neighbours became suspicious and tried to spy upon his nocturnal activity he dressed up as a ghost and frightened them out of their wits. Not even the bravest would dare to walk down by the stream at the witching hour, which of course was the time at which he stole the timber.

One day a fine raft of tree stems came down the stream, but near the smallholding the head of water began to die away and the raft was stranded. Its owner was obliged to leave it until the water had built up again on the following day. About midnight the dealer crept up, climbed upon the raft and began to cut the withies with which it was bound. Further upstream there had been some heavy rain and already the water was rising, and as the man loosed the bindings the stems began to work. Pushing over each other they trapped the thief by the feet, then surged forward and over-whelmed him. When on the following morning the raftsmen came to float the timber downstream they found the logs in disorder, and among the debris the crushed and pounded body of the timber dealer. They worked the corpse loose and brought it ashore for burial, but once again 'providence' was not satisfied merely with meting out a gruesome death. The thief was condemned to haunt the area where once he had assumed the role of a pretended ghost to cover up his robberies – a punishment truly fitting the crime.

Before noon on this ninth day I was on a hilltop from which I could already look over Switzerland and France. Overhead the sky was still and somewhat overcast with broken cloud and down below the Hohe Moor the shadows played in the valleys. I was leaving the heights behind me, for the red lozenges now had no task but to lead me a gentle descent towards Basle. Next morning I came to a barrier across the path, and beside it a notice from which I discovered that the Swiss frontier was only open on Saturdays, Sundays, and Bank Holidays, between eight in the morning and eight at night. I happened to have arrived on a Monday, and as I had no particular wish to make a detour of several kilometres just because the frontier post was closed, I jumped over the bar into Switzerland, and almost into the grounds of the protestant missionary training centre of Chrischona.

Once again I was in Ursula country, for the name Chrischona contained the recollection of a member of Ursula's famous entourage of eleven thousand English maidens. On their ill-fated

G

journey down the Rhine towards Cologne the company had only
reached Wyhlen (opposite the Swiss lock at Augst) when three of
their number had to be landed as sick. These girls settled in the
neighbourhood, where they did a number of useful wonders such
as snake-killing, and when they died (together as it seems), their
corpses were laden on an ox-cart and in the usual fashion a church
was built where the oxen came to a halt under an oak tree. That
was at Eichsel (which means Holy Oak), and in the middle ages
the place became a considerable centre of pilgrimage, particularly
among those afflicted with various kinds of disease.

Another of Ursula's entourage was landed below Basle, a girl
named Christiana (or Chrischona, as it has now become). She died
almost immediately after being put ashore, and she also had her
place of burial decided by cattle. Two young oxen never previously
yoked were chosen 'to do the Lord's will', and they performed
their task with such energy that they trampled down any trees
which stood in their way and hauled their burden right to the top
of the hill overlooking the Rhine valley. There followed the burial,
the church building and the familiar flow of wonders which turned
the place into a centre of pilgrimage. Some said that three little
flames might sometimes be seen dancing along the path from
Eichsel towards Chrischona, and afterwards four flames journeying
back to Eichsel.

Others have told a different tale of Chrischona, saying that once
there was a wicked robber baron in the neighbourhood of Basle
who had three beautiful daughters: Margareta, Ottilia and Chrischona. The girls were courted by three good and handsome young
knights, sons of a neighbouring lord. The wicked baron objected,
and confining his own daughters in the dungeon he had his men
lie in wait for their sweethearts, seize them alive, and bring them
into the keep to be put in chains. The three noble sisters kept up
their own spirits by singing, and the sound of such cheerful songs
emanating from the dark and damp of the dungeon so maddened
their psychopathic father that he next had the girls brought out –
to see their own young men being beheaded. News of this horror
quickly spread, and the friends of the murdered brothers swiftly
raised a force to storm the castle and free the girls. Yet it is not
surprising that after all these adventures Chrischona and her

sisters wanted no more to do with life in castles. Instead of marrying any of their liberators they retired from the world, each with a cell and chapel of her own upon a hill an hour's walk from her sisters.

They seem however to have been friendly girls who liked their solitude broken by a reasonable amount of chat. From their respective hills at the three points of the triangle they would wave to each other with white cloths and talk through loud-hailers. At bedtime each would signal goodnight to her sisters by swinging a lantern. Eventually the girls died, Chrischona being the last of the three. Their names are preserved in their respective places of solitude – Chrischona and St Margareta in Swiss territory and Tüllingen (from Ottilia) in Baden. And just in case any should doubt the tale, in each of the three a giant megaphone is preserved from the days when the girls talked to each other across the intervening country – though another version of their story tells that the girls themselves were so devoted and so holy that God endued them with the power of speaking to each other over long distances without raising their voices, and yet of being heard by their two sisters alone.

Below Chrischona the pines gave up the territory to the beeches, and the steep hillside down which I ran towards the distant glimmer of river might have been a scarp in Buckinghamshire. As I leapt down the woodland slope, scattering the crisp beechleaves of many years and cracking the twigs beneath my feet, I noticed a number of square blocks in the ground, very much like small milestones. They had some carving upon them, weather worn and heraldic, but I did not stop to examine them in detail. Quite suddenly a little gnome in a lichen-coloured uniform and pill-box hat stepped out from behind a tree. He was too large, I thought, to squeeze into a beer bottle for transport to the Feldberg. Besides, I had no bottle with me. If he was a malevolent spirit of the woodland I should have to try and humour him.

'Grüss Gott,' I said. Then, remembering I was in Switzerland, 'Gruetzi!'

The wood sprite looked at me with a gnome-like frown. 'You walked to the right of that stone,' he said, pointing at one of the square ones set in the ground. 'You should have walked to the left. Then it would have been in order.'

'I'm sorry,' I said. I had often read of spirits waiting for release who had to wait another thousand years because their possible deliverer had muffed it all by some thoughtless error of just that kind.

'Go back and walk round it again, but to the left,' the little fellow said, still pointing. I had no wish to be turned into a toad so I did so.

'Like this?'

'Yes, like that.' He tightened his belt. 'You stepped into Switzerland without permission,' he added. 'Those stones mark the frontier. You must not walk on the wrong side of them.'

'No, of course not.' I wondered if the bears would come out and eat me. 'I'm terribly sorry,' I said.

'That is good. We have to be careful you know.'

'Of course.'

'People think that just because it's Switzerland they can do what they like.'

'I would never think that,' I said to reassure him.

'So we watch the frontier. This is my beat, up the hillside in the wood.'

'Ah!'

'Yes. People may walk the wrong side of the stones. What is the point of marking the frontier if people pay no attention?'

'What indeed!' I saw that the man was very serious about his responsibilities. 'Does it happen very often?'

'Not very. You are the only man I have seen in the wood for the last month,' he said sadly. 'It is not as busy a frontier as some, you know. Show me your passport.'

I did so. He examined it carefully.

'What are you doing, running through this beechwood?'

'Catching the evening plane to London,' I said.

'Then it is in order. But don't forget, next time you come you must walk to the left of the stones.'

'I'll promise,' I agreed.

Five minutes later I was on the bank of the Rhine, close by the fine modern barrage and lock of Birsfelden. A glass of beer, and I made my way to the bridge, crossed the river into the city of Basle and walked up to the air terminal.

The journey up from Neuenburg to Basle by water was less interesting, for we were running up the section of the G.C.A. built before the loop system was agreed in 1956, and almost all of our course up to the final lock at Kembs was between the banks of shingle excavated from the bed. Only briefly above each of the great locks at Fessenheim and Ottmarsheim did we have a view over the country to either side before once again the gravel ramparts rose to cut off the world outside.

The lock of Kembs was the only one to be completed before the Second World War, but it had the effect of bypassing the difficult passage of the Isteiner Schwelle (step or threshold) where there was a band of hard rock in the river. The result of this natural obstacle was to prevent the bed being cut down by water erosion at the same pace as the bottom immediately downstream, so that a distinct drop was developed in the river. Even in medieval days there were shipwrecks on the Istein bar, and the Basle archives have a picture of the wreck of a barge there in 1646. The increased flow which came with the Rhine correction of Tulla made the Istein passage quite as formidable as that of Bingen, and it was one of the main obstacles in the way of opening Basle to waterborne trade.

The Kembs barrage also had the result of making the Rhine water back up as far as Basle itself, and at certain times all the way to Birsfelden on the upstream side of the city. Permission to build it had of course to be sought from the Council of Basle, and the city fathers showed themselves to be exceedingly good businessmen in managing to strike a bargain by which Basle itself – whose port was of course greatly improved by the increased depth of water – should be compensated for seventy-five years at the rate of six Swiss francs per horse-power of energy derived from the Kembs turbines.

Istein itself is marked by a great bluff of limestone standing up proudly on the Baden shore, and so abrupt is this cliff where it falls to what was the Rhine before the French engineers stole its water for their huge new canal, that even the railway was unable to negotiate it without a tunnel. Naturally its summit early came to be the safe perch of a castle, and the story told of the romance of a twelfth-century knight of Istein is one of the most horrific of any along the river.

The Isteiner was betrothed to the fair and lovely Jutta of the house of Sponeck, the ruin of which now forms an attractive residence nestling in the trees at the edge of the Kaiserstuhl, but before the wedding he went off, as knights would so often do, to joust in a tournament at the castle of Angerstein on the River Birsig in the Swiss Jura. (The Birsig flows into the Rhine immediately below the Central Bridge, and if today the little tributary is arched over and almost invisible its situation has some importance in this tale.)

No doubt Jutta was alarmed for her lover's safety, for though tournaments were friendly affairs the contestants were sometimes violently thrown in their armour, but the Isteiner survived his bouts of combat well enough to fall in love with the daughter of his host, the fair and lovely Bertha von Thierstein. More than that, he pledged to her his hand in marriage.

It was not long before a rumour of this change in her fiancé's affections reached Jutta at Sponeck, and at once she set off on what she declared to be a pilgrimage to a popular shrine. Her steps were of course directed toward Angerstein, and when she reached the River Birsig at its foot she came upon her lover arm-in-arm with Bertha. Stepping in front of them she pulled out a dagger and plunged it neither into Bertha's bosom nor into that of her deceiver, but into her own. As she did so she flung herself into the Birsig.

The Isteiner had recognised her, and leaving Bertha at Angerstein he sped home in remorse toward Istein. On his way thither he had to cross the Rhine by the ferry at Hüningen, which is downstream of the confluence with the Birsig, and as he did so there came bobbing past him, borne upon the swift current the body of Jutta, her face deadly white and the fatal gash upon her breast turned towards him. The knight was almost in a state of collapse when he reached Istein. He must have travelled at much the same speed as the current, for who should be there to greet him but Jutta, washed up at the foot of the Isteiner Klotz.

The knight galloped up the track to his castle, screamed to the astonished servants that his bride was coming in state, then ran stumbling down the road to the river. The servants rushed in alarm to the walls and saw in the light of the rising moon how their master staggered to the beach, flung his arms around a white figure at the foot of the rock and then threw himself with it into the river. It was several days before fishermen lower down recovered the two bodies locked tightly in the rigor mortis of mutual embrace, and bringing them to land buried the young pair beside the river. But just where the grave may have been I do not know. Perhaps it disappeared under the correcting hand of Gottfried Tulla.

The Isteiner Klotz was just behind us on the port quarter as we chugged out of Kembs lock into the Rhine itself, with the vine-clad foothills of the Black Forest crowding down towards the stream. Basle lay less than one hour upstream, and soon the tall warehouses and silos of the Port of Klein Hüningen were in sight, ranged so close to the German frontier that when the *Thames Commodore* swung round the tip of the mole to lie close beside the *Vogel Gryff* she was no more than twenty yards outside the realm of the Bundesrepublik. All the same, twenty yards was far enough for her to have to haul down the French courtesy flag which she had worn for the Grand Canal d'Alsace, and she now ran up the white cross on red background of the Swiss Confederation.

The *Vogel Gryff* was a powerful tug, painted in the gleaming mustard yellow of one of Switzerland's shipping lines. We soon discovered from her sun-bronzed captain that she would not be putting out. She was port-bound, with girl trouble. The regulations approved by the Central Commission for the Rhine laid down certain minimum requirements for the crew of motor vessels, and a tug as powerful as the *Vogel Gryff* needed, I think, a complement of seven.

'The Binger Loch may be tricky to navigate,' the skipper remarked, 'but nothing will wreck a ship more surely than a girl. Not the Lorelei, but a real one. You have a ship's lad, and he goes and falls head over heels for some girl or other, and before you know what's happening she has lured him off the boat into a town job so she can see him every evening. We've been sitting here in the harbour for more than a month now, and all because of girls. No, the labour exchange can't help. Lads just don't want to know anything about joining a tug crew. The money's good, the life's good, there's only one trouble – no girls, no chance of seeing your true love every evening. God knows what will come of it. Conversion to pushers with a crew made up of lightermen I suppose. Either that, or a whole blinking crew of courting couples. I'm fed up with these damn females.'

Having expressed his views upon women, the captain took me to see the engine room (short of one mechanic) the galley (with no cook) the winches (two lads missing) and his bank of telephones. He had as many of these as a business tycoon. On one instrument he could speak to any of the locks on his route, with another he could call up almost any ship on the inland waterway system. A third was connected by yet another radio link to the land network so that the captain could dial any telephone number ashore that he wished, the fourth was a house system, to call the crew – when there was any.

The *Vogel Gryff* took her name from one of Basle's special fabulous creatures. In the outskirts of the city there are three ancient guilds, not unlike those of Zürich, and in January they take part in a strange festival which goes back to earliest times – and perhaps many hundreds of years before even the guilds were founded. Down the Rhine comes a sort of raft, a platform supported on a pair of boats, and on this stands the Wild Man, an ancient figure decked out with ivy and fruit, and bearing a small pine-tree in his hands. Winter is past, the solstice gone, the days are becoming noticeably longer and the fertility of spring can at least be expected; and when the Wild Man, who must certainly symbolise this fertility, reaches the Central Bridge, he is received there by one or both of the other guild figures, Vogel Gryff (a griffin) or Leu the Lion. As the clock strikes noon and the pale winter sun is at its highest these creatures march to the middle of the bridge, pay their respects to the chapel over one of its buttresses, and perform a ritual dance, careful never to look towards the city but always away from it and toward the Black Forest.

Naturally, the whole affair takes place to the sound of drums. I doubt if there can be any place in the world which has more drums than Basle, and the *Thames Commodore* may well have been fortunate not to arrive in the city during the first week of Lent. Perhaps in the port we should have had some peace, but elsewhere everything would have been in commotion, for at that time an unusual form of madness descends upon the place and it seems as though the whole of Basle is filled with drummers. And so it is.

There are thirty drumming schools in the city, and all the year round the members are practising. Boys of nine, lads, old men, all have been drumming right round the year, just to be ready for four o'clock on this Monday morning. Thirty drumming schools can make a deafening noise, and the authorities have wisely decreed that for forty-eight weeks they have to learn to play without proper drums and in closed rooms, so that their combined din does not drive people demented, but for the last four weeks they are allowed to drum properly and unrestrained, preparing for the great occasion of the Basle carnival.

The tremendous Monday morning drumming is a signal to summon the members of the guilds. Soon they come, with lanterns, and dressed as wild men, or animals, or as people from the middle ages. They are all so masked and disguised that none can be recognised and this of course is all part of the fun, because for three days any masked figure can say just what he thinks to anyone else, whether they are masked or not, and it has to be taken in good humour. There are masked balls, processions, people dressed as animals dancing in the streets and hugging complete strangers, the whole population refreshing itself with onion tarts and flour soup.

Then on the Thursday morning, everything is back to normal. The barges in the harbour are busy unloading, the chemists are rubbing their sleepy eyes in the laboratories. The banks are open. Expresses move out of the stations just as usual, bound for Scandinavia, Italy, Turkey, the Netherlands, or for the channel boats to England. The drums have been put away for another eleven months. But that same night some of the lads will be together again. They will be practising already for next year's carnival. Not on real drums, of course, which is forbidden until another eleven months have passed, but practising just the same.

Klein-Hüningen is a fine port, and a busy one filled to capacity. It is proud of its existence, too, and the upper mole ends in a magnificent silvery pylon marked in the national colours of the three countries which meet in the water close by, and there is a cafe and seats and everything to make a landsman very content to stay awhile and watch the ships unloading in the port, or sweeping down the river outside the basins. There is the shipping museum too, with models of ships from medieval times and the story of the Zürich porringer; and one of the tallest warehouses along the docks has a lift so that visitors can be whisked up to the roof to have an aerial view of the docks below. From this perch one can see up to the old city, across the German suburbs to the Black Forest, and westwards to the trailing end of the Vosges. Below, the giant Rhine lighters are discharging at their bays, beyond the mole with its sightseers the ships are ploughing the current on their way to the refineries further up-river, and on the other shore the remains of the old entrance lock of the French Canal de Huningue can still be seen, though the waterway itself has now been replaced by the new cut some miles lower down. Opened in 1834, it was the route by which the upstream ships reached Basle, so avoiding the difficult and swift river reaches above Strasbourg. In drought the down-goers used the canal also, but when the river was carrying plenty of water they naturally preferred to sweep swiftly down the Rhine itself instead of passing through nearly fifty locks to cover the drop of 350 feet to Strasbourg.

The original port of Basle was a wharf, the Schifflände, at the foot of the bluff on which stands the cathedral and the older quarter of the city. It is even alleged that this was the very place at which St Ursula landed with her eleven thousand English virgins when she came sailing up the Rhine on her way to visit the Pope in Rome. It was there that the first steamers drew in.

Concordia res parvae crescunt; discordia maximae dilabuntur.

So ran the motto of the united shipping companies which ran the steamboat services on the Rhine in the earliest days of mechanical power, and to express in practical terms the idea that cooperation is more profitable than rivalry the first steamship to be built in Rotterdam for the trade of the Upper Rhine was named the *Concordia*. Unfortunately her draught proved too great for the shallows above Strasbourg – for this was before any of Tulla's corrections had been put in hand – and a second ship was built with a flatter bottom. In July of 1827 the *Ludwig* set out upon the first attempt to reach Basle under steam. Puffing up the river she made Kehl without much difficulty, but when the steersman set off by land to take soundings further up the river he found only two and a half feet of water, and the *Ludwig* had to return to Mannheim. Disappointment in Basle was intense, but soon it was the turn of the paddle-wheeler *Stadt Frankfurt* to take up the challenge.

Although this vessel drew less than two feet of water her journey was not easy, for her Brunel engine could only muster forty-five horse-power. However, the shifting shoals had moved favourably and soundings taken ahead of her showed a least depth of three feet. Three days after leaving Kehl she was within sight of Breisach when she was seen to stop, and eventually to float back down the river. She had struck a shoal with one of her paddles. To the general relief her crew managed to repair her, and that same evening she steamed in stately fashion towards the landing stage below the cathedral of Breisach. Next day she almost reached Neuenburg, to which cartloads of coal were brought to feed her. The swift and shallow passage below the Istein cliff nearly proved too much for her, but sixteen brawny farm-workers came running to her aid, and hauled her through the swift passage with a long line from the shore. One more morning of continual stoking as she puffed and wheezed against the current, and the *Stadt Frankfurt* drew into Basle to the accompaniment of a thundering of cannon and a rousing welcome from the town band. The steam route to Basle was open.

Five years later the Oswald brothers, candle-makers of Basle, began to develop a steamer service by which they hoped to offer connections all the way from Basle to London in four-and-a-half days. There was to be one ship daily from Basle, and on the return journey the river steamer would take the recently opened Rhine–Rhône Canal from Strasbourg – a circumstance which severely limited the size of ship that could be used. Unfortunately the service proved too difficult and costly, and only five years from its beginnings the Oswald company failed, and its graceful ships were put up for auction.

It remained for yet another company to introduce ships specially designed to meet the conditions of the river itself. Connections to London were again arranged, and for one hundred and eleven

Swiss Francs one could travel first class all the way. And first class really meant first class on these 'Eagles of the Upper Rhine'. Drunks and mentally deranged travellers were not allowed aboard, but facilities were provided for more respectable passengers to play draughts, chess and dominoes. Card-playing was allowed provided there was no gambling, and an English newspaper was provided in the first class saloon. The captain had full authority to have recalcitrant or objectionable passengers put in the life-boat and immediately dumped upon the river bank with their luggage.

Great care was taken over the furnishings. The table-cloths had to be of pure linen, the cutlery of solid silver and the cruets only of the finest cut crystal. The cuisine was exceptional, and one can well imagine that those who travelled in such luxury could easily become so engrossed in the seven course dinner that an occasional bumping on the river bottom did not fill them with apprehension, and they had little objection to the delay when the ship dropped anchor to wait for the mist to disperse, or for the moon to come over the horizon and shine a little light upon the difficult course ahead. Occasionally a traveller fell in when disembarking, but that was just part of the adventure, at no extra charge.

It was the increased pace of the Rhine resulting from Tulla's reconstruction of the bed which finally prevented the development of shipping on the upper reaches. When in 1903 the tug *Justizia* arrived in Basle at the end of a successful trial run, she was the first steamship to be seen there for nearly sixty years, and as great a novelty to the land-bound Baslers as the *Stadt Frankfurt* had been to an earlier generation. This time the steamer was indeed the first swallow, and the very next year a cargo of coal was hauled up to Basle in the 300-ton lighter *Christine*, pulled by a Dutch tug. The *Christine* unloaded at the city gasworks, but she was never to reach her home port of Mannheim again. When the discharging was complete the tug began to turn her in the river, and swinging too wide was washed against the opposite shore. The towing line snapped, and the empty lighter drove down the swift river towards the bridge of boats. Some watermen raced to their small boats and rowed swiftly out to rescue the steersman and his family just in time, for the *Christine* struck the ice-breakers of the bridge with

such force that she sank and could only be removed from the fair-
way by dynamiting her.

Yet the *Christine* and her tug had opened the way for goods to
pour into Basle from the ports of the lower Rhine. Within twenty
years the graceful two-funnelled paddle-wheel tugs were hauling
up to the new harbour of Klein–Hüningen more than three million
tons of cargo annually, the list including consignments of Egyptian
cotton, chemicals, fertilizers, bricks and timber, petrol and tobacco,
American wheat and Danish butter. At last Switzerland had
an outlet to the sea and was developing shipping lines of her
own.

The port of Klein–Hüningen was not the limit of navigation on
the Rhine, so next afternoon the *Thames Commodore* set off up the
river again, passing the hills of black coal dust and yellow sulphur
as she chugged up towards the Bridge of the Three Roses, the
first of six which span the stream in Basle. Just below it and on the
port hand the tall, slender metal finger of CIBA's chimney pointed
proudly upward as though to remind us that as far as the chemical
industry of Basle was concerned, the sky was the limit.

Basle is certainly the pharmaceuticals centre of the world, and it
became so in a peculiar way. Centuries ago, when the Edict of
Nantes was revoked and freedom of worship vanished overnight
from France, the Catholics began to attack their Protestant fellow-
men, sometimes murdering them but at least driving them to flee
for their lives. Many escaped as refugees to Britain, or Germany,
or the Netherlands, but those who lived closer to Switzerland fled
across the frontier to Basle. Many of these refugees were weavers,
and they set up little workshops for making silk ribbons. Ribbon-
making soon became a great business in Basle.

As time went on, ladies' fashions changed and new colours were
needed for the ribbons, so a dye-making industry followed hard on
the heels of the ribbon-makers, but its tremendous expansion was
stimulated mainly by the discoveries of Perkin, the young London
student who set up a simple laboratory in his parent's house and in
the Easter Vacation of 1856 actually succeeded when he was still
only eighteen years old in elaborating the synthetic dye mauveine.
With his brother he set about the manufacture of the first artificial
colouring materials derived from coal tar, and in so doing he laid

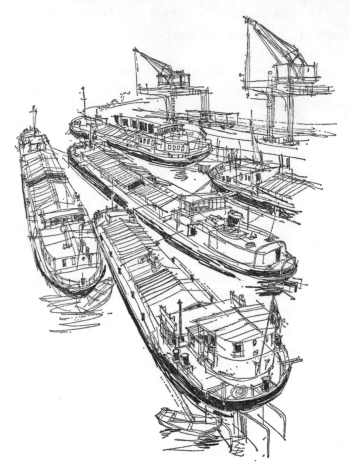

Klein–Hüningen Harbour

the foundations of organic chemistry. The colour-makers became organic chemists.

Now it so happens that dyes are very complex chemicals, and once a firm has all the know-how to make them it is well placed to step out into other products too. The industry expanded into the drug field, and many drugs in everyday use were first perfected in the laboratories of Basle. All across the world tablets and pills from Basle are in daily use, and the Swiss are very conscious of their prowess in this field. 'Every disease has a cure already growing in Basle,' they proudly declare, and this is hardly an exaggeration.

Basle was well placed to develop its trade beyond mere colour-making, for it also had a chemical industry of long standing. The famous firm of Geigy had been there since the 1750s and now it was joined by others, particularly by chemists emigrating from France – not on this occasion for religious reasons but because of the very restrictive patent laws. The forerunners of CIBA were soon established in Basle, and those of Sandoz also. These firms were originally concerned with dyes alone, and sometimes they came up against unexpected difficulties – as when a chemist in the Müller aniline works (later united with Geigy) elaborated an excellent new dye in a strong shade of blue. So pleased was Müller that he at once gave the man a reward of one thousand francs and sent him off to Paris to enjoy himself. This the worthy research-man did, but he was so swept off his feet by the entertainments of Paris that he somehow lost his notes of the process and Müller was unable to manufacture the dye. At least that is what is related, but I have always found it difficult to believe that a man could really make such a discovery and within a few days entirely forget how he had done it.

CIBA extended into plastics, water-proofing, paint pigments and almost every possible branch of chemical synthesis, but per-haps it is most famous for its pioneer production of hormones. These complex substances are normally manufactured in endocrine glands such as the pituitary, thyroid or adrenal glands, and the simplest way to obtain them is by extraction from the tissues con-cerned. Yet a simple method is not always a sensible one. To produce a mere tenth of a gram of adrenalin it would be necessary to obtain two tons of adrenal glands from a slaughter-house and render them down. Much better, thought the CIBA chemists, to find a way of building up the right molecules from less complex ones. Besides, the medical consumption of hormones is now so great that the slaughter-houses could hardly produce enough bits and pieces of cattle to keep up the supply.

Geigy became interested in mothproofing, then moved from the clothes moth to insects in general and became specialists in pest control. One of the Geigy products must have saved many millions of lives around the world – though cynics might add that this has merely made the population explosion detonate earlier than it might have done. The substance was of course the famous dichloro-diphenyltrichloroethane, which may be just a greenhouse aid in Britain, but elsewhere has almost exterminated the insect carriers of some of the greatest killer diseases – malaria, yellow fever and plague. Dr Paul Müller of Geigy certainly earned the Nobel Prize which was awarded to him for producing that first of the great insecticides, known for short as DDT.

There is no end to the chemical conjuring of Basle. The Sandoz company specialised in plant drugs, and long ago isolated the active principles in the purple and yellow *digitalis* (foxglove), and the deadly poison in the arrow-tips of South American Indians. Once a chemical has been analysed in its molecular structure there is a chance to make it artificially, yet drugs are not such an easy way to wealth as one might think. Out of every thousand complex substances built up in the laboratory, only one will have properties which are medically useful.

Last of the great drug names of the Swiss City by the Rhine is Roche. Hofmann La Roche specialised in vitamins, and it was Roche who developed the manufacture of Vitamin C – something that might have been most useful to the crew of the *Thames Commodore* if they had voyaged centuries earlier and found their teeth dropping out from scurvy. Vitamin A later appeared on the Roche line, and B_1, B_2 and E have all been run to earth in the Basle research laboratories. Altogether the chemists of Basle spend some ten million pounds annually on research, and every now and again a real winner is found which will bring in money from all over the world. It may be a new anti-depressant for the suicidal, or perhaps a systemic poison which can be spread on the ground so that plants take it in by the roots and are made poisonous to insects. One bite at a leaf, and a bug falls down dead – unfortunate if one is the bug, but very good if you are a gardener or a shareholder in the chemical enterprise of the city and involved in the export of drugs and biologicals and pesticides, which together flow out of the factories to the pleasant melody of more than 700 million Swiss francs a year.

Amid all these chemical musings the *Thames Commodore* has been plodding up against the current. Three Roses Bridge, then St Johns Bridge, and at the Central Bridge or Mittlere Brücke she is forging past the Birsig and the landing stage where the dignitaries of Basle once welcomed the approaching boats of the cardinals and envoys bound for the Council, the craft moving elegantly and extremely slowly up the rippling stream as the horses of their towing-troops plodded step by step to haul them up the shore toward the Schifflände and the ancient guildhall of the Worshipful Company of Boatmen of Basle. Dignified, the prelates stepped out where Ursula is said to have done so long before, then made their way to the rooms they were to occupy through the years of theological and ecclesiastical discussion.

Yet Basle did not always lie happily under the yoke of the Roman Church, and the people once showed their independent spirit by chasing a papal diplomat out of the city. The man showed considerable courage in coming back again, whereupon the citizens threw him into the Rhine. In return the Pope, or the Almighty, visited an earthquake upon the city and the shaking felled the cathedral tower so that part of the masonry collapsed into the river, taking with it Lucia. This lady was the sister of Susanna of Schönau. They were identical twins, and they were bells.

Deprived of their own bell the Baslers decided that rather than recover Lucia from the Rhine it would be easier to cross the river and snatch Susanna away from her home church in Schönau. This they did, but before the Baslers could drag her up to their own cathedral the law intervened and Susanna was taken home by her own people. As for Lucia, she may still lie buried somewhere among the gravel banks of the river, and legend says that she will stay there until the city becomes Catholic again. In that case I suspect she has a long time to wait.

We are now in the centre of the city, most of the chemical factories left far astern. Somewhere to starboard lie hidden the buildings of the forty financial houses which have made Basle famous for banking, their business proceeding with a rattle of IBM type-heads and the silent lightning-speed calculations of computers hidden away in smooth modern office blocks. Most famous among them is the Bank for International Settlements, created under the Young Plan in 1930, when Germany was having difficulty in meeting the reparation bills imposed upon her at Versailles. The new bank was charged with managing the Young Plan, and also

with arranging all kinds of international financial transactions, but
its operations are so specialised that when someone kindly undertook to explain them to me I found my attention beginning to
wander.

The passage of Basle is a fascinating one, for this Swiss city is
the only one upstream of Cologne to lie fairly astride the water.
Below the cathedral cliff a traditional type of ferry which resembles
a sampan takes people swiftly across the river by no other means
than a long rudder which enables the steersman to set the bow at
an angle to the current, which here is once again very swift. The
boat hangs on a long line from a pulley on a cable stretched high
above the Rhine, and the ferry angles across the river with a gentle
rocking but no other sound than that of the Rhine swashing
against her flank.

Apart from the cluster of buildings in the cathedral quarter, I do
not consider Basle a picturesque city. Certainly it is rich in museums
and galleries, but the buildings of the place itself are too brash, too
prosperous, too Edwardian for my taste. Yet somehow the whole
is redeemed by the Rhine itself, which swirls noisily through the
city, flowing faster than at Cologne, more purposefully than at
Mainz, cleaner by far than beside Mannheim's wharves, its water
steely grey and cold, with still a flavour of the Alpine snows far
away in the St Gotthard mountains. And right in the centre of the
city stands the Mittlere Brücke with its chapel, a romantic sight
even if the present structure is a twentieth century one whereas
the former bridge was for hundreds of years the only one between
the Lake of Constance and the North Sea. We have plenty of time
to regard this bridge with awe, for the broad buttresses reduce the
channel and cause a fast passage. Our progress is slow here, but
once past the medieval port the channel begins to broaden out, and
the river runs between tree-lined banks where salmon-nets dangle
over the edge of the stream. Beyond the railway bridge the honey-
comb structure of the power station of Birsfelden is already in view,
as good a piece of industrial designing as is to be seen on all the
river. To its right is the first of the Swiss locks, and as the gates
are closed, the signal lights red, we draw over to a pleasant quay
with a lawn of well-cut grass and a background of flowering shrubs,
to have tea on deck while we wait for the two empty tankers to

enter the lock from the upstream side and be lowered to the reach below, the first step on their long journey as they run swiftly down on the wings of the current to the refinery jetties of Vlaardingen, three countries distant.

The Rhine at Basle

XI

The Rhine above Basle – Lock of Augst – Augusta
Raurica and Kaiseraugst – Rheinfelden, town of Kilowatts
– the end of navigation

AT BIRSFELDEN lock the city of Basle lay astern of us. The
Port straggled on spasmodically, for the Klein–Hüningen docks
were long ago filled to capacity and the refinery jetties and other
newcomers had been crowded out to find a home on the reach
above the barrage, but the Rhine was quickly taking on a new
character. As the heaps of brilliant chemicals, pink and grey and
canary yellow glinted in the evening sun behind us, the course
ahead was leading into a quiet stretch of river between meadows.
Heavy well-fed cows looked up from their supper of green grass
and scabious to watch us as though not quite sure why we were
coming up their river at all. Ducks scampered over the surface to
the edge of the stream, a buzzard soared up from behind the bluff
of the Grenzacher Hörnli on the port hand, called to us, and swept
away over the woods in search of something more digestible.

To the left the land rose up steadily to where the dark domes of
the Black Forest rested in the warm glow from the west, ahead and
to starboard the purple lines of the Swiss hills lay faint and
mysterious as though on a faded water-colour painting, and far away
in the sky beyond them a saw-edge of palest pink showed where the
giants of the Alps towered above the summer mist of this gentle
evening in June, proudly displaying their eternal snows in the
horizontal light.

As the glow of evening took on its tint of celestial green and
began to tinge with violet we came in sight of a barrage with a
power station at either side, one German, the other Swiss. The
run-off foamed in hues more subtle even than those of the dye-men
of Basle, and as we bobbed upon it to wait for the signal to enter
the lock on the Swiss side a fine fish leapt clear of the water like

some spirit of the upper Rhine, revelling in the beauty of the late evening. A flash and he was gone again, the broken water leaving no trace of ripples where he made his re-entry. Very slowly the black rectangle of the gates beneath the bridge split and folded back, the light winked green, and a rather surly keeper stood on the wall to watch us glide through the entrance and look around for some place to lie. I soon understood why he was not the most cheerful of men. The design of the lock was enough to drive any keeper demented, if only because of the language it must have induced in the exasperated skippers of ships passing through.

This lock was the first built by the Swiss, and if anyone deserved to be drowned in his own pen that man was surely the engineer who thought up the details of Schleuse Augst. (So far as I am aware he came to no such end, probably he retired after a long and worthy life of which his one lock was the great fulfilment.) The lock itself was more square than rectangular, and the upper gates were near one corner. So were the paddles, and one did not need to be a hydraulic engineer to guess that if the water shot in along one side of the lock it would soon start the entire pool stirring to rotate as a giant aquatic merry-go-round. This would not have mattered if we could have drawn alongside, but the designer evidently thought this an unnecessary luxury for ships and he had built the banks at such a flattened angle that the lock-side was altogether unapproachable.

Unable to make fast in this witches' cauldron, I thought our only course would be to run up against the further gates, set the *Thames Commodore*'s nose against the mitre and put her engines full speed ahead in the swirl – a favourite method when dealing with ill-designed locks. But this idea did not appeal to the keeper, for the designer had made special provision for boats whose captains had a foolish irrational desire not to have their ships made a total loss claim at Lloyds. Across the centre of the lock a steel hawser ran from side to side, on the bottom. All one had to do was to bring out a grapple, fish for the cable, haul it up over the bow, make it fast forward and go full speed ahead on that instead.

The lock took long to fill, but with the wheel hard over and the Perkinses pushing against the hawser that crossed our fore-deck we rose slowly and steadily until the time when I could ease off and

Miriam dropped the cable over the bow with a splash. We chugged out into a reach which disappeared into the gathering darkness but a short way ahead on the starboard side the lights of a scatter of houses glinted above the steep bank. I could see in the water the stolid legs of a pier, and quickly making fast we climbed the path to emerge from an alley into the main street of a picture-book Swiss village. After dealing with the eccentricities of Augst lock my brain cannot have been working to full capacity, or else I would not have reached the third course of our supper in the Gasthaus Lamm before realising that the name *Kaiseraugst* boldly painted on the jetty was nothing more nor less than the barely disguised title *Caesar Augustus* given to every Roman emperor from the year 27 B.C. onwards.

In fact the few miles of navigable Rhine above Basle are extremely rich in remains of Imperial Rome, for the river once formed the final barrier between the Roman empire and the fierce German tribes to the north. More than forty watch-towers have been discovered upstream of Basle, each in sight of the next so that news of impending attacks could be passed down the line by some primitive sort of semaphore. Several forts strengthened the line, and the *castellum* of Kaiseraugst was one of them. Parts of its wall lie scattered about the village, but these are as nothing compared with the vast remains of Augusta Raurica, beyond the railway-track and the noisy main road which divides the little waterside village of Kaiseraugst from the newer and larger Basel–Augst, in the edge of which this important Roman colony was set.

Augusta Raurica was established by L. Munatius Plancus, whose tombstone in Italy establishes the fact boldly and beyond doubt. 'Lucius Munatius Plancus, son of Lucius, grandson of Lucius, great-grandson of Lucius, Consul, Censor, twice fieldmarshal and a member of the Council of Seven, triumphed over the Rhaetians, built the temple of Saturn out of the war booty and founded the colonies of Lugdunum (Lyon) and Raurica.' The inscription omits to mention the date, but it is believed to have been on mid-summer's day in 44 B.C. – the lay-out of the town being orientated towards dawn on that day. Three hundred years later the violent Alemanni stormed and destroyed the place, but enough remained to show that it was the most impressive Roman development in

Switzerland, with two bridges across the Rhine. The fort of Kaiseraugst was built after the Alemanni attacked Raurica, to prevent further invasions from over the river, and was a massive strong point with a heavy wall and numerous watch-towers and sally-ports. On the Baden shore a smaller fort completed the defences.

Much has been done to excavate the remains of Augusta Raurica, with its theatre which could hold ten thousand spectators and was specially equipped with a water supply to end upon the stage, which could be filled to the brim for pageants involving naval battles. The house of a Roman businessman has also been reconstructed and filled with many of its original pieces of domestic hardware and furniture, and the temples and forum and the baths laid bare. As always, many of the stones of the ruined Roman buildings have long since been removed and used in later houses, but the amount of Augusta Raurica remaining is astonishing. We walked over the stage of the theatre, sat in the auditorium, climbed the ascent to a temple on a knoll and found our way to the court where once justice had been dispensed. Only a stolid Swiss cow now sat there on the grass, chewing the cud and gently ringing its bell as it nodded its head and twitched its ears to rid itself for a moment of the buzzing flies of summer.

Above Kaiseraugst the Rhine is nearing the end of navigation, but this final reach is more beautiful than any since the castled gorge below Bingen. The broad gravel plain has gone, and the river runs in a bed which it has sliced through the rock. There are no groynes of correcting engineers, no dikes or stone-clad banks, nothing but a stream running deep and irresistible between the cliffs of its own making. On the German shore the fisher village of Warmbach is perched high above the water, and on the Swiss side the steep rocks are topped with little summerhouses or platforms, each with its derrick from which a dropnet can be lowered into the clear water. Patient fishermen sit there in armchairs, winding away at their cranks, looking with resignation into the empty nets, lowering them again and leaning back to enjoy another two minutes of cigar before looking again to see if a salmon has been slow-witted enough to let itself be trapped.

It was only half an hour before the bridge of Rheinfelden came

into view, a long greyish stone structure of low arches connecting
Rheinfelden (Germany) with Rheinfelden (Switzerland) by way
of a small mid-stream island which had once borne a castle to
control the crossing. The Rhine foamed swift through the arches,
bouncing towards us over the shallows. Cautiously we edged up
towards the island but after two gentle bumps on the bottom I let
our good ship float away again. I had no wish to lose a propeller
so far away from her home yard on the Thames, just for the sake
of landing on an island in the middle of the Rhine; and as there was
no other facility on the Swiss shore I waited till she had bobbed
away into deeper water and then brought her over to where the
potash barges lay against the commercial jetty on the German side
of the river.

German Rheinfelden is not the most attractive of towns. It is a
new settlement, not in the sense of a planned piece of architectural
virtuosity, but merely because it was built in modern times. It owes
its existence to the Frankfurt Exhibition of 1891, where visitors
witnessed the miracle of electric lighting produced not by a local
steam-engine but by water pouring through machinery at Heil-
bronn, more than one hundred miles away on the River Neckar.
Awe-struck, they stared at the unethereal glow of the orange
filaments, which owed their brightness to nothing more mysterious
than the flow of the river beside the Swabian vineyards, but whilst
the public gazed in astonishment the electrical engineers were
pondering what might or might not be done with the Rhine.
Above Rheinfelden the river ran down a considerable flight of
rapids, and if the stream could be dammed then the kilowatts
could hum merrily along the wires. To put a hydro-electric plant
in such a turbulent river as the Rhine was a hazardous undertaking,
but a consortium of German and Swiss firms decided to take the
risk. Four years later the power plant at Rheinfelden had its
twenty turbines purring contentedly, and even if by modern
standards they were not very efficient the work was to be the fore-
runner of another twelve power-stations between Basle and the
Lake of Constance.

An army of workmen of every conceivable nationality streamed
to the construction site at Rheinfelden, and their numbers were
swelled by land speculators, tradesmen, pub-keepers and all the

usual construction-camp followers. Ugly houses and blocks of flats for the workmen sprang up all along the river's edge and as this was before the days of planning or control the result was – Rheinfelden. As soon as the main work was finished the boom town fell on hard times, and half a century later the final phase of the Second World War razed much of its more hideous aspect to the ground. Today it is hygienic, airy, planned, spacious, and unbelievably dull.

The Swiss town also has an industry of its own. Switzerland happens to be one of those lands which used to have to import its salt from elsewhere. In the sixteenth century a small deposit was found, but the country was far from being self sufficient in this useful chemical until the 1830s, when boring brought to light the salt beneath the ground in the Rhine valley. Salt mines were soon developed at Kaiseraugst and Rheinfelden, where the beds lie some 400 feet beneath the surface. And because Rheinfelden was already a pleasant little town it now also became a spa where one could bathe in the brine which was the bringer of health. Had not the great Paracelsus of Basle once extolled the virtues of salt?

Yet Rheinfelden has escaped becoming a sophisticated colony of hypochondriacs. One can be steeped in brine there, salted like a cod or made to sit in a steamy mist until one feels suitably befogged, but all this happens in a discreetly withdrawn area outside the old town itself, which is so tightly cramped against the edge of the river that it has the appearance of trying to fling itself into the stream. It has the best waterfront of the whole river from Rheinfelden to the sea, the steep-roofed houses bursting out into balconies over the water which races grey beneath them, churning and wrinkled like the great salmon stream that it is. Along the railings and in the window-boxes of these unpretentious buildings from an earlier age of prosperity the geraniums and pelargoniums glow brilliant in the intense sunlight of a clean unclouded atmosphere. Swiss Rheinfelden has the air of a happy place, and probably it always was so unless one happened to be a prisoner in the Messerturm (Knife Tower) which still stands forward from the walls, its foot washed by the Rhine. This was once a keep where starving prisoners were tempted to leap out to snatch food, but inevitably failed in the attempt and fell to their death in the river below, where the rocks were specially studded with knife-blades in order to assist their demise.

Here, at the upper limit of navigation, the Rhine still shows every facet of its history. The Romans had a tower there, part of the first intensive 'Watch on the Rhine'. Along the bank the houses of the merchants stand above forgotten landings where in medieval times the servants would unload the bales of goods slowly dragged up the river in small barges horse-hauled all the way from the Low Countries, or floated down from Zürich. Tight among them are the church towers which speak of the great religious struggles of Europe as the Reformation, born beside the Rhine and wordily fought out at Worms, swept across the countries. The greying Messerturm stands mutely in the water's edge, an ageing silent witness of the cruelty and horror of an era when human life was held of as little account or value as it is in our own, and at either end of the bridge are the huts where uniformed customs men, green on the right bank and grey on the left, casually glance at the papers of travellers and vehicles, a reminder that medieval boundaries still exist and national entities cannot disappear over-night, even if archiepiscopal marksmen no longer hold the shipping to ransom.

The Rhine is a bringer of contentment, too. Along its verge the week-end fishermen recline dreamily by their drop-nets, glad to be finished with another week in the laboratory or banking office, while at home their very practical wives prepare a meal of veal or steak, confident that once again the men will return home relaxed, happy, but with a long and technical explanation of just why it was that the salmon never came. In the shallows of a bay across the river a group of cows cool their feet, watching the boys who daringly swim out to be swept down the stream to another beach nearby. A pair of young lovers stand by the bridge parapet between the two customs posts, watching from their no-man's-land above the water as the river steamer comes surging up the stream, white and graceful and with power enough to make the run from Basle, however capricious the Rhine may be.

She is not the only ship to be seen. Above the bridge a speed-boat criss-crosses swiftly between the shoals before shooting over the bounce of water under one of the bridge arches. Across the

Rhine on the German shore another trailer lorry bumps dustily down to the loading jetty where a trio of barges are lying part laden, one from Duisburg and two from Rotterdam. Astern of them another vessel strains at her two stout bow-lines in the powerful pull of the Rhine. She is of a type and nationality rarely seen on the upper reaches of the great river. Shining in her blue paint and with the Red Ensign fluttering in the river breeze she bobs a little on the water, which is still resilient from thrusting round the buttresses of the bridge that marks the end of the shipping channel.

In the evening she is still there, but as the summer dawn brightens and the sun climbs over the hills to cast a fiery glow on the turbulent water the *Thames Commodore* is already drawing away from the jetty to let the Rhine push her bow downstream, towards Alsace, the Rhineland, the Netherlands and the far North Sea.

INDEX OF NAMES

(For ease of reference people and legendary creatures or beings are printed in italics)